Called to One Hope

Called to One Hope

The Gospel in Diverse Cultures

Edited by Christopher Duraisingh

WCC Publications, Geneva

Cover design: Edwin Hassink

Photos: WCC/Chris Black

ISBN 2-8254-1235-X

© 1998 WCC Publications, World Council of Churches,
150 route de Ferney, 1211 Geneva 2, Switzerland

Printed in France

Impressions Dumas – Dépôt légal : Juin 1998
N° d'imprimeur : 34468

Table of Contents

Foreword *Ana Langerak* vii
Preface *Christopher Duraisingh* x

Part I

The Route to Salvador *Guillermo Cook* 2

"Laudate Omnes Gentes": The Conference Begins
Christopher Duraisingh 10

Part II

CONFERENCE MESSAGE 20
ACTS OF COMMITMENT 26
REPORTS FROM THE SECTIONS 29
    Preamble 29
    I: Authentic Witness within Each Culture 30
    II: Gospel and Identity in Community 40
    III: Local Congregations in Pluralist Societies 53
    IV: One Gospel – Diverse Expressions 64

THEME ADDRESSES
    Gospel and Culture
        Metropolitan Kirill of Smolensk and Kaliningrad 77
    Called to One Hope: The Gospel in Diverse Cultures
        Musimbi R.A. Kanyoro 96

vi   *Table of Contents*

THEME PANEL I: "FOR SUCH A TIME AS THIS –
EVANGELISM AND CULTURE"

A German Perspective	
Cornelia Füllkrug-Weitzel	111
An Australian Aboriginal Perspective	
Wali Fejo	121
A Brazilian Perspective	
Robinson Cavalcanti	127
A Jamaican Perspective	
Marjorie Lewis-Cooper	131

THEME PANEL II: "EACH IN OUR OWN LANGUAGE –
THE BIBLE IN CONTEXT"

The Bible in Context: An Indian Story	
K.M. George	137
The UK: A Post-Christian, Post-Modern Context	
Kristin Ofstad	145
Interpreting the Bible in a Central African Context	
Jean-Samuel Hendje Toya	152
The Bible in the African American Cultural Context	
Prathia Hall Wynn	158

Part III

From Each Culture, with One Voice: Worship at Salvador	
Jean S. Stromberg	166
Sharing the Riches of the Bible across Cultures: Bible Studies at Salvador	
Sister Monica Cooney	177
"Thuma Mina" – "Send Us, Lord": The Conference Closes	
Christopher Duraisingh	186
Salvador: A Signpost of the New in Mission	
Christopher Duraisingh	190

Appendices

Participants	214
Contributors	233

Foreword

It is a distinct privilege to present this report of the conference on world mission and evangelism that took place in Salvador, Brazil, 24 November-3 December 1996, under the theme "Called to One Hope – The Gospel in Diverse Cultures". The Salvador meeting, standing in the tradition of world mission conferences held under World Council of Churches auspices, embodied a constitutional mandate that provides for regular (once between assemblies) intentional deliberation by the global Christian community on the nature of the proclamation of the gospel of Jesus Christ and the dimension of unity that this proclamation is intended to nurture and express.

Salvador came at the close of a century of debate, study and cooperation in mission that, with the historic Edinburgh conference of 1910, became a characteristic feature of the modern ecumenical movement. At the end of this century, how appropriate that the joys and challenges brought about by the fact that the gospel has been proclaimed in cultures around the world should become a theme for ecumenical discussions and, taking another vantage point – the dawn of a new millennium – how pertinent to focus on the calling to one hope that is addressed by the fullness of God's love in Christ to all the world!

The 574 participants at the conference in Brazil grappled with the implications of a gospel that by definition seeks to be incarnated in a myriad of authentic ways. They shared their stories, worshipped together, listened to one another, dreamed, debated and grew. The reports of their work in four sections (frequently rich and insightful, sometimes indicating the need for further study) on such crucial contemporary issues as religion and culture, culture-sensitive evangelism, the message of the gospel in situations of crushed identities, accountability in mission, the phenomenon of globalization, and authentic diversity in expressing the gospel, are included here so that their usefulness may extend beyond the direct participants to the wider Christian community engaged in witness.

This "official" report of the conference contains not only the documents arising from the conference and the major plenary presentations, but also a number of commissioned chapters that discuss aspects of the programme or provide the background or some interpretative keys for studying the material. In this regard the editor of the report, Christopher Duraisingh (who played a fundamental role in designing the conference), provides the readers with a creative integration of the "text" and a helpful interpretation of the "moment" of this ecumenical gathering.

Responsibility for the conference was lodged in the commission of Unit II – Churches in Mission: Health, Education, Witness, whose oversight of the development of the meeting was commendable, not only in bringing together a number of distinct processes – including the Gospel and Cultures study process – but also in facilitating proposals for a clearer structural place for mission in the WCC. It did this without losing sight of an integrated vision of mission, and stimulated its expression by the unit as a positive contribution to the ecumenical discussion on the vision and vocation of the WCC.

The task of coordinating the various facets of the conference was headed by the conference officers: the co-moderators of the commission, Erme Camba and Sigrun Mogedal, and myself. Naturally, the process required extensive work by the entire staff of Unit II and by many in other parts of the WCC, as well as the skills, support and collaboration of individuals, churches, agencies and councils of churches – who together turned it into a very memorable joint effort. Thanks are due to all of these.

From April 1995 to April 1997, the unit enjoyed the collaboration of Guillermo Cook, from Costa Rica, as the conference administrator. I wish to express tremendous gratitude to Guillermo for contributing his wide-ranging skills, his ample knowledge of the Brazilian context and his passion for mission to the common task. Special recognition should also be given to the members of conference-related committees – including the conference planning and worship committees, the group who produced the Bible study materials and the national and local host committees in Brazil, together with the local organizing secretary, Gérson Meyer – who, working at international, national and local levels, made the meeting possible.

Foreword ix

The response to the conference message, acts of commitment and section reports has been extremely encouraging. It now remains to assess the thinking that Salvador produced and to relate it critically to our practice of mission. In a spirit of expectation, therefore, I commend this official report to the churches and to individual Christians, trusting that it will constitute an important resource for their study and involvement in the *missio Dei* in the years to come.

ANA LANGERAK
Executive Director
Unit II – Churches in Mission: Health, Education, Witness
World Council of Churches

Preface

The eleventh ecumenical conference on world mission and evangelism, which took place in Salvador, Bahia, Brazil, from 24 November to 3 December 1996, was a unique event. No printed report could ever fully capture the tone or texture of such a gathering nor adequately portray the depth of encounter among the participants. Nevertheless, the printed word still functions as a permanently available instrument which enables further study and reflection on the deliberations and findings of such an event and, to some extent, on the profound experiences of those who were part of it. With the hope of engendering continued thought and action by Christians and churches everywhere upon foundational mission issues for the next decades, the Salvador conference produced a *message*, a set of *acts of commitment* and extensive reports of the deliberations by the participants meeting in *sections*. For the stated purpose of a conference on world mission and evangelism is "to assist the Christian community in the proclamation of the gospel of Jesus Christ by word and deed to the whole world, to the end that all may believe" – in continuity with the first ecumenical mission conference, held in Edinburgh in 1910, the deliberations of which ran to several volumes!

For the representatives of the churches, mission agencies and groups on the frontiers of mission brought together in Salvador by the World Council of Churches for "reflection and consultation leading to common witness", the theme "Called to One Hope – The Gospel in Diverse Cultures" provided the focus for analysis of the mission situation today, identification of urgent mission issues and articulation of the nature of Christian witness at the turn of the century and indeed of the millennium. What better "umbrella" theme could there be? Is not a singular characteristic of our times (as one of the main speakers at the conference put it) the temptation to "flirt with hopelessness"? Is not a central element of the Christian vocation and the church's mission to be and to set up signposts everywhere that God in Jesus Christ is the hope for a world torn by violence and fragmentation and the destruction of community? The theme, too, was well suited for the fresh articulation of perennial mission topics such as the relationship between Christian witness and culture, the relevance of the gospel to structural issues, the equipping of local congregations in increasingly pluralist societies, and the developing of responsible ecumenical relationships in mission in a context of rampant proselytism. These issues were explored at the conference under four section themes: (1) authentic witness within each culture; (2) gospel and identity in community; (3) local congregations in pluralist societies; and (4) one gospel – diverse expressions.

These long-standing mission issues come with challenging relevance today, for at the end of this century we may boldly claim that the church is truly global, not merely in a geographical sense but also in the plurality of culturally influenced ways in which Christians live their faith, worship and witness around the world. The voices of (for example) Christians in the South, indigenous peoples, women and youth are now being heard as never before; the Salvador meeting was a clear testimony to that fact.

Salvador was also a reminder in no uncertain terms that the process of the "vernacularization" of the gospel – the inevitable embodiment of the gospel in particular cultures, for the understanding and articulation of the Word-become-flesh – which began on the day of Pentecost, continues today in myriad ways. In some instances, the understanding of the gospel is illuminated by local cultures; in others, the gospel seems to have become captive to – or critiques – cultural values and norms. What then constitutes an authentic relationship between the gospel and cultures as Christians seek to live and witness to the good news? The urgent need for and the manner of evangelism – the unequivocal witness to God's love in Jesus Christ – and the offer of hope in culturally relevant and sensitive ways were clearly on the agenda of the Salvador conference. These central *missiological* questions regarding the content and message of the gospel of hope and its contextual proclamation were addressed in Section I.

Salvador also recognized that the gospel of Christ as bringing "life in all its fullness" is intrinsically related to *the structural dimensions of cultures* as well – for culture is not only a vehicle of meaning but also a structure of symbols through which people express relationships of power and status. Salvador heard stories of how cultures are used to justify oppressive practices, and also how they provide powerful symbols for liberation. Images from the "killing fields" in places such as Rwanda and the former Yugoslavia were fresh; the locale of Salvador itself evoked memories of past linkages between colonialism, the slave trade and Christian mission. What are the structural factors in societies that lead people to lose hope? What role do the search for local or narrow group identities and the process of globalization play in promoting the fragmentation of human community on the one hand and the destruction of local cultural identities on the other? How may Christians witness to the gospel of Christ as the power of God which frees and unites? How may they proclaim the gospel as the relevant word of hope to the public structures of society? These were among the questions addressed by Section II.

Local congregations are the crucial hermeneutic, the test case, of the transforming power of the gospel. Their life has tremendous capacity to witness to the "one hope". As migration brings culturally and religiously different people into proximate relationship more than ever before, many congregations do not seem to be equipped to witness to the inclusive love of God in Christ. Some withdraw into themselves and become "comfort zones for the familiar"; some identify and support the "identity politics" and ethnic sentiments of society at large. Christians are not free from the demon of xenophobia. In the context of a culture that tends to exclude that which is unfamiliar and different, what are the ways to further *the equipping and nurturing of local congregations for witness* to the good news of God's love and embrace, of a God-intended human community of love and justice, thus promoting a culture of dialogue? These critical questions were the focus of Section III.

The conference was itself a sign of a polycentric church in all its plurality of cultures. Diverse voices and stories were heard. But the more diversity is encountered, the more unsettling it becomes for many, particularly those who are accustomed to conceive of one or another culturally shaped expression of the gospel as normative. The very process of inculturation challenges the churches to discern and celebrate the rich diversity of ways of Christian witness and worship as a blessing bestowed upon the church by the Holy Spirit. Salvador therefore witnessed both excitement and frustration in seeking mutual understanding and appreciation among Christians across cultures. What process and criteria, what language – in short, what intercultural hermeneutics – will enable Christians to understand and accept each other's formulation and proclamation of the gospel? Moreover, recent years have seen an increase in expressions of aggressive evangelism leading to proselytism – competition in the name of mission, in an almost free-market spirit. This has resulted in unhealthy relationships between churches and the deterioration of common Christian witness. If the unity of the church and its witness to the gospel of reconciliation are inseparably related and if the hope to which Christians are called is one, how may the churches promote responsible relationships in mission that witness to God's purpose to reconcile all things into unity in Christ? The urgency of these *ecumenical* questions in a world that "flirts with hopelessness" and distrusts even the possibility of human community cannot be overstated. The Salvador conference engaged with some of them, albeit in a somewhat limited and tentative manner, in Section IV.

The exploration of the conference theme was undergirded by vibrant and uplifting daily worship, which used culturally plural symbols and expressions. The discussions and the very life of the conference were enriched by daily Bible studies in small groups around selected passages from the book of Acts. The exploration of the theme and the process towards the renewal of the participants and their churches in mission were further enhanced by a number of special events. The following report seeks to share some of these inputs and discussions and their fruits. It falls into three parts.

The first part consists of two brief essays: the first, by Guillermo Cook, conference administrator, describes the preparatory processes for the conference and gives some details about the nature and composition of the gathering; the second attempts to convey the flavour of the opening moments of the conference, primarily in the words of some of the speakers, and sets out in brief compass the overall flow and dynamics of the event. The second (and most extensive) part includes the conference message, the seven acts of commitment, the reports of the four sections and the texts of the main plenary presentations. The third part consists of four essays, each seeking to describe a particular aspect of the conference. Jean Stromberg writes about the worship experience, and Sister Monica Cooney describes and summarizes the discussions in the Bible study groups. Then follows a description of the closing moments of the conference, identifying some of the special events intended to further the cause of mission in the next decades. The final piece is an attempt to interpret the significance of the eleventh conference on world mission and evangelism.

Behind the production of this volume lies the labour of love and wise counsel of many, two in particular, to whom a debt of gratitude is owed: Dawn Ross for her tireless and painstaking assistance in finalizing the text of not only this report but virtually all the conference documents; and Marlin VanElderen for his patient and skilled accompaniment – editorial and otherwise – of the publication processes for various texts related to the conference, including this report.

The outcome of a large gathering such as the Salvador conference cannot be measured solely by what it generates as printed documents. Given the scope of the conference, it is entirely normal that its statements are unfinished, its findings limited. The lasting impact of Salvador will depend to a large extent on the mission impulses and fresh evangelistic commitments that its reports trigger in the minds and hearts of those who study them. It is with that hope and prayer that this report is offered to Christians and churches everywhere.

May the eleventh conference on world mission and evangelism inspire and enliven Christians in every culture as they give an account of the hope to which God calls all in Jesus Christ, to the glory of the triune God.

CHRISTOPHER DURAISINGH

Part I

The Route to Salvador

Guillermo Cook

The eleventh conference on world mission and evangelism (CWME) in this century was the result of a five-year process. The conference was called together by the commission of Programme Unit II – Churches in Mission: Health, Education, Witness, under the direction of the central committee of the World Council of Churches. Working through an able conference planning committee, the commission organized this major event which brought together 574 persons from 98 countries.

The conference venue
In ecumenical history the venue of a conference on world mission and evangelism takes on historic significance. All such conferences since the first one in Edinburgh, 1910, are known by their location – we speak of Jerusalem, Tambaram, Mexico, Bangkok and San Antonio, for example. The venue is chosen, at least in part, in relation to its appropriateness to the theme. Certainly the choice of Salvador was closely related to "Called to One Hope – The Gospel in Diverse Cultures".

Through a long history of colonization, forced importation of Africans as slaves and subsequent immigration, Brazil has a rich diversity of races and cultures. That part of the population which is of African descent is larger than any African nation other than Nigeria. Although around ninety percent of the population is Roman Catholic, there is a significant presence of other mainstream Christian traditions. Pentecostal churches and those in a charismatic tradition are growing at a phenomenal rate. There is also a wide variety of popular religious expressions arising from a blend of Afro-Brazilian, Christian and indigenous spirituality. The largest country in Latin America, Brazil also reflects many of the issues and social dynamics that would be discussed at the conference. All these elements of diversity are present in Salvador, the third largest population centre in the country.

Founded in 1549, Salvador was the colonial capital of the far-flung Portuguese empire and the principal entry-point in Brazil for the slave trade from West Africa. Since colonial times it has been a centre of jurisdiction for the Roman Catholic Church; the archdiocese of São Salvador da Bahia, dating from 1551, is the oldest in the country. Salvador has the highest concentration of people of African origin in Brazil, and many of its (nominally Roman Catholic) inhabitants practise Candomblé, a religion which is deeply rooted in West African spirituality. Given such a wealth of cultural diversity and spiritualities in Salvador the potential for engaged deliberations at the conference was clear. Thus Salvador became the place that will be associated with the last world mission conference of the second millennium.

Another important consideration in the choice of the venue was the ecumenical context in Brazil. The churches in Brazil through their ecumenical fellowship, CONIC (National Council of Christian Churches in Brazil), issued an invitation to the WCC to hold the conference in that country. In addition to many of the "mainline" churches, CONIC includes in its membership the Syrian Orthodox Church as well as the National Conference of [Catholic] Bishops of Brazil (CNBB).

Under the guidance of CONIC, a national host committee was appointed with official representation from the ecumenical family of churches and NGOs, together with two representatives of non-CONIC Evangelical and Pentecostal churches. The national host committee assumed general oversight of the conference preparations in Brazil, in regular and full consultation with the WCC. In Salvador itself the conference benefited tremendously from the logistic support of CESE (Ecumenical Services Coordination), which was founded in the 1970s to provide a prophetic voice during the years of military rule. A significant portion of CESE's infrastructure – personnel, offices and equipment – was placed at the disposal of the local organizing committee during both the preparation phase and the conference itself.

Under the capable leadership of the local organizing secretary, Gérson Meyer, the local committee handled many of the day-to-day responsibilities of organizing the conference in Salvador. The local committee worked closely with the Geneva staff, especially with the conference administrator, who made several lengthy visits to Salvador during his two years of work.

The venue choices in Salvador for an event of this nature and size were only two: the vast and austere national convention centre on the outskirts of the city – expensive and far from hotels and other accommodation; and the Ondina conference centre and hotel complex – a consortium of proximate tourist hotels with ample accommodation and adequate meeting space at no additional cost. In spite of the relatively luxurious surroundings, the latter was chosen as the venue for the conference because in the end it offered the more economical and useful package.

Participants

The Salvador conference was indeed a global mission gathering, with some 98 nations being represented. The variety of cultures, languages and denominational backgrounds of the participants augured well for a rich sharing of experiences and insights on the impact of the gospel in diverse cultures. This broad participation was the result of an arduous process of selection and processing that began in November 1994. The process sought to ensure adequate balances in terms of region, denomination, gender and generation. It also sought to provide for an appropriate representation of church leaders, theologians, ordained and lay persons, and persons working and witnessing at the grassroots. The WCC central committee had set 500 as the upper limit for the number of participants (excluding press and visitors), including 300 with voting rights. Of the 300, 200 were to be representatives of the churches and 20 to be representatives of the CWME affiliated bodies (mainly ecumenical mission agencies and national/regional councils of churches); the remainder were to be people from the "frontiers of mission" (some named by the churches). In the light of the emphasis on the gospel in diverse cultures, the "frontiers of mission" category included a number of those who had been involved in the four-year WCC gospel and cultures study process. The organizers were acutely aware that it would not be possible for all WCC member churches to send delegates to the conference; priority was thus given to churches which had not been represented at the previous world mission conference (San Antonio, 1989).

For a variety of reasons, the number of persons who officially participated in the conference was somewhat under the ceiling of

500 that had been set by the central committee. Out of a total of 400 official participants, 247 were voting delegates and 153 non-voting participants (members of the central committee in leadership positions, resource persons, consultants, delegated and host country observers, national/regional coordinators of the gospel and cultures study, advisors, guests, staff and stewards). The following table indicates the breakdown of the 400 official participants by region:

Region	%
Africa	11%
Asia	16%
Caribbean	4%
Europe	30%
Latin America	21%
Middle East	4%
North America	12%
Pacific	2%

The commission and conference planning committee worked towards having 50 percent women, 20 percent youth and 25 percent Orthodox participation. In spite of concerted efforts and extensive consultations with churches and mission agencies, women constituted 43 percent, youth 16 percent and Orthodox 22 percent of the voting delegates. Among the participants were a number of differently abled persons. Of the 400 official participants, 57 percent were ordained and 43 percent lay.

An additional 174 participants included 49 journalists, 61 accredited visitors, 42 coopted staff and 22 seminarians from the USA and Canada. Thus the total number of registered participants in the Salvador conference came to 574.

The quality of the conference was enhanced not only by the *number* of participants who attended the conference, but by their *diversity* in terms of background and commitments. In this respect the presence of a number of Evangelicals and Pentecostals was significant, leading to a highly positive contribution from them.

There were 29 Roman Catholic participants, including a 10-person delegation named by the Vatican. A few had been named to represent national or regional councils, and others came as consultants, staff or accredited visitors.

Furthermore the theme of the conference called for active participation by indigenous people, and at least 22 – from almost all regions – were enabled to be present in a variety of categories. In addition to a number of significant consultations and studies on gospel and cultures organized by indigenous peoples particularly in Latin America as part of the preparatory process, 37 persons participated in a consultation in Salvador just prior to the conference, coordinated by the WCC indigenous peoples' programme. A statement from that meeting was offered as an input into the conference proceedings.

A similar preparatory process was organized by young people (coordinated by the WCC youth desk), including a series of regional and global gatherings on gospel and cultures issues and a pre-conference meeting in Salvador of youth participants, designed to orient and equip them for maximum participation in the conference.

The gospel and cultures study process had, of course, involved many women – both in special women's groupings (a pamphlet on women's perspectives on the issue, for example, had been published prior to the conference) as well as in broader contexts. While it was decided not to hold a women's pre-conference event, space was provided for women participants at the conference to meet together from time to time to articulate their insights and concerns.

Conference finances

Almost inevitably, finance became one of the most daunting challenges for the Unit II commission. Preparations had barely gotten under way when the WCC found itself in difficult financial straits (as were most of the member churches). The question could reasonably be asked, and indeed was posed by some: How could a major world conference take place at a time like this? Apart from the constitutional stipulation that a world mission conference be called between two WCC assemblies, there was the strong conviction that if the WCC failed to convene a mission conference at this juncture in its history, the credibility of the ecumenical movement's commitment to mission and evangelism among large segments of its constituency would be sorely tested. Since the San Antonio conference the unit had annually set aside funds towards the next one, eventually amounting to about half of the projected cost of the conference. It was recognized that the shortfall would have to be made up by fresh pledges, those who would cover the costs of their own participation, and the reserves of Unit II. Indeed, such was the commitment of the Unit II commission to moving ahead with the conference that, at its

Coventry meeting (June 1995) it both rejected a proposal that the number of participants be reduced and recommended that a portion of the Unit's reserves be made available, as necessary, to ensure the financial viability of the conference. The strong commitment to the conference among the CWME affiliated bodies also became evident as a number agreed to pledge additional monies.

In the end, with careful monitoring and fiscal discipline by all those who staffed the conference both in Geneva and Salvador, and with the lower-than-planned attendance, the budget of the conference was covered in full.

Programmatic preparations

A unique feature of the preparations for Salvador was the WCC's four-year study process on the relation between the gospel and cultures in many parts of the world. The study, undertaken by churches, ecumenical agencies, special groups, theological institutions and interested individuals in over sixty countries, contributed to the reflection on the conference theme in a variety of ways, including the production of a significant body of materials on gospel and cultures issues both within the WCC and in many parts of the world. In fact, the study process provided the basic framework for the exploration of the theme at the conference itself, since the four foci of the study eventually became the sub-themes of the four sections.

In many instances, the gospel and cultures study process culminated in national or regional consultations on the subject. The substantial preparatory papers for conference section work were in large part a fruit of the synthesis of the findings of more than sixty reports received from these consultations and from other groups/bodies engaged in the study. Furthermore, those who had coordinated the study at the local, national or regional level offered to share their findings in imaginative presentations at the conference itself (in the *Encontros* programme). Therefore, as will be seen below, a significant part of the conference was an outcome of the study process.

It was envisaged that the entire life and work of the conference would be undergirded by worship and prayer. A small international and interdenominational group of highly talented women and men worked long and hard to prepare the worship. At the conference itself the worship, which took place every morning in a beautiful canopied area overlooking the azure waters of the "Bay of All

Saints", was richly symbolic. In tune with the context of Salvador, the worship "had a rhythm, a harmony, a beat... of the drum".

Following the decision of the commission, seven Bible studies were prepared on passages selected from the first 17 chapters of the Acts of the Apostles. The booklet *Spirit, Gospel, Cultures: Bible Studies on the Acts of the Apostles* was used both in the preparatory period by churches and groups as well as during the morning Bible study sessions in Salvador. For many the Bible studies, where diverse cultural insights on particular passages from Acts were shared in small groups, constituted a major highlight of the conference.

In addition to the preparatory papers for the section work and the Bible study booklet, several issues of the *International Review of Mission* were devoted to exploring the four sectional themes. A further *IRM* issue introduced the life and mission of the churches in Brazil and the particular milieu of Salvador.

Together with some of these preparatory materials, a poster and prayer brochure were circulated widely among the WCC member churches and those who had been named to participate in the conference. The churches and prospective participants were encouraged to prepare for the conference by making use of a specially written prayer which asked for a vision of God's love in Jesus Christ "that embraces within its transforming power the rich plurality of the human race", that both at the conference and beyond, churches and Christians may be inspired for "a rich sharing across cultures so that the heritages of all peoples may be offered" to the triune God.

Issues and dialogue

Both the life of the conference and the deliberations were enhanced by the diversity of the participants. Given the very different understandings among the churches of the content of the gospel and its relationship to culture, the Salvador conference could have become a time of confrontation. Issues such as proselytism (a concern raised by many, including some Orthodox churches), syncretism, the effects of cultural imposition accompanying the missionary enterprise (especially in relation to indigenous peoples) and religious pluralism (as, for example, in the relations between the churches and the Afro-Brazilian religions in Brazil) were clearly on the agenda. The different perspectives and interactions of church leaders, theologians and grassroots people made this conference an event where, in the words of one mission executive, "the cultural context was described by everybody".

There was a conscious attempt to facilitate a dialogue between representatives of evangelical bodies as well as selected representatives of an ecumenical persuasion. While the desire expressed at San Antonio that future WCC and evangelical mission conferences should take place simultaneously and adjacently remains unfulfilled, the evangelicals at Salvador (unlike previous conferences) decided to address their concerns primarily to fellow evangelicals and not to the WCC.

The conference message expresses the "profound hope" of the participants that "this last great mission conference of the 20th century" may serve to re-emphasize that "the gospel to be most fruitful needs to be both true to itself and incarnated or rooted in the culture of a people".

"Laudate Omnes Gentes": The Conference Begins

Christopher Duraisingh

"To the glory of the triune God and for the renewal of the churches in mission, I declare the eleventh conference on world mission and evangelism in Salvador, Brazil, open." These words from Sigrun Mogedal, one of the co-moderators of the conference, were followed by a thunderous singing of "Laudate omnes gentes, laudate Dominum" ("All peoples, praise the Lord!"). Earlier, in the opening service, well over 800 persons had joined in the hymn "All people that on earth do dwell". "Omnes gentes"... "all people" – what fitting words with which to begin the last of the series of ecumenical conferences on world mission and evangelism in this century.

An *omnes gentes* indeed it was, gathered together "from every corner of the earth" – rich in plurality of colours, cultures, languages, church traditions, etc., but with a common intent to "open our hearts and minds to God" and to each other. At the opening worship this *omnes gentes* was reminded that "from our diverse cultures we are called to one hope. We have seen with our eyes, we have touched with our hands the word of life in our diverse cultures. But it is in our sharing within the community of the church that we shall discern the fullness of God that fills us all. Come then with joy to give and receive the word of hope in Christ and to be strengthened in our mission!" The loud beats of the *local* drums of Salvador, combined with the words of welcome repeated in the many languages of those who gathered from around the *globe* and the sharing of the coconut milk as a sign of affirmation of one another and a commitment to "nourish us with the gifts of many cultures", set the stage for the exploration of the theme of the conference: "Called to One Hope – The Gospel in Diverse Cultures".

During these first few moments of the conference, the participants gathered in worship were reminded also that they were surrounded by a cloud of witnesses, a company of the pioneers in faith and missionary obedience to the one hope to which all are called. A powerful and moving litany of remembrance bonded those present at the Salvador conference with their ancestors in mission reflection and practice who had gathered in each of the ten previous conferences, beginning with Edinburgh 1910.

The interplay between the local and the global in such an international gathering was further accentuated at the opening plenary by the presence on the platform of a representative of the civic authorities, and the greetings brought by an indigenous person from Brazil, the chairperson of the Brazilian host committee, the president of the Latin American Council of Churches (CLAI) and Konrad Raiser, general secretary of the World Council of Churches. Greetings from the Roman Catholic Church – the largest Christian community in Brazil and in Latin America as a whole – had already been extended during the opening worship by Cardinal Lucas Moreira Neves, the Roman Catholic archbishop of Salvador and president of the National Conference of Bishops of Brazil.

From the front

Dr Raiser reminded the participants of both the richness of the theme and its vital significance for the future of the ecumenical movement, as had been seen from the WCC's four-year "study process on gospel and culture,... which has shaped the theme and the content of this conference... and the preparatory papers for section work, which build on the reports of the study groups".

He spoke of "genuine progress and a deepening of insight since the question of gospel and culture was first put on the agenda of the WCC at Vancouver":

> Beyond the earlier discussion about inculturation, we now see cultures as dynamic configurations which change as people's lives in community change. We understand more clearly the ambiguity of all cultures, which provide meaning and identity but also become oppressive and exclusive. We recognize that, in most cases, culture and religion are inseparable; in fact, religion provides the inner coherence of the culture of a given community. This explains the dangerous mix which can emerge where religion serves to legitimate an exclusive culture of ethnocentrism and nationalism.
>
> The processes of rapid globalization which have dissolved many hitherto homogeneous cultures, leading to fragmentation and exclusion, make it an urgent task for us to understand the gospel as the power

which creates true human community, a viable human culture. The study invites us to rediscover and reaffirm catholicity and contextuality as inseparable dimensions of any authentic witness to the gospel, and it is here that the truly ecumenical challenge of the study emerges: how can we be sensitive to God's presence everywhere in the world of diverse cultures and religions and yet affirm the "one hope of our calling"?

Dr Raiser indicated that the nature of the city of Salvador da Bahia gave to the above questions particular significance.

> This city, which was the first colonial capital of Brazil, has also been the centre of the colonial slave trade and today is one of the cities of the world with the largest population of African descent. What is the criterion for authentic witness to the gospel in this place of cultural and religious plurality? If God is present also in the Afro-Brazilian tradition and cultures, how should we live our gospel-based commitment to building inclusive communities? Certainly, the setting in which this conference takes place will challenge our understanding of gospel and culture.

He also reminded the gathering that the ecumenical calling embraces the call to unity, to mission and to service as an inseparable whole. The gospel and culture dialectic is therefore at the heart of the dynamic of the ecumenical movement, which is not – and must never become – an end in itself, a closed affair of the churches as organized bodies.

It is the missionary vocation which places the ecumenical movement in the midst of the world, loved by God in all its plurality of cultures and religions, and which challenges it to go beyond all established boundaries. This must find its visible expression in the place given to common witness and to the work of mission and evangelism in the structured life of the ecumenical movement, especially in the World Council of Churches.

Pointing to a very particular link between the theme of this conference, "Called to One Hope", and the theme of the 1998 WCC assembly in Harare, which invites the churches to "Turn to God" and "Rejoice in Hope", Dr Raiser affirmed that "the ultimate test for the authenticity of our witness to the gospel [is] whether we become agents for building communities of hope in a world of uncertainty, loss of meaning and despair". His prayer for the conference was that it would become "a source of inspiration and encouragement for all who witness to this hope in the many places where there is no hope, and who struggle to maintain or create a culture of life".

Erme Camba, one of the co-moderators of the conference, introduced some contemporary issues in mission as well as expectations for the conference.

> Recognizing the diversity and plurality of response to the gospel and our mission task, this conference was planned to give space for many individuals – especially new voices – to tell their stories, for the issues are much more alive in actual life experiences. It is our hope that in this conference these experiences in mission are shared in the "Rainbow – Festival of Gospel in Cultures" and *Encontros* as well as in the worship, the Bible studies, the section discussions and personal conversations among the participants.

Rooting his comments in specific experiences in his home country, the Philippines, Bishop Camba touched upon some of the pressing mission issues that demanded the attention of the conference. He spoke, for example, of how young Filipino Christians who are recruited as contract workers in countries of the former Soviet Union inadvertently become involved in proselytistic activities, without being aware of the existence of the Orthodox churches. This issue was further highlighted later in several moments of the conference.

Bishop Camba referred also to "the resurgence of world living religions who have become 'mission'-minded" and the challenge they pose for responsible dialogue and witness. Christian indigenous communities in the Philippines and elsewhere use cultural symbols and practise their religious cultural heritage, adapting them in Christian worship – and leading some theologians to "cry syncretism". How should the conference address this issue, since Christians are also called to "repent for the excesses of the past where the church may have participated in the destruction of cultures, resulting in the alienation of Christians from their own people"?

Bishop Camba also spoke of the process of globalization – "that worldwide movement of restructuring economies into a new economic order of the market". How might the conference take seriously

> ... this new idolatry: the worship of the new god of globalization with its own promise of "abundant life"; its own "high priests" – the financiers, the super-executives and economic planners of the conglomerates; its own "theologians" – the market economy ideologues;

its own "temples" – the mega-malls, industrial sweatshops and high-rise modern offices and executive apartments; and its own "sacrifice" on the altar of consumerism and individualism – the poor of the land...? Should this conference speak to this new phenomenon, this challenge of a new god whose "evangelists" are driving the peoples of the world into a crisis of human community?

Alongside the process of globalization, Bishop Camba identified the increasing forces of fragmentation "happening not only among nations and peoples but also among families". He spoke specifically about the increasing problem of migration for economic reasons which has led to the dispersion in various parts of the world of about six million Filipinos (a large majority of them women) who receive very low wages and undergo untold problems – contributing to the fragmentation of families at home. He asked whether this phenomenon of "overseas contract workers" was "a revival of slavery, the shadow of an old god with a new face".

He hoped that the conference would be "a time for setting new visions in light of contemporary realities". He pointed to the Christian understanding of God as triune as a source for such a new vision. Quoting some Filipino theologians, he suggested that Christians need to promote "values which nurture community following the trinitarian paradigm of a plurality in communion and a mutuality in relationship... [to build] a community of a plurality of peoples under a common humanity and to form right relationships with one another and with earth..., a global community wider than the church... where the positive meaning of globalization becomes concrete..., a community reflective of the reign of God (Luke 4:43)."

Finally the executive director of Unit II, Ana Langerak, addressed the conference. She pointed to the rich diversity of the participants, the comprehensive and multifaceted nature of the countries, cultures, traditions and experiences represented, as well as of "the longings, achievements, sufferings that we bring from the life of our societies, communities and churches". This very diversity provided an appropriate setting for the exploration of the theme of the conference; participants were not asked to leave their identities behind. "But in bringing them, will we at the same time allow others to ask us critical questions? Will we listen and learn? *Will we be honest in our disagreements?* Our conference is an *ecumenical* conference. Will we affirm our unity in the body of Christ or will we be tempted to drift further apart? Are we ready to give tangible expression to the oneness of the hope to which the churches, humanity and the cosmos is called?"

She reminded the participants that the Salvador conference was a *mission* conference and therefore that the deliberations were to be undertaken "in the light of the churches' witnessing vocation". She further urged: "Will we be open enough to discern the shape of the commission addressed to the churches in our time? Will we be open to a new Pentecost, a pouring out of the gifts and power to witness to the gospel so that the knowledge and love of God may fill all peoples and cultures?"

Drawing the participants' attention to the integrity and wholeness of both the conference and its theme, she called for great care in exploring the theme in its totality:

> This will not always be easy, for we tend to separate the two aspects of the theme. This diminishes its fullness. The theological affirmation that humankind, the churches and the cosmos are called to one hope through the reconciling and uniting love of Christ provides a lens through which to read the focus on gospel and cultures. Similarly, the dynamic interaction between gospel and cultures is an expression of and a search for the one hope offered by God in Christ Jesus. It will be important for us to keep the fullness of the theme before us.

Ms Langerak then provided an overview of the dynamics and flow of the conference, calling attention to the holistic nature of the programme, with each part intended to strengthen the other. The purpose of it all, as she put it, was to point to ways of concrete "engagement" in mission. It was hoped that the closing worship would be a decisive moment in the life of the conference, leading to fresh commitments in missionary obedience. "We anticipate that this will be a memorable act, a service in which we formally commit to God the fruits of the conference and in which we personally commit ourselves to carry back the spirit of our sharing and learning."

From exposure to engagement – the conference moves on

It was clear that any commitment to fresh engagement in mission would be the fruit of a process over the entire ten days of the conference. The nature of the theme clearly called for exposure to diverse cultural expressions of the gospel – and, indeed, *exposure* became the first of four phases of the conference. As the participants entered the conference venue they were drawn into an exhibition (in almost 30 booths) of the variety of ways Christians worship, witness and live out their faith, put together mainly by participants who had been involved in national or regional groups engaged in the gospel and cultures study process. This "Rainbow – Festival of Gospel in Cultures" included faith expressions of indigenous peoples; traditional (often non-Christian) art and music used in worship; icons and other powerful expressions of the liturgical heritage of Orthodox churches in different cultures; photographs, literature and other articles testifying to gospel witness in multireligious and intercultural contexts – some of which were painful signs of the cultural captivity of the gospel – and so on.

Exposure to cultural expressions of the faith, which continued throughout the conference in a variety of ways, led to the second phase of serious *encounter*, through dialogue with people from different cultures. To enable this, a series of 27 *Encontros* ("encounters") took place – in-depth presentations of the interaction between the gospel and specific cultural contexts by national/regional groups involved in the gospel and cultures study as well as by youth, women and indigenous people.

In the third phase of the conference, the participants began the *exploration* of the theme, "Called to One Hope – The Gospel in Diverse Cultures". This exploration began with theme addresses from two very different persons and perspectives: Metropolitan Kirill of Smolensk and Kaliningrad (Russian Orthodox Church) and Musimbi Kanyoro, a lay woman Lutheran theologian from Kenya. These were followed by two theme panels: "For Such a Time as This – Evangelism and Culture" (moderated by Emilio Castro, former WCC general secretary), in which four persons from diverse cultural contexts explored the nature of evangelism in relation to culture; and "Each in Our Own Language – The Bible in Context" (moderated by Konrad Raiser, current WCC general secretary), in which four others explored the task of interpreting the Bible in different cultures.

The participants then moved on to more sustained exploration of the theme through work in four sections, each considering a different aspect of the theme: (1) authentic witness within each culture; (2) gospel and identity in community; (3) local congregations in pluralist societies; and (4) one gospel – diverse expressions. Each section met in plenary and in sub-sections and most met in small groups as well, in nine sessions altogether. The report from each of the sections was discussed and adopted by that section and then presented to and received by the conference plenary.

As indicated above, the purpose of exploring the theme – and, indeed, of the entire conference – was to lead the participants to commit themselves and the churches and agencies they represented to fresh missionary obedience and to take new directions in mission in the next decade and new millennium. Thus the fourth phase of the conference, during its last two days, was that of *engagement*. The conference message and the seven acts of commitment – specific and "do-able" affirmations pointing to possible concrete mission actions – adopted by the plenary and used in the closing worship service, are indications of the participants' resolve to give a culturally relevant account of the hope to which they are called in Christ Jesus.

The entire flow and programme of the conference were thus envisioned so that – in the words of the prayer for the conference – "through it [God's] people may be strengthened in their cultural identity, renewed in their Christian life and equipped for authentic witness in each context" and led to "discern and celebrate the wondrous variety of expressions of the Christian faith and the unity that binds them together". The following sections of this report seek to witness to that intention and hope.

Part II

Conference Message

The conference on world mission and evangelism has met in Salvador, Bahia, Brazil, at a significant moment in history – the approach of the end of the century and of a new millennium.

Soon after the start of this century, the first comprehensive ecumenical mission conference took place in Edinburgh. It stated: "The work [of mission] has to be done now. It is urgent and must be pressed forward at once." The work of mission, however, did not turn out to be straightforward. Within four years of that conference the world was engulfed in war. Since then it has known massacres and mass deportations, another world war, the development of new forms of colonialism, life under nuclear threat, the destruction of ecosystems by human greed, the growth and collapse of the Soviet bloc, violent and separatist ethnic struggles, rampant capitalism leading to an ever-greater gap between rich and poor.

We believe that it is still the church's primary calling to pursue the mission of God in God's world through the grace and goodness of Jesus Christ. Yet this mission, history-long, worldwide, cannot be seen today in narrow ways – it must be an every-member mission, from everywhere to everywhere, involving every aspect of life in a rapidly changing world of many cultures now interacting and overlapping.

In conference here in Salvador, we have sought to understand better the way in which the gospel challenges all human cultures and how culture can give us a clearer understanding of the gospel. It would be difficult to find a more appropriate venue for such a conference. Brazil has the second largest population of people of African origin of any nation. Salvador is a microcosm of the world's diversity of cultures and spiritualities. Yet this very place made us aware of the pain and fragmentation that comes from the racism and lack of respect for other religions that still exist in sectors of the Christian churches.

The theme of the conference was "Called to One Hope – The Gospel in Diverse Cultures".

The hope of the gospel is expressed in the gracious coming of God in Jesus of Nazareth. From the day of Pentecost this hope manifests itself as the fruit of faith and in the struggle of the community of faith. It reaches out to all people everywhere. This conference has been a foretaste and impulse of this hope.

In the conference we have experienced much which has given us such hope:

- the wide diversity of peoples and churches represented (in Edinburgh in 1910 the large majority of the participants were European or North American; in Salvador over 600 Christians of a wide spectrum of cultures from almost 100 nations participated in the life of the conference);
- the genuine attempt which has been made to listen and to share ways and wisdoms across cultures;
- the thrill of participating in the life of a community where the voices of young and old, women and men from Christian churches around the globe have all been speaking out;
- the willingness of the churches and mission agencies to admit past failures and to refuse to engage in stereotyping, and the determination to stay together and work together for the good of our common mission;
- the solidarity of standing at the dockside in Salvador where, for 300 years, the African slaves who were still alive after their capture and deportation were unloaded. By the "Stone of Tears" together we wept tears of repentance;
- the encouragement of participating in the rhythm of daily worship where the honouring and use of different sounds and languages did not result in a divisive and confusing "babel", but rather gave a hint of the unity and inspiration of a Pentecost;
- the privilege of sharing for a short time in the life of a continent and people with a rich cultural history and a diversity of religious spirituality, whose churches are responding to the challenges of social change and poverty through the embodiment of gospel hope.

It is our profound hope that this last great mission conference of the 20th century has clearly illuminated that the gospel to be most

fruitful needs to be both true to itself, and incarnated or rooted in the culture of a people. We have had a first-hand experience of seeing and hearing Christians from many diverse cultures expressing their struggles and hopes.
- We have heard the cries of pain from indigenous peoples who have faced the near extermination of their communities and cultures, and we have marvelled at their resilience and their determination to make connections between their indigenous spirituality and their Christian faith so that their identity is not divided.
- We have heard the longing of women around the world for a real partnership in church and society.
- We have listened to the voices of young Christians telling us that they do not wish to be objects of the church's mission but full partners in the work of mission, particularly in relating the faith to the energy and aspirations of youth culture today.
- We have learned from our Latin American hosts the importance of "doing" theology which seeks to create a "community called church", which is rooted in the life of the people amongst whom the church is set, and which shows itself, for example, in their response to the plight of the street children in their cities.
- We have heard the voices of Christians in the Pacific who seek mutuality with their Christian partners from the West, insisting that full partnership in mission is reciprocal, not paternalistic.
- We have heard the anger of African people, Afro-Caribbean people, Afro-Latino people and African people of North America at the horror of slavery, and we have heard how the faith, though presented to them in distorted forms, became the hope of liberation. We have admired their determination not to be trapped in a lament over history but to cooperate together in a strengthened partnership between African people and people of the African diaspora.
- We have been moved by the stories of disaster and disease which led one speaker from Africa to say, "Times are ripe for flirting with hopelessness", and we have been astonished at the strength and determination of African Christians, women in particular, to share the pain of their people and to combat despair and plant the seeds of both food and hope.
- We have benefited from hearing of the long-term experience of Asian Christians of living a life of Christian discipleship in multifaith societies, sometimes as vulnerable and threatened minor-

ity groups. We have also heard of a surge of grassroots missionary activity.
- We have been moved by the experiences of Christians in the Middle East living with the privilege and pain of life in a "holy land" torn apart by division and injustice, and their indignation at the way in which biblical texts are misinterpreted so that their culture is blemished and some are made to feel strangers in their own land.
- We have admired the commitment of those from the Orthodox and other local churches in the former Soviet Union and Eastern Europe now determined, in the new atmosphere of religious freedom, to serve their people in such a way that the faith which sustained many through times of persecution might now be an equal blessing in times of new challenge. We have heard their protest at the ways in which rich foreign Christian groups are seeking to proselytize their people.
- We have recognized the caution of Christians in Germany about being too ready to see God's spirit in all human cultures, growing out of their painful memories of how the churches risked becoming captive to Nazi ideology in a previous generation.
- We have heard how the churches, against the background of the post-modern culture influencing much of Western Europe, are studying the phenomenon of secularism and engaging with those turning from traditional faith and seemingly seeking a private "pick-and-mix" spirituality.
- We have heard reports of the growing localism of North American churches which, while strengthening their commitment to mission and evangelism in their own context, may lead to an isolation and insulation from global realities.
- We have shared the concern of many at how the global free-market economy seems to exercise sovereign power over even strong governments, and how the mass media disseminate worldwide images and messages of every description which influence – and, some believe, undermine – community and faith.
- We have discussed how, perhaps as a reaction to these developments, new fundamentalisms are emerging in all world faiths, adding to the divisions in an already fractured world.
- We have heard how Christians in many places around the globe are engaging in serious dialogue with people of other faiths, telling the Christian story, listening attentively to the stories of

others, and thus gaining a clearer and richer understanding of their own faith and helping to build a "community of communities" to the benefit of all.

In such ways we have recognized how the church engages in mission with cultures around the globe today. What then would we want to emphasize from this conference?

- The church must hold on to two realities: its distinctiveness from, and its commitment to, the culture in which it is set. In such a way the gospel becomes neither captive to a culture nor alienated from it, but each challenges and illuminates the other.
- Perhaps as never before, Christians in mission today need to have a clear understanding of what God has done in history through Jesus Christ. In this we have seen what God requires of individuals, communities and structures. The biblical witness is our starting point and reference for mission and gives us the sense of our own identity.
- We need constantly to seek the insight of the Holy Spirit in helping us better to discern where the gospel challenges, endorses or transforms a particular culture.
- The catholicity of a church is enhanced by the quality of the relationships it has with churches of other traditions and cultures. This has implications for mission and evangelism and calls for respect and sensitivity for churches already located in the place concerned. Competitiveness is the surest way to undermine Christian mission. Equally, aggressive evangelism which does not respect the culture of a people is unlikely to reflect effectively the gracious love of God and the challenge of the gospel.
- Local congregations are called to be places of hope, providing spaces of safety and trust wherein different peoples can be embraced and affirmed, thus manifesting the inclusive love of God. For congregations in increasingly plural societies, inclusion of all cultural groups which make up the community, including those who are uprooted, marginalized and despised, is important. Strengthening congregations through a spirituality which enables them to face the vulnerability involved in this openness is critical.
- Small steps which involve risk and courage can break through barriers and create new relationships. Such steps are available to us all. They can be the "miracle" which changes a church or community's self-image and enables new God-given life to break forth.

Music at the conference has had a rhythm, a harmony, a beat. In a place with a deep African tradition it is natural that in our worship the beat of the drum has frequently been the vehicle to carry our souls to resonate with the beat of God's love for us and for all people. With hearts set on fire with the beat of mission and a prayer on our lips that many will share with us in being "Called to One Hope" and take and find "the Gospel in Diverse Cultures", we commend the fruits of the conference to Christians and churches everywhere. Our profound hope is that they too may be renewed in mission for the sharing of the knowledge of Christ, to the glory of the triune God.

Acts of Commitment

1

We, the participants in the Conference on World Mission and Evangelism in Salvador, Brazil, affirm that the truth of the gospel is challenging and relevant to all dimensions of life.

We therefore commit ourselves to unequivocal and cooperative witness to the gospel of hope in Jesus Christ in all contexts.

We shall continue to explore the truth of the gospel and its public relevance, particularly in cultures where religion continues to be relegated to the private sphere.

2

We affirm that it is only as churches seek the truth of the gospel in dialogue with each other that they may discern the fullness of God's reconciling work in Christ and the one hope to which they are called.

We therefore commit ourselves resolutely to continue in dialogue together even when we substantially differ in the way we comprehend and use the term "gospel" and understand the work of the Holy Spirit in all cultures.

We shall continue to strive together in mutual respect for greater clarity about and common understanding of the relation between the gospel and culture.

3

We rejoice that many churches are increasingly engaging in new forms of local and global mission. At the same time we note with pain that many new expressions of mission lead to unethical forms of coercion and proselytism which neither recognize the integrity of the local churches nor are sensitive to local cultures – and hence run counter to God's reconciling love in Christ.

We therefore commit ourselves to promote common witness and to renounce proselytism and all forms of mission which destroy the unity of the body of Christ.

We shall continue to seek together with others a framework for responsible relationships in mission.

4

We affirm that the Spirit poured out on the day of Pentecost makes all cultures worthy vehicles of the love of God and that no culture is the exclusive norm for God's relationship with humans. We also affirm dialogue as a vital mode of developing relationships, cultivating understanding and growing towards the unity to which all creation is called in Christ.

We therefore commit ourselves to seek out dialogue with others from diverse cultural and religious contexts, to subject our own culture to the critique of the gospel, and to be unwavering in our determination to sustain dialogue, even in the face of differences and disagreements.

We shall continue to explore the inter-relationship between our commitment to witness to Christ and our determination to dialogue with people of other faiths and cultures.

5

We affirm that God's inclusive love embraces and endows all people with inherent dignity on the basis of their creation in God's image, including those who have been stigmatized and discriminated against and those who have been marginalized and excluded from participation and self-expression. Many persons in oppressed groups internalize negative images of themselves, yet the Holy Spirit enables a real awakening of the image of God in them, and empowers them to live as persons of dignity and worth.

We therefore commit ourselves to confronting and working to transform oppressive structures and dynamics in the churches and in society which ignore, desecrate or assault the divine image in persons.

We shall continue to explore ways of resolving the tensions and overcoming the divisions which arise when churches are confronted with the legitimate aspirations of oppressed people.

6

We affirm the sovereignty of God and the Lordship of Jesus Christ over all areas of life, including economics, the media and the environment.

We therefore commit ourselves to the search for alternative models of community, more equitable economic systems, fair trade practices, responsible use of the media, and just environmental policies, in the perspective of the coming of God's reign of justice and peace.

We shall continue to explore ways in which the church can counteract the negative impacts of globalization and seek ways to place it at the service of all humanity and all creation.

7

We affirm that all Christians are called to participate in the mission of God in their various callings. Equipping the saints of God in local congregations for the work of mission and of ministry is crucial.

We therefore commit ourselves to ensuring that resources and relevant processes of formation for mission are available for all persons, especially youth.

We shall continue to explore fresh ways of drawing out the gifts of the Spirit in all members of the body of Christ, that they may fully participate in the total life and mission of the church.

Reports from the Sections

PREAMBLE

The section work of the eleventh conference on world mission and evangelism in Salvador, Bahia, Brazil, was informed by the WCC gospel and cultures study process, the conference preparatory papers, the "Rainbow – Festival of Gospel in Cultures" and "Encontros" (in which conference participants shared with each other the encounter of the gospel with their respective cultures), the Bible studies and the plenary sessions. It was against such a rich background of experiences that the section discussions took place and the section reports were written.

The purpose of world mission conferences is to assist the churches in the proclamation of the gospel of Jesus Christ and to contribute to their permanent renewal in mission. The conference theme, "Called to One Hope – The Gospel in Diverse Cultures", challenged each participant personally, calling for repentance, faith and a commitment to dare to confront, in the light of the gospel, the forces that deny hope and even life itself.

In the face of the forces of death rampant everywhere, the Christian hope which is rooted in the resurrection of Christ is the hope of new life that God in Christ promises to all. In a context of increasing fragmentation of human communities through narrow loyalties, the Spirit of unity poured out at Pentecost promises the hope of a new community in justice and peace, particularly for excluded and marginalized people. As creation continues to be defaced and sullied, the whole creation groans in labour waiting for its release from bondage (Rom. 8:21-24). The hope to which Christians are called will find its fulfilment in the fullness of the coming reign of God.

The theme was studied in four inter-related sections:

1) authentic witness within each culture;
2) gospel and identity in community;
3) local congregations in pluralist societies;
4) one gospel – diverse expressions.

Each section explored a cluster of issues, attempting to hold together the two parts of the theme: one hope, and the gospel in diverse cultures.

The reports use "gospel" in many different senses: the first four books of the New Testament; the message witnessed to in those four books; the experience of the story of Jesus as good news. Some use the term to refer to the liberative elements within their culture before they heard the gospel of Christ – "the gospel before the gospel". For others, "gospel" is equivalent to Christianity or to the whole Bible. In reading the reports it is important to discern how the word is being used.

The mission of the church is grounded in a vision of the triune God – Father, Son and Holy Spirit – the source and sustainer of the church's mission. This mission "cannot but flow from God's care for the whole creation, unconditional love for all people and concern for unity and fellowship with and among all human beings" (San Antonio, 1989, p.25). This theological affirmation offers an appropriate foundation for an exploration of the relationship between the gospel and cultures in the context of the church's calling to mission and evangelism as it approaches the new millennium. The reports are intended to serve not as definitive theological statements but as an invitation for continuing reflection as Christians seek to be faithful to the church's missionary calling into the 21st century.

I: Authentic Witness within Each Culture

A. DISCERNING THE SPIRIT AT WORK IN ALL CULTURES

Theological understanding of cultures

Speaking of "culture" evokes many different words, terms and concepts: food, environmental influence, architecture, art, language, relationships, sexuality, humour, sports, education, communication, politics, economics, power structures, conflict management, traditions, values, rituals, religion, worship, spirituality – indeed all aspects of human effort. There is no way of being human without participating in culture, for it is through culture that identity is created. Culture is both a result of God's grace and an expression of human freedom and creativity. Culture is intrinsically neither good nor bad; it has the potential for both – and is thus ambiguous.

Some Christians emphasize that culture is an aspect of God's creation and others that cultures are of human creation. This difference of viewpoint clearly allows for differing perceptions of gospel and culture issues. Common ground includes the following affirmations:
– Creation is the work of the triune God.
– Human beings are created in the image of God.
– Language, thought-forms and expressions are shaped by culture.
– God's word always reaches people through culture.
– The human response to God is always through culture.
– The gospel cannot be identified with particular cultures.
– Culture is not to be regarded as divine.
– No culture can claim to have grasped the fullness of God.
– As cultures increasingly interact with each other, it is possible for human beings to belong to more than one culture or to leave one culture and enter another.
– In the encounter between cultures a richer understanding of the divine mystery may unfold.
– As cultures change, new dimensions of God's presence and work may become known and expressed.

To celebrate God's presence in human cultures is to express the encounter between the human and the divine in all its richness and diversity.

The ambiguous nature of culture raises the question of discerning the work of the Spirit within culture. Most people would affirm that in many cultures the fruit of the Holy Spirit – "love, joy, peace, patience, kindness, generosity, faithfulness, gentleness and self-control" (Gal. 5:22-23) – as well as the pursuit of justice in human affairs, can be identified. Do these not testify to the presence of the Holy Spirit? All cultures, however, also exhibit evil: there are life-denying and oppressive elements in cultures which run counter to the fundamental values of human relationships. Sin is present in everything human, including culture. This does not mean that God is absent from these cultures; God is present in both judgment and grace in the midst of pain and suffering. The ultimate goal of God's activity in cultures is to bring about liberation, life and the knowledge of God for all (John 10:10; 17:3).

Religion, culture and gospel

How do religion and culture relate to each other? Religion – a system of beliefs and practices – is part of culture. Culture is related to religion in many different ways: religion can be imprinted in or intertwined with culture; culture can grow out of a particular religion; religion can be a directing dimension of culture, alienated from culture, in conflict with culture, denied by culture, rejected by culture or concealed in culture.

The biblical testimony concerning the relation between religion and culture is diverse. In the Hebrew scriptures we find on the one hand the influence of elements from other ancient cultures and religions, such as wisdom literature from other parts of the Old Testament world, and on the other hand strong rejection of some elements of the religions and cultures of Israel's neighbours. In the prophetic tradition, Israel's worship itself is sometimes denounced for its emphasis on religious rituals coopted from its neighbours, to the neglect of justice (cf. Amos 5:21-24).

Many testify to having seen glimpses of God's presence and activity as well as having recognized the fruit of the Holy Spirit in people of other religious traditions, and can with confidence sing the ancient hymn, *Ubi caritas et amor Deus ibi est*, "Where there is charity and love, God is present". However, we can never say exactly how God is at work in any religious community.

If God's work in other religio-cultural traditions is affirmed, there are consequences for Christian mission. The followers of other religious traditions should be listened to as they express their relationship to God in worship and witness.

This, however, does not diminish the missionary vocation of the church. Christians are called to witness to God's revelation in Jesus Christ and their communion with God in Christ in the fellowship of the Spirit. We are also called to give testimony to liberation from oppression and death through the resurrection of Christ, who in self-giving love became powerless and was tortured and killed so that all may have life. We cannot keep this to ourselves; God's Spirit urges us to invite people everywhere to share in this life.

The triune God has not left creation without a witness. As the San Antonio conference stated: "We cannot point to any other way of salvation than Jesus Christ; at the same time we cannot set limits to the saving power of God" (San Antonio, p.32). Christians prayerfully and humbly ask: To what extent may other religions be acknowledged as being expressions of God's mercy and grace found in Christ? At what points do these expressions appear to run counter to God's fullness, life and love in Christ? Some do not doubt that people of other faiths experience decisive moments of deliverance, integration and communion which come to them as gift, not achievement, and that these experiences are akin to what Christians experience as salvation in Jesus Christ. Others question whether such experiences attest to the fruits of the Spirit, the presence and grace of God in them. Can a distinction be made between a spirit which is present in the whole of creation, including forms of culture and religion, and the Holy Spirit? Herein the Christian understanding of the very identity of God is at stake. The Christian faith affirms that God is one, and therefore the spirit present in the cultures and religions of humanity in mercy and judgment may be said to be none other than the Holy Spirit, that is, the Spirit of God who is eternally united to the Son and to the Father. Such convictions lead some to ask whether the triune God is redemptively present even where the gospel is not preached and Jesus Christ is not named as Saviour and Lord.

All creation comes to be through the Word (John 1), coheres in him and achieves its restoration and perfection in him (Col. 1:15-20). The gospel is the good news that the light that enlightens all took on our human condition in the person of Jesus Christ; and that in Jesus Christ is given the gift of God's very self, sharing the joy and misery of all humanity, freeing from all forms of domination and condemnation, and inaugurating the restoration of all creation.

The missionary task is both to proclaim the good news of Jesus Christ and to invite people to recognize and experience his presence and work among them and to respond to him. In this way some aspects of other religions may be seen by Christians as preparation for the proclamation of the gospel (Acts 17:16-34). However, at times the proclamation of the gospel may lead to open conflict with other religious traditions. It is of utmost importance to discern whether this conflict is the result of a genuine confrontation with the gospel message or of missionary insensitivity to other cultures. The fact that many people have experienced the gospel as "bad news" – not least when Western cultures are seen as examples of Christian ideals – must not be forgotten. On the other hand, there are numerous examples of communities and individuals, especially women and marginalized groups in many societies, who have heard the gospel as a call to conversion to Jesus Christ, and have experienced this as a conversion to greater freedom and a new hope.

B. DYNAMIC INTERACTION BETWEEN GOSPEL AND CULTURE

The incarnation of Jesus Christ, as testified to in the gospel according to John (1:1-14), is basic to an understanding of the dynamic interaction between gospel and cultures. In becoming human, Jesus affirms, fulfils, challenges and transforms cultures. It is the life of Jesus the incarnate, lived out in the realities of a particular context, that illuminates the very nature of God's way of salvation, the gospel. But within the mutual interaction between the gospel and cultures, the gospel functions as the new and inspiring principle, giving rise to the renewal of cultures through the transforming work of the Spirit.

Gospel illuminating and transforming cultures
In identifying the gospel's role in illuminating and transforming cultures, "transformation" is understood in various ways:
– Transformation means that the gospel becomes incarnate in the culture in which it is proclaimed, just as the Word became incarnate in human flesh (John 1:14).
– The gospel gives culture an orientation towards the glory of God. Such transformation opens up both those who witness to and those who receive the gospel to turn towards the mystery of God and the reality of others, drawing out what is best in them and in their cultures.
– Transformation means being freed from the oppression of particular aspects of culture; for example, Paul on the road to Damascus (Acts 9:1-19) is freed from deeply rooted religious prejudgments and undergoes conversion.

- Transformation means purification of certain elements of cultures in which the gospel is proclaimed.
- Transformation implies the empowerment of people to gain deeper insights into both the gospel and their own culture.
- Transformation further implies that a missionary entering a different culture to proclaim the gospel must begin a journey of conversion in knowing, living and loving that culture.

The transformation brought by the gospel may be described as a lamp "that gives light to all that is in the house" (Matt. 5:15). Such transformations are taking place in different parts of the world, bringing new meaning to religio-cultural activities such as marriage ceremonies, funeral services, liturgical rites and rituals related to health and healing.

There is diversity of opinion regarding the distinction between the gospel and the cultural expressions of "gospels". For some, the gospel can only be derived from the person of Jesus Christ; there is only one gospel. For others, the gospel is accessible only through cultural forms, and human understanding of the gospel differs from person to person; any human talk about the gospel is therefore an articulation of one of the "cultural gospels". This matter requires further consideration and exploration.

Culture illuminating and incarnating the gospel

Biblical faith recognizes cultures other than the Hebraic, indicating that God can work through and within any culture. Yet there is only one gospel, manifested in many cultural expressions. Christian mission involves people gaining access to God's word in scripture in their own language and culture, and being empowered to interpret that scripture through the guidance of the Spirit.

The gospel may be made more accessible and given a deeper expression through human cultural activities. To affirm that cultures illuminate the gospel is to hold that culture, manifested in art and other forms of human creativity, enlightens and enhances our understanding of the gospel.

As Christians discern the gospel/culture dynamic, some cultural and cultic activities will be joyfully affirmed, others abandoned, others retained with changed meaning. God being active in judgment and in giving life, new dimensions of meaning will emerge so that each Christian community develops its particular worldview, lifestyle, cultic practice and ecclesial structures.

Not only can culture be used to express the meaning of the gospel but also, in a deeper sense, it can create values and give birth to new forms of human community.

Problems in the relationship between gospel and culture

The dynamic interactions between the gospel and cultures in human history have been both constructive and destructive. In many cases the gospel has illuminated and transformed particular cultures and has received illumination from and become embodied in them. But there are also cases in which the style of proclamation of the gospel has caused cultural alienation, because the culture has not been allowed to illuminate and give genuine expression to the gospel.

Because culture is constantly in flux and cultural expressions change from generation to generation, the interaction between the gospel and cultures must be a continuous process in every place.

Christians must be aware of the limitations of any culture, for there is always the danger of the gospel being domesticated and made captive to that culture. Similarly, there are situations where the gospel has been abused for political purposes or to exploit people.

Authentic interaction between gospel and cultures

Authenticity in witness has to do with the witness of persons of one culture to persons of another culture as well as the witness of a Christian community within its own cultural setting. In witness across cultures, those who witness must be faithful both to their own experience of Christ and to the cultural values and symbols of those to whom witness is given. The witness of a local church in its own community must be rooted in the culture of that community. The danger of inauthentic witness arises also when a church manifests loyalty to its cultural identity such that the gospel is made to serve the cultural interests of that church.

Different situations create different problems of identity. Some people live in places where numerous cultures interpenetrate and mix, and therefore their sense of cultural rootedness is confused (this "culture" is one that leaves people feeling rootless and in search of identity). Others come from a more clearly defined cultural background that gives a more secure identity.

All Christians have an identity and rootedness in Christ. Along with the need to understand the particularities of their different cultural locations, Christians need to affirm and strengthen the universal church, in which a common Christian identity is found.

True identity – the gift of the triune God – is strengthened as the scriptures lead Christians to a common faith in God, a common experience in the Spirit and a common hope in Christ, all expressed in diverse forms. The one hope portrayed in the scriptures includes both present liberation and the consummation of all things in Christ in glory.

C. VOICING THE GOSPEL: EVANGELISM TODAY

Christians today have much to share about evangelism that is either culturally sensitive or culturally insensitive. Culture-sensitive evangelism is facilitated by the task of pre-evangelism – a careful laying of the proper groundwork for discerning the appropriate time and place for proclaiming the gospel message.

A number of biblical texts offer helpful insights for the discussion on culturally sensitive evangelism. In Isaiah 61:1, for example, preaching and healing are brought together. The nurturing and selfless love of the evangelist is expressed in 1 Thessalonians 1:7-8: "We were gentle among you, like a nurse tenderly caring for her own children. So deeply do we care for you..." The motive of the evangelist is expressed in 2 Corinthians 5:14, "the love of Christ urges us on", and the humility of the evangelist in Philippians 2:5-8. The latter passage reminds us of the intimate relationship between "the messenger" and "the message" in evangelism as elsewhere. The events on the road to Emmaus (Luke 24:13-35) provide further insight into drawing alongside people in their journey. And in Mark 7:24-30, Jesus learns from a woman who remains in her own culture and religion; he does not ask her to change her religious loyalties – an example of living dialogue.

Greater discernment of the nature and values of a particular culture is important for Christians, especially in communities where there appears to be no separation between spirituality and culture. Some suggest that the integrity of the human person might be a more appropriate criterion for cultural discernment than the integrity of culture.

In the exploration of culture-sensitive evangelism, dialogue and cooperation in community development are seen as socially and culturally appropriate ways in which the gospel can be "made real". Dialogue does not, however, displace proclamation. As the San Antonio conference affirmed: "Witness does not preclude dialogue but invites it, and... dialogue does not preclude witness but extends and deepens it. Dialogue has its own place and integrity and is neither opposed to nor incompatible with witness or proclamation. We do not water down our own commitment if we engage in dialogue" (San Antonio, p.32).

Some suggest that a way of making non-intrusive contact with communities of other cultures is that of "presence". An effort is first made to get to know and understand people in that community, and sincerely to listen to and learn from them. A general sharing of interests, questions, objectives and priorities might follow. At the right time people could be invited to participate in the story of the gospel. In some cases silent solidarity may be the most appropriate form of Christian witness.

Others insist that there is no substitute for preaching the word. While acknowledging that Christian presence within communities is important, they also see the need for witnessing to the signs of the dynamic movement of the Spirit and actively voicing the gospel. What sometimes deters people from proclamation includes feelings of guilt about past styles of evangelism.

In contexts where the dominant culture is hostile to the proclamation of the gospel message, some suggest the need to provide a "safe space" for spirituality to germinate, where the Jesus story can be revealed.

In this connection the nature of the relationship between words and works in authentic evangelism is to be considered: whether witness or unconditional loving service can alone constitute authentic evangelism, or whether they always belong together. As San Antonio affirmed: "The 'material gospel' and the 'spiritual gospel' have to be *one*, as was true of the ministry of Jesus... There is no evangelism without solidarity; there is no Christian solidarity that does not involve sharing the message of God's coming reign" (San Antonio, p.26).

Honesty and openness are integral and vital to the process of evangelism. Of crucial importance is the integrity of all involved: the person offering the witness, the congregation or faith community to which the witness or messenger belongs, and the community to which witness is being offered, the social and cultural integrity of which must be carefully respected.

In relation to the authenticity and integrity of the missionary messenger, it is important that he or she act in a spirit and manner appropriate to the gospel, in a Christ-like way. For some, integrity is synonymous with faithfulness to the language and meaning of the scriptures and therefore has to do with the content of the gospel message. For others, integrity means a more general faithfulness to Jesus Christ.

Often missionaries present differing interpretations of the gospel. To the extent that this represents a faithful endeavour to address particular communities in ways appropriate to their differing (sub)cultures and understanding, this diversity may be healthy.

Some, however, find such differing interpretations problematic and contrary to the ideals of common witness. When Christians apply what has been learned about cultural sensitivity in the mission of the church to relationships between sister churches and among different parts of the same church, this diversity can be enriching and can promote unity.

Other problems in voicing the gospel may also be identified – for example, the manner of issuing of "the invitation" often used in popular/mass evangelism, which for some has misleading theological implications. In such situations it must be clear that it is Christ who extends the invitation and calls for a response.

CONCLUSION

Each culture has its own hopes. All such hopes are expressed in particular cultural perspectives. Any witness to God's offer of the eschatological hope in Christ must relate to the present hopes of the culture in which the witness is given. The gospel proclaims the victory of life over death through the risen Christ who has defeated death; our hope is to participate in "the power of his resurrection" (Phil. 3:10). The hope which underlies Christian mission is to help all people to come to know Christ and find salvation in him. Today hope has a face and a name and is alive. Christ is our hope.

II: Gospel and Identity in Community

INTRODUCTION

The gospel addresses all aspects of human life, including the structural dimensions of culture. In understanding the relationship between the gospel and cultures, the focus has often been on the symbols and values of particular cultures. In an exploration of the structural elements of culture in relation to particular groups within a society, it is necessary to hold together two reference points: identity (which may be defined in many ways, for example in terms of race, gender, ethnicity, age) and community.

Power has often been misused to crush the identities of marginalized and excluded persons and groups. The gospel – the good news of the saving love of God for all people made known in Jesus Christ – has also been misused by dominant groups to deny or distort the identities of people and to perpetuate marginalization. Many of these marginalized people, however, have found in the gospel empowerment for their struggle against life-denying forces.

Increasingly, tensions arise between different ethnic groups in a multicultural and multi-ethnic context. These ethnic tensions are often exacerbated by religion. The Christian faith has sometimes been misinterpreted and misused to reinforce the identity of one ethnic group over that of another, thereby leading to the fragmentation of community. But the gospel clearly promises community across ethnic and other boundaries. The imagery of "the body" in the New Testament undergirds such an understanding of community.

A further element of the structural dimensions of culture is globalization. Economic globalization promotes a single economic community focused on the accumulation of wealth – creating increasing poverty and unemployment and leading to the further marginalization of the poor and the exclusion of many. Economic globalization seeks to impose a single consumer identity throughout the whole world through corporate control, the media and technology. This process leads to a loss of self-identity. This form of homogenizing economic community which enriches the few and excludes many is contrary to the values of the gospel.

The conference theme speaks of the one hope to which Christians in their diverse cultures are called. This is a hope both for the restoration of creation and its liberation from bondage to the abuse to which it has been subjected (Rom. 8:19-23), and for the gathering up of all things in Christ (Eph. 1:10). In the early church in Jerusalem (Acts 2:42-47), people from diverse backgrounds experienced a foretaste of the hope which is to come within the new community, the church. There are today situations in which solutions seem impossible and hope is dim. In such cases Christians are called to a missionary presence, sharing in the suffering and thereby witnessing to the cross and to Christ's conquering of death.

It is the power of the Spirit which enables mission. This mission proclaims God's intention that all – with their languages and their cultural and spiritual heritages – should be affirmed as people of worth. Christian mission also has to do with identifying and even suffering with those whose identities have been denied. The liberating message of the gospel is not only that *the identity of each* is affirmed but also that all are taken beyond their own identity into *the one new community of the Spirit* (Acts 4:32-35).

Greater clarity is needed in describing this new community of the Spirit. Is it identical to the visible church as seen in the Acts of the Apostles? Or is it a wider community in the world, whose hallmark is love?

A. GOSPEL AND CRUSHED IDENTITIES

Marginalization through economic, political, social, cultural and religious forces is a reality in all societies. People are marginalized because of, for example, their age, gender, class, caste, race or ethnicity, and experience mutilation of their identities.

Groups which have been excluded and oppressed include the following:
- indigenous peoples;
- Africans in the diaspora;
- women;
- children (especially street children), youth, the elderly;
- persons who are casualties of economic, social and political wars (immigrants/migrants, refugees, those who make their living

from the garbage heaps of big cities, prostitutes, single and teenage mothers, drug-users, alcoholics, child labourers);
- poor, illiterate, unemployed or underemployed people, and those with skills inadequate for the high-tech demands of the current global market;
- persons living with HIV/AIDS;
- persons who are physically or mentally differently abled;
- persons with sexual orientations other than that of the majority in their society, and their advocates;
- religious minorities.

Many who suffer oppression are running out of hope because they continue to be exploited, excluded or ignored, and have internalized negative images of themselves projected by dominant groups within the culture. However, some of those who are denied full self-expression in society nonetheless live the Christian virtues of faith, hope and love. They find hope in the living Christ. Their struggle against oppression lies in their faith and hope that God loves them, sees their suffering and cares for them. They seek respect for their identity, to be understood and taken seriously. They do not see faith and hope as passive waiting for the future. Rather they believe that faith and hope give them power and creativity in their struggle for justice and fullness of life, both of which are central to the witness and mission of the church. As Christians they believe that all this *will* happen, because of power from God and from each other as they join in solidarity.

Indigenous peoples

Indigenous peoples in all parts of the world have suffered the decimation of their population by colonization and the loss of their culture and spirituality, which emphasize interconnectedness, solidarity and reciprocity with the whole of creation. These peoples, once so closely related to the land, today have only limited access to land and other resources, as well as to vital representation and decision-making within societal and church structures. The gospel communicated to these peoples was distorted insofar as its interpretation emphasized elements such as separation of the body and soul, and individualism rather than community.

We call on the churches to respect indigenous identities and to work towards the full participation of indigenous peoples in all aspects of church life. We affirm the following recommendations of the (November 1996) indigenous spirituality consultation, which called on the World Council of Churches and its member churches, ecumenical bodies and other churches to:

- be in solidarity with indigenous peoples, Afro-Latinos and Afro-Caribbeans irrespective of faiths and traditions and to walk with us in respect;
- work in partnership with indigenous peoples, Afro-Latinos and Afro-Caribbeans to re-examine their history of absolutism, verticalism and intolerance and to reconstruct the spiritualities and theologies of the church, eliminating all expressions of Christianity that practise aggression against indigenous spiritualities;
- promote the meaningful participation of indigenous peoples, Afro-Latinos and Afro-Caribbeans within all church structures and decision-making levels, allowing for full and equal partnership among indigenous and non-indigenous members;
- promote the development of curricula and the teaching by indigenous people of their own spiritualities and theologies in church-related educational institutions;
- empower indigenous peoples, Afro-Latinos and Afro-Caribbeans and accompany them in advocating indigenous social justice issues for self-determination and land rights.

We affirm that many of the above recommendations apply to other marginalized groups as well.

Youth

Young people (especially young women) searching for their identity and role in the church and society have often felt ignored and patronized by older people, who sometimes refuse to enter into dialogue on matters of faith and other issues relevant to youth.

We call on the churches to commit themselves to full ministry with young people, to teach them and learn from them, to trust them and accept them as active partners in the church and its mission, rather than treating them as objects of mission.

Many young Christians live out their faith in alienating cities and fragmented cultures and struggle with the fracture between generations. Only as churches become fully rooted in their societies will they be able to address the issues that particularly affect youth today. Increasing numbers of young people in this post-modern era are afraid of the future, unemployed, manipulated by the media and market forces, bewildered by the competing/conflicting Christian cultures and unable to reconcile the gospel of Jesus Christ with the traditional practices of the churches as they experience them. In this context we call on the churches to bear witness to the resurrection hope.

Young people are distressed by the past sins and present failings of Christian community and Christian mission. They call for a church which not only knows how to use words but which loves the living Word, and so includes and loves young people. Indigenous young people especially are often torn between their cultural identity and their Christian calling.

We call upon the churches to act concretely insofar as they are able, to support (financially and otherwise) the training and education of young people to equip them for the demands placed upon them.

Women

Men and women in the churches are encouraged to recognize each other's worth and identity and to work in partnership. We affirm the work of the Ecumenical Decade of the Churches in Solidarity with Women, which has raised awareness of structures and practices in church and society that have prevented the full participation of women. The churches need to denounce violence against women and children and to be aware that most acts of violence take place in the home.

The churches are called to commit themselves to developing women leaders who will take responsibility and exercise leadership within the church. They are also encouraged to help create space where women's voices can be heard, both as women and within the community of men and women. For reconciliation to take place the pain that women have borne for generations must be shared and heard. Where possible, collaborative relations should be established with secular agencies which are working with and for women.

* * *

As churches seek to relate to marginalized people and to enable their empowerment, they are called to:
- encourage such people to see themselves as sons and daughters of God rather than as victims;

II: Gospel and Identity in Community 45

- enable Christians to affirm all people in their community as "beloved of God";
- welcome into the life of the church community people living with HIV/AIDS, providing support for them and their families and friends especially in times of sorrow and grief;
- act in solidarity with groups excluded from their economies because of policies of the World Bank, International Monetary Fund, etc.;
- establish ministries among peoples devastated by inter-ethnic strife;
- develop styles of leadership that foster community.

It is also important to place emphasis on programmes that enable Christians, especially marginalized groups, to reread the Bible from the perspective of their own cultural context. Such programmes may include:
- enabling other members of the church to hear the Bible interpreted from the perspective of oppressed people;
- helping Christians to understand that certain biblical texts have been used to justify oppressive practices, and to deal with them in such ways that the Bible becomes a force for liberation and life.

In relation to the above, we commend again to the churches for study and action the sections of the WCC document "Mission and Evangelism – An Ecumenical Affirmation" (1982) which deal with doing mission "in Christ's way".

B. GOSPEL, ETHNICITY AND IDENTITY POLITICS

Migrations and other movements of people throughout history and up to our time have made homogenous societies a rarity. Nearly every society today is becoming increasingly multicultural, multireligious, multi-ethnic and multilingual. This has led in many cases to a renewed and intensified claiming of ethnic identities, with a rise in mutual suspicion, tension and hostility. Often this manifests itself in efforts by people belonging to one ethnic group to dominate another politically... Ethnicity refers to a collective group awareness shaped by factors like ancestry, homeland, language, culture and religion...

Most often, perhaps, ethnicity becomes divisive and conflictual when a group feels its identity and survival threatened by social, economic and political forces. The sociological make-up, demographic realities and geographical location of a group may evoke memories of old historical conflicts and bring about new ones. Distorted images of those who are ethnically different, portraying the other as dangerous and even demonic, exacerbate such conflicts. Religious symbols and myths reinforce the divisiveness of ethnicity (Salvador preparatory papers, p.31).

The church is called to proclaim the gospel in such a way that people of different ethnicities are invited to respond in faith and are invited to receive the gift of the Holy Spirit, who incorporates them into the body of Christ. Each is given a new identity as a daughter or son of God. Each is bound by love to the other as parts of one body. Yet each part has its own identity. If one part hurts, the whole body feels pain. The whole body shares Christ's openness and vulnerability.

Identities thus ought not to be constituted defensively, in competition with or in fear of others, but rather must be understood as being complementary and of intrinsic value, for all people are children of God. Christians are called to see the face of God in others, as all are called to be part of the one body.

The gospel reconciles and unites people of all identities into a new community in which the primary and ultimate identity is identity in Jesus Christ (Gal. 3:28).

Ethnicity and identity politics

Identity politics exists when elements constituting the identity of one segment of a society are used as leverage for political power and socio-economic advantage over against other segments. Identity politics is problematic because this way of using identity is based on exclusivity. Identity politics leads people to understand identity as static and impermeable rather than fluid and open to change. This is particularly the case when, for example, ethnicity is used as a highly politicized concept by one ethnic group to organize itself and to perpetuate its own interests at the expense of other ethnic groups.

Ethnicity is a valuable gift of God. The varieties of ethnic belonging and identity – when they remain open to and respectful of others – are to be affirmed and valued.

Some churches, however, have supported identity politics, legitimizing community-destroying concepts of identity which have led to violence and war. Churches identified with a particular ethnic group should not allow this to reinforce the controlling, dominating and destructive effects of identity politics. Rather, the churches are called to raise their voices on behalf of minority identities – specifically, vulnerable groups of marginalized people, including women, youth and children. We condemn utterly the use of systematic rape as an instrument of war and of identity politics.

The mission of the church in relation to ethnicity is to enable every person to experience love and acceptance as a child of God. This will be helped by:
- creating space in worship, pastoral care, education and other areas of church life for experiences and encounters to enable people to see the face of God in "the other";
- enabling personal encounter and intercultural learning processes among people of different ethnic belongings;
- providing authentic information about "the other", particularly in situations of tension and conflict;
- enabling processes of non-violent resolution of conflict;
- advocating and allocating resources for peace research and training for mediation in areas of conflict.

God wills fullness of life for all people. The church's understanding and actions related to ethnic identity must therefore be measured by criteria of justice, freedom, participation, non-violence and self-reliance. As in the body of Christ special honour is given to the weaker parts, justice for the poor, neglected and marginalized and protection of the human rights of people of all ethnicities are a precondition and sign of the community for which the church yearns.

Nation-state, nationalism and ethnicity

The boundaries of modern nation-states have been defined through war, conquest, colonization and treaties. For many countries in Latin America, Africa and Asia these boundaries were drawn by colonial powers, often with support from the churches, in a way that separated tribes, ethnic groups and even families. As a result these national identities are often artificial; and attempts to maintain them have sometimes involved the dominance of a single ethnic or religious group or the creation of a homogenized "national" culture which denies the rights of other groups... Many minority peoples have had their sense of "nation" violated by the influx of a new majority (Salvador preparatory papers, pp.34-35).

While the identity and integrity of some nation-states is threatened by divisive internal forces, the major threat in other cases comes from international or global forces. Since the process of globalization seems unavoidable, the churches should work to ensure the preservation of ethnic values which enrich life in community. The positive values of ethnicity and sovereignty of peoples and nations in the face of the forces of globalization are to be affirmed.

Actions which the churches and ecumenical bodies could take in this respect include:
- Churches in which there are ethnic minorities and/or indigenous peoples should be encouraged to include study of ethnicity and ethnic values in their programmes of theological formation, and to include people from such minorities in decision-making structures and delegated representations.
- The human rights desks of the churches and councils of churches should be encouraged to develop strategies of advocacy for indigenous groups who have lost their lands to economic exploitation.
- The churches should become familiar with separatist movements and challenge or support them as appropriate through international networking and advocacy for the rule of justice and peace.
- The WCC should study political situations involving ethnicity with the aim of strengthening the peace-making and human rights efforts of the churches, giving special attention to the resolution of violent conflicts.
- The WCC should support international agencies in mediating boundary disputes through dialogues and referenda involving regional and local government representatives, leaders of the ethnic groups concerned and the general public.

Uprooted peoples

The movement of people for political and economic reasons has been a continuing phenomenon for centuries. Wars, natural and environmental disasters and long-term political and economic upheavals continue to create millions of refugees, migrants and asylum-seekers... Many people whose religious and cultural background is different from the majority in the country in which they now live represent the second and third generation in their adopted countries. But the response to their presence has been increased xenophobia, hatred and violence, along with ever more restrictive laws to control immigration as governments throughout the North close their borders. These people of different cultures experience many kinds of oppression and exploitation (Salvador preparatory papers, p.36).

The church's involvement with uprooted people has largely focused on social services and assistance. While affirming the importance of this role, the churches should also exercise a prophetic role, analyzing the causes of uprootedness and engaging in advocacy.

In view of the large numbers who are uprooted by war, interethnic violence, persecution and natural disasters, the churches are called:
– to exercise constant vigilance to enable uprooted peoples to cross national frontiers for the sake of survival;
– to listen to, learn from and be changed by uprooted people, their stories and experiences, praying for and with them, and welcoming them into the community;
– to stand with and aid those who have been deprived of their basic human rights due to lack or denial of legal documentation;
– to bring together representatives of immigrant groups and governments to work for the improvement of the lives of uprooted people;
– to make special efforts on behalf of immigrant youth, who often find themselves straddling two cultures and having to take on parental responsibility for younger siblings.

Even those deemed by the authorities to be in a country illegally are children of God. The basis for rule of government must be justice for all, protecting the welfare of the poor and ensuring that the basic needs of all are covered. "The alien who resides with you shall be to you as the citizen among you; you shall love the alien as yourself" (Lev. 19:34).

Questions and tensions

Diversity of denominational and theological backgrounds leads to a variety of responses to questions such as the following:
– What constitutes Christian identity? What are the marks? What are the criteria for membership in the body of Christ?
– Are all people called to be part of the body of Christ? Are there ways other than through Jesus to answer God's call?
– What does being members of the one body imply for relations between churches of different ethnic backgrounds?

C. GOSPEL, GLOBALIZATION AND LOCAL COMMUNITIES

People everywhere are increasingly faced with the impact of globalization. The churches need to discern those elements of this process which are liberative and those which are destructive. On an economic level globalization is likened to invasion and colonization, controlled mostly by policies of bodies like the International Monetary Fund, World Bank and World Trade Organization. At the base of globalization is the liberalization of the economy at both the national and international levels – more or less voluntarily in the North, and forced by structural adjustment programmes imposed on the nations of the South, particularly those with crippling external debt. Globalization is accompanied by intensified competition which privileges the powerful and further marginalizes and excludes the weak, who are blamed for the circumstances resulting from this exploitation.

Not only is globalization an economic matter but it furthers the racial divide, creating global "apartheid". The policy-makers of the transnational corporations and international financial institutions are largely from North America, Europe and Northeast Asia. Those who suffer the most violent and devastating impact of globalization policies are the peoples and nations of the South, and the South in the North. The market enriches a few and makes many poor. Large numbers of people are excluded.

Greater economic polarity is the result, with increasing violence, political instability, migration and displacement. Economic migration often leads to xenophobic backlash, manifested in tougher immigration policies and the sanctioned oppression of all who can be placed in the role of "the other" by virtue of race/ethnicity/indigenous status, age, gender or sexual orientation. These dislocations in national economies lead to the break-up of families, as breadwinners (female and male) receiving bare subsistence or below-poverty-level wages are forced to relocate for survival. Recognizing the negative impact of the policies and conditions of the international financial institutions does not release from responsibility those in the South who are the beneficiaries of these decisions. By their silence and acceptance of these privileges, they become co-conspirators in the sin of exploitative globalization.

A further aspect of globalization has to do with the degradation of the environment, which calls for urgent strategizing and action.

Increasingly people are recognizing that they live in a world in which "what goes around comes around". Globalization has led to a situation in which one country's pollutants create death in other countries. Communities everywhere are facing the effects of, for example, the excessive use of fossil fuels and problems related to the production of nuclear energy. Attention must thus be given to the development of alternative renewable fuel resources. The dearth of firewood in many countries of the South, partly as a result of deforestation, has put stress on women who have to search farther and farther afield for fuel for cooking and to provide warmth. Deforestation also affects the course of rivers and the availability of water. This in turn affects community life, contributing to the rural-urban exodus, particularly of young people.

Information technology is the most powerful instrument of the process of globalization. Information and messages communicated through the media – satellite television, advertising, films and computer technology (including the World Wide Web and electronic mail) – shape the identity of the world community as a whole and influence the identity of local communities and cultures. The media globalization effort and its message are driven by those who control the world market. That message suggests that there is redemption through consumption, that the ability to consume means success, and that "being connected" means "being community" – in contradiction to the gospel's understanding of a community of live connectedness as being God's hope for God's people. More importantly the media often objectify and commodify women and stereotype racial/ethnic groups and gays and lesbians, debasing and degrading all. They tend to give youth a false image of being invincible, portraying technology as a source of wisdom.

The Internet and other communication systems hold the potential of enabling communication and solidarity among oppressed peoples. We call upon the churches to work towards a new communication order which challenges unjust power structures and allows the voices of the people to be heard.

We call upon the churches to examine the meaning of the gospel and its values vis-a-vis the destructive forces of globalization and the market. The Christian claims concerning the sovereignty of God stand in opposition to the totalitarian pretensions of the market economy. Christians must declare their opposition on theological grounds to any idolization or absolutization of the market. The messianic claims of the market and the consumerist life-style are in sharp conflict with the Christian confession that Jesus Christ is Lord. The churches should not be intimidated by globalization and cultural imperialism, but rather should confront the "centres of power" with the power of the gospel.

The churches need to reaffirm that God's purpose includes liberating all people from all forms of exploitation and exclusion so that they can live and share their lives in freedom and justice. We call upon the churches to support communities and groups which are resisting the exploitative and exclusionary dimensions of globalization.

We call upon the churches to work towards alternative models of community development, economic systems and fair trade practices, and to strengthen bodies such as the Ecumenical Church Loan Fund and the Ecumenical Development Cooperative Society.

We call upon the churches to be ever mindful of the biblical calling to care for the creation. Christian stewardship demands a just sharing of the earth's resources.

We call upon the churches to examine ways of counteracting the globally conveyed cultural images which have a homogenizing effect on homes, communities and churches the world over. The churches should work towards a more equitable balance of power in communication, with genuine two-way cultural sharing, in which the weaker parties are neither exploited nor their identity distorted. Moreover, the churches must do all they can to counteract negative images of oppressed people, for such people carry within them the image of God.

We call upon the churches to affirm the value of face-to-face contact. They should avoid being seduced into using the methods of the market in the church and in evangelism. The nature of the church's participation in the communication process within the global culture and economy should be carefully considered.

We call upon the WCC to re-examine its policy of providing translation/interpretation into only European languages, in order to make its work accessible to people who do not know these languages and to enable them to participate more fully in ecumenical gatherings. We are reminded that the churches at times have themselves been involved in imposing a single culture on other parts of the world, for instance during the colonial mission period, thus participating in the process of cultural imperialism.

CONCLUSION

The churches need to be empowered for culture-sensitive evangelism which takes seriously people's history and cultures. Thus will the gospel be proclaimed through people's own cultural symbols, myths and rituals, stories and festivals.

When Christians are prepared to cross cultural frontiers in openness to the Spirit, the mission of God in Christ advances as they meet each other in giving and receiving, teaching and being taught, understanding and being understood.

III: Local Congregations in Pluralist Societies

INTRODUCTION

After long years of encounter between a visiting pastor and a prisoner, the latter decided to accept Jesus Christ as Lord and Saviour. When the man was eventually able to leave his cell and recover freedom, the pastor was worried: would the congregation accept the former prisoner and include him fully in its life? The same kind of question had already been raised by Paul in his letter to Philemon and the church meeting in his house: would Onesimus feel that the liberating power of the gospel he had discovered in prison with Paul was real when he came back to the place from whence he had fled?

These examples show how essential is the role of each local congregation in God's mission. Like the early church in Acts, it has the privilege to live in joy the presence of the risen Christ and is called to embody as community the priorities set by Jesus in his own life. For many people, acceptance or refusal to become members of a church is linked to positive or negative experiences in or with a local congregation, which can be either a stumbling-block or an agent of transformation. It must be added, however, that Christian networks, solidarity groups, student and youth movements, urban rural mission-related groups, women's movements and others often play as important a role in the front lines of mission as do local congregations. The personal witness of Christians in family, workplace and society is also irreplaceable.

Exploration of the conference theme includes a consideration of the role of the local congregation in inculturating the gospel, making the gospel meaningful in its own context and expressing the inclusive nature of God's mission in the world to reconcile and unite all creation and humanity with God.

A. INCULTURATING FAITH IN LIFE

The conference theme speaks of a common hope, implying that our common hope is in Jesus Christ. We work together towards a renewed understanding of our common mission. As witnesses to the good news, we understand that our worship plays a crucial role in the building of strong spiritual community.

We begin with the humble statement that the scriptures are a divine source of good news. We encourage a wider dissemination of the Bible in many languages, placing in people's hands and hearts the tools for understanding and growing in faith. The moment scripture reaches its audience it is contextual. From the language in which it is read to the methods of interpretation employed and the kinds of authority attributed to it, scripture offers rich variety to a diverse humanity. From our distinct cultures and with a commitment to making the Bible accessible, we would promote its reading in an intercultural way. In our rich diversity, we may also find a richer understanding of the sacred texts.

In the church's liturgical life, culture and gospel interact and transform, illumine and challenge each other, shaping people for mission. People come to worship God using the eyes and ears of their culture, and through these same eyes and ears they may glimpse God's smile and hear the echo of God's voice. Along with the scriptures and worship, the sacraments mediate the real presence of the Holy Spirit in our worshipping communities – a presence which is also experienced in funerals and other rites, on pilgrimage, etc.

Symbols speak to the heart and to the mind. They are windows to heaven and help us relate to the divine. When we speak of symbols we recognize two rough overlapping categories: cultural symbols and cross-cultural symbols. We share a variety of symbols and images throughout Christianity, and at the same time cultural specificity dictates how these and other symbols will be incorporated into the environment of worship. Cultural history, values and aesthetics will influence the incorporation of these elements into meaningful worship – for example, the arrangement and ornamentation of worship space.

In exploring worship and cultures, there are two perspectives which are both complementary and contradictory. On the one hand, it is essential that Christian communities be (re)educated to receive anew the ancient and universal symbols. Too often Christians are unable to understand the fullness of the rich tradition with which they have been gifted. Many worshippers are unaware of the full meaning of the symbols which adorn their sacred spaces, and do not reflect on the significance of, for example, the hymns; thus they are not fully prepared to meet God in the traditional symbols and rituals. For many, learning to read icons and understanding liturgical forms and rituals can be greatly enriching and empowering. The churches must take seriously the task of education – particularly of children and youth (much of this has been taken on by laywomen) – so that liturgical symbols and theological concepts might become more accessible and better understood.

On the other hand, churches which have emerged from a colonial history have much work to do in reclaiming the symbols of their own cultures and relating them to their present experience of the sacred. For centuries, Christian societies conquered territories and used violence against local peoples, destroying their life and culture and taking their land. Too often what was holy for many communities – music, gesture, language – was put away from the churches. This calls churches today to repentance for a history in which the indigenous experience of encounter with the divine has been suppressed and rejected. Any missiology which encourages encounter with another culture, tradition or local church without showing respect for the relationship to the divine which is already at work there, must be critiqued. Even within a specifically Christian context, if the gospel is to penetrate and take root in the society it must be grounded in the people's own sense of holiness. The churches are therefore called to participate in the dismantling of all unjust structures which depreciate and dehumanize people.

With regard to the task of liturgical renewal, many Christians struggle to maintain a creative tension (particularly in worship) between the preservation of traditions and their meaning, and the renewal of liturgy relevant to the context, including freedom for spontaneity and expression of emotions. Those who have contributed to and are engaged in the task of liturgical renewal are to be commended, and need the prayers of all that their work will remain Spirit-filled.

In many congregations there exist power structures which diminish the place and influence of women, youth, so-called lower classes, ethnic and immigrant groups. Among those who are least respected are children and differently abled people. Even when potentially important decision-making positions are held by women, young people or members of minority groups, what they say is often not really taken into consideration because of the inferior status given to their input. This also affects the powerful oppressor, for example, men in male-dominated systems, who by their attitudes and actions dehumanize themselves.

It is essential for the church's renewal that steps be taken towards the empowerment of youth. Youth need to be engaged in mission, in liturgical renewal and in decision-making processes, thus sharing in the task of discerning the movement of the Spirit. The proposal to ensure 25 percent representation of youth in church bodies and related activities must be borne in mind. Their place within decision-making bodies at local and other levels must also be guaranteed, even if this requires structural changes and amendments to rules. What are the ways in which space can be provided for young people in the churches at all levels so that they feel fully part of Spirit-filled communities? Many elements of youth cultures should be recognized as valid cultural expressions. To encourage young people to remain in their countries and cultivate strong links with their church, people and culture, it may be helpful for the churches to participate in programmes creating employment for youth.

The inculturation of the gospel also involves enabling the empowerment of oppressed people both within and beyond the church, such as women and the Dalits in India. Dominant groups such as men who hold power in a local congregation may need to question their styles of leadership and change their ways of relating, in order that renewal of the common life and healing of relationships may be made possible. The role played by church leadership in the discernment of the Holy Spirit should be carefully examined. How can the congregational leadership become stepping-stones rather than stumbling-blocks in the process of renewal in the power of the Holy Spirit?

The Holy Spirit can touch anyone in any culture and context. Yet the fact that so many Christians have left their church communities because they have not been able to see the Spirit at work there is troubling. How can the church both prepare people for meeting God and also remove the stumbling-blocks which any culture – but specifically dominant and colonial cultures – has placed as obstacles to the movement of the Spirit?

Important missiological work into the next century will include giving more attention to the discerning of the presence and work of the Holy Spirit. Through this the church may become more self-critical in relation to its use of symbols, its practices and its presence in the world. A set of criteria for discerning the presence of the Holy Spirit is found in 1 John 4. They include the fact that the Spirit bears witness to Jesus Christ as Lord, that the Holy Spirit must be discerned *in community*, and that Spirit-inspired actions build up community, bearing fruits of love, unity, justice and peace.

B. BECOMING SIGNS OF GOD'S INCLUSIVE LOVE

The challenge to transform the life of the local congregation faces individual Christians as they function in this primary unit of faith expression. The challenge of facing the inconsistency between the verbal expression of faith and its practice in each person's own experience is often uncomfortable. However, provoking a healthy and challenging discomfort in this respect in the life of local churches everywhere is desirable.

The local congregation is meant to be a community of fellowship flowing from the all-embracing love of the God it serves. In the African "economy of affection", receiving the other is to the benefit of all: you are because I am – I am because you are. Each is enriched by receiving and affirming the other. The stranger may be the one bearing the gifts, even the very gift of the Holy Spirit.

For the church to become inclusive, it must recognize that its hopes are not the only hopes expressed in the world. In a world filled with hopelessness, people everywhere desire hope. Jesus Christ

embodies hope for all the world. What is the content of this hope in the concrete realities in which local congregations live?
- It is the hope in the mystery (surprise) of resurrection, the renewal of life in which strength can be found for all needs.
- It is the hope that each human being will recognize his or her worth before God and will strive for the healing and wholeness of each person and of the community.
- It is the hope that God's reign of righteousness, justice and peace will be experienced on earth as human beings undergo a fundamental transformation wrought through God's grace and become Christlike.
- It is the hope, founded in Christ's triumph over evil, that the principalities and powers will not triumph but that the will of God shall prevail.
- It is the hope of Christ's coming in fullness and of the final unity of all things in God, who is "all in all" (1 Cor. 15:28).

Christians have a specific calling, but the hope God offers is for all. This truth provides the missionary imperative for the church in the 21st century. The church is called to be the vehicle through which this hope is communicated to the world.

Evangelism is the joyful communication of hope, the proclamation and sharing of a life of hope; people both inside and outside the church need to hear this gospel of hope. Evangelism is a reaching in and a reaching out, proclaiming the gospel in words and actions. Through the witness of congregations and of individual Christians, the gospel can penetrate society and transform culture – even secularized culture – acting as a liberating force in contexts of hopelessness or of struggle for dignity and justice.

Though local congregations are called to be people of promise, witnessing to a common hope for all humanity, in reality they often express fear of the unknown and uneasiness with those who are racially, ethnically or culturally different. Some of these fears are born of ignorance as well as people's need to preserve their own identity. Churches, like many other social organizations, desire homogeneity and often find groups that are different "threatening". Such situations arise as communities become increasingly multicultural and the needs of migrant groups, for example, confront them, or when the community has to relate to persons with a sexual orientation other than that of the majority. The church must be willing to confront cultural arrogance or racism, especially within its own body. Christians can learn from the encounter of Peter and Cornelius in Acts 10 how those who are "different" can be God's instruments as well.

Trust is not possible where fear reigns. Some churches long for sufficient trust to be able to embrace the unknown or the different. This trust is the gift of the Holy Spirit, who has the power to transform and unite.

Individuals and groups need to feel that they are fully respected as the persons they are and that their identity is affirmed – particularly when they are different from the majority in a local situation. When it is evident that congregations have merely "accommodated" or "made provision for" those among them who are different, the latter are likely still to feel unaccepted. Therefore care should be exercised by the majority to demonstrate true acceptance and an inclusivity which witnesses to Christ's all-embracing love.

In this the church is challenged as to whether its raison d'etre is more its mission of sharing and living the gospel, which includes serving the needs of humanity, or rather the preservation of its own identity. In what ways are these – the call to share the gospel and serve humanity and the desire to preserve the church's identity – in tension or in symbiotic relationship with each other? What are the values by which the church lives? What standards must be upheld at all cost, including the cost of self-giving love?

Before the church – and the local congregation – can become a household of joyful cooperation in accomplishing its task within the mission of God, walls will have to be dismantled. One way to start doing this is by entering into authentic contact with those who have been excluded. In many places the young people may already have indicated their frustration by refusing to be part of the worshipping community. By taking the youth seriously, engaging in authentic dialogue with them and learning from their openness to those "outside", local congregations may break down some of the walls.

Other ways have been suggested:
– Where distinct communities exist along racial or ethnic lines within a local congregation, encouraging them to celebrate together the multicultural richness of the church as a privilege and as a gift of God.
– Encouraging different language groups in a congregation, though they may worship in separate parts of a church building or at different times, to come together for social interchange.

- Developing various forms of church membership to accommodate people from different backgrounds.
- Making provision for language training for clergy (appropriate to the context), including time spent in other cultural milieus.
- When change in a congregation is called for, ensuring adequate discussion among all sectors concerning what is essential and what may be negotiable.
- Promoting intercultural Bible-reading among Christians from different backgrounds, in order for them to be enriched mutually in their understanding of the gospel of Jesus Christ – thus demonstrating how other cultures throw new light upon the scriptures.

Living with people from many different cultures is an emerging ministry which recalls the life of the early church, and is a foretaste of the "household of God" towards which we all move.

Churches giving common witness in an ecumenical spirit of mutual respect and accountability is yet another sign of God's inclusive love. As the WCC document "Mission and Evangelism – An Ecumenical Affirmation" (1982) states: "Witness that dares to be common is a powerful sign of unity coming directly and visibly from Christ and a glimpse of his kingdom" (para. 24). Congregations are called to cooperate locally in mission and not to compete. It is imperative for churches and local congregations involved in cross-cultural witness in another context to cooperate with churches in that context, recognizing that all are part of one ecumenical family. Such cooperation has become more and more urgent in recent years, as the free-market ethos increasingly influences the mission practice of Christian communities and individuals.

C. WITNESSING IN RELIGIOUSLY PLURAL SOCIETIES

Local congregations everywhere are called to give account of the hope of a restored human community in Christ, especially in situations of increasing religious plurality. Exploring facets of this call and ways of equipping Christians for this ministry is thus vital.

Issues confronting human communities open up opportunities for people of different faiths to enter into dialogue. In central India, for example, people came together to rebuild after an earthquake, in spite of the then-prevalent communal tensions between Hindus and Muslims following the destruction of the Babri mosque by Hindu

III: Local Congregations in Pluralist Societies

militants. In contexts such as so-called post-modern societies, all religions are faced with the challenge posed by a culture which has rendered neutral the question of truth, understanding pluralism in itself as *the* truth. In such cultures, religion is relegated to the private sphere. We affirm that the search for justice and peace and the search for truth are at the core of human life and community relations. Dialogue is thus essential where people struggle to remain human.

Before entering into dialogue with other religious communities, with individuals searching for meaningful religious experience or with those of no faith, a local congregation should be clear about its own identity in Christ, for dialogue implies that Christians bear witness to their experience of the good news of Jesus Christ.

But mission must be "in Christ's way" (San Antonio, 1989). People were called by Jesus to *follow* him; but not all were called to *respond* in the same way. There were many types of relationships with Jesus, depending upon one's commitment, humility, faith, etc. In mission there is place both for announcing the name of Jesus Christ and for dialogical relations with people of other faiths.

To dialogue is to witness to the love of God revealed in Christ. This requires mutual respect and openness to learn from others. It is wrong for Christians to pass judgment on partners in dialogue – just as they cannot impose conversion, which is the work of the Holy Spirit. Furthermore, witness has to do more with the reign of God than with affiliation to particular denominations.

Dialogue is about reconciliation where there is alienation, about building up a community of communities. The motivations for dialogue should be clear. These motivations may vary among Christians, and the emphases may differ from one context to another. Dialogue may be seen as a search for truth on both sides. Some Christians enter into dialogue with the desire to call others to discipleship practised within the Christian community. Others see dialogue as an opportunity to foster among the partners discipleship in a larger sense, referring to the dynamics of God's mission and its priorities. In contexts of conflict, the primary significance of dialogue may be to bring or maintain peace between religious communities. In such contexts, dialogue can be seen as a foretaste of the ultimate hope for the unity and reconciliation of all things in God (cf. Eph. 1:9-10).

The increasingly multireligious nature of many societies raises major theological questions which are reflected also in the reactions of people in local congregations. The presence of God in societies, cultures and religions independent of the presence of a church is one such issue. Aboriginal people in Australia, for example, witness powerfully to such experience. Early Christian theologians such as Justin Martyr spoke of "the seeds of the Word" among the cultures of the world. Many today recognize that Christ transcends time and space and reveals himself to those whom he chooses. In turn, people respond to Christ in their own cultural ways. This makes it possible for Christians to become open to the truth revealed in other cultures and traditions. The journey of Christians thus takes place in a process of both continuity and change, integrating the revealed truth that Christians encounter on their pilgrimage. But in so doing, a Christian community should never lose the centre of its faith: Jesus Christ, crucified and risen. To tell this story is the specific privilege of the churches within God's overall mission.

It is important to reaffirm the statement of the San Antonio world mission conference that "we cannot point to any other way of salvation than Jesus Christ; at the same time we cannot set limits to the saving power of God". With San Antonio, we affirm that "these convictions and the ministry of witness stand in tension with what we have affirmed about God being present in and at work in people of other faiths; we appreciate this tension, and do not attempt to resolve it" (San Antonio, pp.32,33).

On the journey of dialogue, Christians – as well as their partners from other religions – may be surprised, for Christ may encounter them where they would never have expected him (cf. Matt. 25:31-46). This raises the question: to what extent is it possible to discern the presence of the Holy Spirit among people of other religious convictions? It is recognized that values such as humility and openness to God and to others and commitments to solidarity and the way of non-violence are found also – and sometimes more so – among people of other faiths. Galatians 5:22-23, which speaks of the fruit of the Spirit, can guide the minds, hearts and intuitions of members of local congregations as they search for marks of the Spirit in the world. The capacity for such discernment is itself a gift of the Holy Spirit.

A number of factors may prevent the local congregation from entering into dialogue with neighbours of other faiths:
– Though there may be plurality in their community, many people in local congregations prefer the comfort of their own particular cultural group.

III: Local Congregations in Pluralist Societies

- People in local congregations often feel embarrassed meeting strangers or facing people from unfamiliar cultures, partly because they have not been exposed to diversity.
- Some people are not at all interested in dialogue and seldom think about the meaning of being a church and about the church as a "family of families".
- Church leadership is often unprepared and ill-equipped to motivate the members for dialogue.
- Christians often have difficulty engaging in dialogue when they are a minority in their particular society or when they are or feel threatened by other religious communities and/or fundamentalist groups.
- Dialogue may be difficult in contexts where a church supports or identifies itself with the dominant culture influencing all sectors of social and economic life, where people of other faiths are a minority.
- People of faith often hesitate to enter into dialogue in situations of conflict or where religious freedom is denied.

Nonetheless there are many examples and expressions of dialogue, such as the following:

- A congregation in Indonesia is encouraged to have a positive attitude to marriage between people of different faiths.
- A congregation in Sweden lets Muslim neighbours who come to various church activities use its parish hall for their meetings and prayers.
- Muslims in Bulgaria are helping Christians to build churches and schools.
- The inner-city religious council in the UK is helping members of the different religious groups to come together to discuss and advise government on matters of common interest.
- Programmes such as the Programme for Christian-Muslim Relations in Africa (Procmura) help the churches enable their members to relate constructively to Islam.
- Christians in, for example, the Caribbean have lived from birth in religiously plural societies. Members of the same family or community may belong to different faiths and hold differing religious convictions. Yet they live as a single family or in a harmonious neighbourhood without conflict, even participating in each other's religious ceremonies, celebrations and worship. In fact, individuals' ideas of God may be drawn from more than one religious tradition.

The following practical steps are suggested to encourage dialogue in the local neighbourhood:
- training members of local congregations to be sensitive to the religious practices of people of other faiths. Christians in Lebanon, for example, were keen to help Shiite refugees fleeing from the Israeli bombs and brought them food – which the Muslims refused, since they were not sure that it had been prepared according to Islamic custom. Some of the Christians felt terribly frustrated because they did not understand the nature of the problem. Awareness programmes concerning customs and beliefs are needed: how to meet people of other faiths, how to behave in ways that will not shock, how to build bridges rather than walls. Experience shows that initiating such training requires specialists who can in turn train multipliers;
- initiating dialogue among leaders of religious groups;
- teaching about other religions in schools and theological seminaries;
- holding conferences and seminars where people have the opportunity of hearing leaders of other religions;
- publishing or publicizing for local congregational use educational materials (in print and other media) on interfaith relationships;
- recognizing the gifts of young people to encounter others in an open-minded way, and giving space to the abilities particularly of women to reach out with sensitivity to others – thus using these gifts of God positively to break barriers to dialogical relationships.

Genuine sharing can take place only when partners in dialogue encounter each other in a spirit of humility, honesty and mutual respect, ready to take risks in becoming exposed to one another and sharing one another's view of life, its meaning and purpose.

IV: One Gospel – Diverse Expressions

INTRODUCTION

The "call to one hope" comes to churches living and witnessing to the gospel in a variety of ways, each in relation to its local culture.

Through the Holy Spirit churches are led to recognize such marvellous diversity as a gift for their mutual enrichment and to discern within it the unity that binds them together, reflecting the triune God whose inner life is a fellowship of three persons. As churches share life with one another across cultures and engage in mission together, God is glorified and God's love in Christ made known.

A. SHARING DIVERSE EXPRESSIONS OF THE ONE GOSPEL ACROSS CULTURES

Contextuality and catholicity

Any authentic understanding of the gospel is both contextual and catholic. The gospel is contextual in that it is inevitably embodied in a particular culture; it is catholic in that it expresses the apostolic faith handed down from generation to generation within the communion of churches in all places and all ages.

The gospel or good news of the reign of God announced by Jesus Christ is addressed to all human beings irrespective of race, gender, class, religion or culture. It is the Holy Spirit who helps the church to make known this gospel of life to all nations. It is by the power of the same Spirit that Christians are called to one hope in Christ. In sharing this hope with all humanity the church recognizes the work of the Holy Spirit, who inspires and guides and who perfects the creation.

All human cultures in their diversity are part of God's creation. Cultures are formed as a result of the task and responsibility given by God to all humankind to cultivate and take care of God's gifts (Gen. 1:28-30; 2:15). All human beings understand reality in terms of their own particular cultural perspectives constituted by their collective memory, experience, creativity, interpersonal relationships, religious beliefs and practices and physical environment, and expressed in their own particular language.

The gospel of Jesus Christ encountering any given culture becomes incarnate in and illuminated by that culture, but also transforms and transcends that culture. A fuller understanding of the catholicity and contextuality of the gospel must take into account the complexity of diverse cultural groupings, their historical and theological traditions, their interactions and particular perspectives, while at the same time centring on the simplicity and transparency of the gospel of love that invites all human beings to recognize that they are children of God, called to community with God and with each other.

The local churches in early Christian history expressed their faith through their own cultural media. In their different liturgical traditions, for example, they expressed the one faith in diverse linguistic, musical and symbolic ways. These churches manifested the catholicity of the faith through their diverse cultural resources and identities and through their communion with one another.

Identity and context on the one hand and communion and catholicity on the other are not opposed to each other, but are complementary. Cultural contextuality in the Christian sense does not mean isolated and self-contained expression of the gospel but affirmation of the gifts of each culture for the proclamation of the gospel in communion with other contexts. Catholicity does not mean a universality that sweeps away particular identities, but is the expression of the fullness of truth that can be experienced in each particular context. The Greek *kata-holon* (from which "catholic" is derived) means "according to the whole" and so indicates the holistic quality of truth rather than any geographic or quantitative dimension. Catholicity requires that different contexts be in communion with each other and respect and challenge each other in the freedom of the Spirit. Together, contextuality and catholicity become signs of authenticity for the local as well as the global reality of the church.

New Testament narratives illustrate that the gospel refuses to be monopolized by one culture – for example, Jesus' encounter with the Syrophoenician woman (Mark 7:24-30) and the understanding of the gospel across language barriers at Pentecost (Acts 2). The ministry of Jesus Christ and the giving of the Holy Spirit at Pentecost are evidence of how God has claimed all persons and situations as the context for God's healing, justice and love.

"Seeds of the Word"

The gospel is the word of God communicated to all humanity in the incarnate Christ, testified to in the biblical scripture and proclaimed by the church; it is not limited to an interpretation of particular biblical texts. Gospel values are present in all cultures in the form of life, justice, freedom, reciprocity and holistic relations with creation. Therefore the gospel is not the property of any particular culture. The spirituality of different people must be respected as an expression of their integral faith. As such, particular language, interpretative devices, symbol systems or forms of Christian worship in one culture are not binding in other cultures. However, in mutual respect and in a transparent act of communion and love, these may be shared among cultures without coercion, enriching the expression of the gospel.

An early Christian understanding of the "seeds of the Word" in all human cultures is derived from the way the fourth gospel used the Greek concept "logos" to communicate the mystery of Christ to the Greek-speaking world. This was a significant landmark in the passage of the gospel from its Jewish matrix to the Hellenistic world. In the history of the church this concept reminded Christians that no cultural situation in itself can be labelled as closed to the presence of Christ. Within all cultures are found insights and wisdom that can be understood as expressions of the word. The diverse forms in which such expressions might be found are to be fully respected. Christians individually and in community continue to explore how the gospel can best be expressed in their own cultural forms; these attempts deserve the respect and support of other Christians. They will at the same time want to test the appropriateness of their findings in the mutual relationship of catholicity with others.

Criteria for testing the appropriateness of such contextual expressions of the gospel in mutual relationship with other churches include:
- faithfulness to God's self-disclosure in the totality of the scriptures;
- commitment to a life-style and action in harmony with the reign of God;
- openness to the wisdom of the communion of saints across space and time;
- relevance to the context.

Use of power

The secular power of the church in its human institutional dimension is undeniable. Money, material possessions, state connections, history, etc., affect the way churches relate to each other and with cultures. Only when the power of the church is used in the service of the gospel is the apostolic authority *(exousia)* granted to the church by Christ manifested in the world.

The apostolic power of the gospel is expressed by the church in word and sacrament for healing, forgiveness and reconciliation and against death and destruction. The nature of the gospel's power is self-emptying, expressed fully through the cross and resurrection of Christ (Phil. 2:6-8). Churches should take the example of Christ in the exercise of their secular power (Matt. 20:25-28).

It is recognized that imbalances in temporal or secular power exist and can impede even the best-intentioned encounters among churches and with cultures. A dominant force has the potential to intimidate, coerce or end interaction with a less powerful counterpart. The dominant force may be unaware of the impact of its words or actions on the other.

The authority to teach belongs to the apostolic commission given to the disciples by Christ (Matt. 28:19-20). In faithful witness to Christ, Christians exercise this authority in interpreting the scriptures and transmitting the life-giving gospel to all people. A conciliar exercise of the teaching authority as exemplified in the ecumenical councils of the early church is desirable at all levels of the present life of the church. Since this authority is located in the whole body of Christ, any personal or structural expression of faith should be judged by the whole body using appropriate structures of dialogue and participation.

The mechanism for settling disputes varies from church to church. Resolving differences among churches is complicated by the various polities and ecclesiologies that have evolved in the churches. Deciding what is the proper interpretation of a biblical text or an ethical issue depends on the conciliar dialogue among the churches against the backdrop of the spiritual and theological heritage of the whole church.

Syncretism

Dynamic interactions between the gospel and cultures inevitably raise the question of syncretism. From one perspective, syncretism is merely a mixture of elements from different sources. In that respect, any cultural expression of the gospel is syncretic. Theologically, syncretism has tended to mean a blending of elements of different origin or which are in conflict, hence a perceived failure to maintain a faithful correspondence to the gospel. Clarity and care are needed in the use of this term in Christian relationships, since its application is closely linked to the reality of power imbalances among the churches.

Accusations of syncretism have been made by both larger and smaller churches. Powerful historic churches have sometimes accused small and newly emerging Christian communities of syncretism. Accusations have also come from minority churches, as in the case of the Confessing Church in Germany during the Nazi period taking a radically critical position against the mainstream church, which had mixed nationalistic political ideology with Christian faith. It is important that syncretism be judged apart from the relative "power" of the accusing body.

Authentic witness to the gospel is threatened when Christians, knowingly or not, align their faith with life-denying and exclusivist ideological, political and socio-economic schemes, or when their actions betray Jesus Christ crucified and risen – the ultimate source of and standard for human faith and hope. The criteria to discern syncretism must be centred on Christ and grounded in a Christian witness characterized by life-affirming, inclusive, liberating and community-building attitudes. These criteria are to be applied sensitively within particular local contexts.

Some practices and customs which were once negated and rejected as "pagan" and "superstitious" are now recognized as authentic elements of people's spirituality. The use of certain musical instruments and forms of traditional worship are cases in point. The profound need of many peoples to include the living presence of their ancestors in an organic and holistic vision of reality is not seriously considered in some Christian churches. Other Christian traditions, however, provide for this need through commemorative feasts, prayers, liturgical celebrations or visual arts. It is the task of the church to give theological meaning to this profound need through the incarnate Lord, crucified and risen from the dead, who gives the promise of eternal life.

In rediscovering the catholicity of the church in each cultural context it is the incarnation, life, death and resurrection of Jesus Christ that together constitute the known standard for such discernment. Destructive and death-dealing elements in every culture are judged in the light of that standard.

Intercultural communication

Grappling with the complexity of cultural diversity and the simplicity of the gospel of love raises the question of mediating the meaning of the gospel across cultures. Many elements can prevent the genuine communication of the good news from culture to culture, including fear of other cultures, arrogance about one's own culture, prejudices against others, and stories and jokes about others.

The assumed cultural "superiority" of some cultures has sometimes made "bad news" out of the good news. The Bible interpreted through certain cultural norms in some so-called Christian societies has been used to suppress and marginalize indigenous peoples, women and youth and to perpetuate racism, slavery and other evils.

The need for community at a personal level as well as at the level of social cultural groupings is a gospel imperative that binds cultures in the Spirit, who leads all into sharing and fellowship, speaking and listening, challenging and supporting each other (John 17). Christians need each other to discern the one gospel of Jesus Christ in their diverse cultures. Each can help the other in the struggle to live out the gospel in any particular culture. Mutual respect and receptiveness to one another's gifts are essential for genuine communication. True communication of the gospel does not create a false hierarchy between persons. The encounter becomes a special moment of grace, revealing new possibilities of communion free from self-serving interests. Intercultural communication of the gospel is not a one-time event but a continuous dialogue of love and mutual exchange of the life-giving message. In this ongoing dialogue the power of language, gesture, art, image and symbol should be fully explored and utilized.

B. TOWARDS RESPONSIBLE RELATIONSHIPS IN MISSION

The theme "Called to One Hope – The Gospel in Diverse Cultures" reflects the recognition that this one hope is expressed in different ways and within different cultural contexts. This compels the church to face the challenges of responsible relationships and methodologies in mission. These challenges are even more pronounced with the end of the cold war, when the dominant forces of the world seem to be imposing on all cultures values driven by a free-market economy. In today's world a critical appraisal of the form and practice of mission is crucial so that competitive and divisive mission methods may be avoided. In the light of this danger, the San Antonio declaration that "to be called to unity in mission involves becoming a community that transcends in its life the barriers and brokenness in the world, and living as a sign of at-one-ment under the cross" (San Antonio, p.28) rings with renewed urgency.

Being united in mission is therefore an imperative as churches respond to the call to one hope and live and witness to the one gospel in its multiple facets.

Mission and unity

Past mission conferences and WCC assemblies have yielded a number of ecumenical missiological insights, many of which continue to be relevant to the work of mission today. Since at least the Whitby world mission conference (1947), partnership in mission has been understood as an essential way of following Christ's call; and a number of documents have been produced on "common witness". The WCC document "Mission and Evangelism – An Ecumenical Affirmation" (1982) states:

> Common witness should be the natural consequence of [the churches'] unity with Christ in his mission... In solidarity, churches are helping each other in their respective witness before the world. In the same solidarity, they should share their spiritual and material resources to announce together and clearly their common hope and common calling (para. 23).

While many of the convictions and commitments made in recent years have been put into action, much remains to be done. Nevertheless, churches and mission agencies agree that:
- "Mission is *the mission of God* whose 'love has been poured into our hearts through the Holy Spirit' (Rom. 5:5), inviting the community to become God's co-workers (cf. 1 Cor. 3:9) in God's continuing act of re-creating and uniting the whole of creation" (Salvador preparatory papers, p.76). The *missio Dei* takes place in multiple directions in the whole world and results in the transformation of human communities.
- A holistic understanding of mission as including both evangelism and service leads the church to faithfulness to God's continuing act in Christ. Indeed mission challenges "the whole church to take the whole gospel to the whole world" ("The Lausanne Covenant", 1974, para. 6). Such mission is engaged in by and for persons of all races and social strata, women and men, young and old, lay and ordained, poor and rich, and persons with different abilities.

Mission and unity are inseparably linked; mission in unity remains a goal to which the church aspires. Visible signs of commitment to the goal of unity include collaboration, cooperation and networking among churches and mission agencies in the same area, across cultural and denominational boundaries, and across national and regional boundaries.

Traditionally, some parts of the church have understood mission as an activity outside their own borders, while others have understood mission as primarily focused on their own contexts. In recent years it has been said that "the primary responsibility for mission rests with the local church". Some suggest rewording this to read: "The primary responsibility for mission, where there is a local church, is with that church in its own place." Local congregations are thus called to be missionary congregations.

Since the task of evangelism is primarily the responsibility of the local church in each place, any international mission effort must recognize and respect this. Sister churches can however assist each other's local mission. Where churches are not actively engaged in evangelism efforts, there may be need to challenge each other, in affirming ways, towards authentic proclamation and living out of the gospel.

Mutuality in mission

Churches need each other both locally and globally. This need has been expressed in a variety of ways in mission history.

In recent years the structures of various mission agencies – such as the Communauté évangélique d'Action apostolique (CEVAA), the Council for World Mission and the Vereinigte Evangelische Mission (UEM) – have been transformed to reflect more adequately mutuality in mission and increased commitment to South-to-South relationships. Many other models undoubtedly exist.

No matter what the structures, churches, mission agencies and local congregations should be called to the practice of a common discipline of mutual cooperation in mission, taking into consideration various experiences and new models. In the search for such a discipline, a number of key insights and core values have been identified in recent ecumenical discussions. They include:
- mutual challenge and encouragement;
- the creation of "safe spaces" in which honest speaking and real listening occur;

IV: One Gospel – Diverse Expressions 73

- the sharing of resources in ways that promote genuine interdependence;
- shared decision-making in the context of mutual respect for each other's priorities;
- patience and appreciation for the dynamic nature of relationships;
- openness and a continuing search for greater solidarity;
- transparency and mutual accountability.

Some forms of global partnership have been a hindrance to local ecumenical partnerships. Bilateral denominational mission relationships have sometimes distracted churches from fostering local ecumenical relationships and ignored the local ecumenical instruments already in place. Churches everywhere should value, strengthen and utilize ecumenical mission relationships at all levels. Ecumenical institutions should also be challenged to place mission and evangelism among their priorities.

The WCC and its member churches and affiliated bodies should intensify dialogue with non-member churches, agencies and associations, formally and informally and at all levels, in order to share visions and practices for mutual challenge and encouragement in mission – for the challenge to mutuality in mission in response to the call to "one hope" applies to all churches everywhere. Through conscious effort to share experiences and explore common issues in mission in a prayerful spirit, the churches may be helped to avoid repeating mistakes of past unilateral and colonial patterns of mission.

Towards common witness

The (draft) WCC document "Gathering into Unity: Affirming Mission in Fidelity to the Gospel" (1996) is a commendable framework for addressing issues of common witness and proselytism.[1] Among the affirmations in that document which undergird authentic common witness are the following:

> Participating in God's mission is an imperative for all Christians and all churches, not a specialized calling for individuals or groups. It is also an inner compulsion, based on the profound demands of Christ's love, to invite others to share in the fullness of life Jesus came to bring (cf. John 10:10)...
> The ground for our common witness is that:
> - we proclaim and worship one God and Creator;
> - we confess the same Jesus Christ as Lord and Saviour;

- we are moved by the one Holy Spirit who empowers us;
- there is one gospel which we proclaim and to which we witness;
- there is one mission of God in which we share as God's co-workers (1 Cor. 3:9; 3 John 8).

As Paul says: "There is one body and one Spirit, just as you were called to the one hope of your calling, one Lord, one faith, one baptism, one God and Father of all, who is above all and through all and in all" (Eph. 4:4-6) ("Gathering into Unity", paras 6,18).

The new contexts in which the churches are called to common witness today expose increased obstacles to such witness. One major obstacle is proselytism. The (draft) document asserts:

> Different churches understand proselytism in different ways. Here it is taken to mean the encouragement of Christians who are considered members of one church to change their denominational allegiance through ways and means that "contradict the spirit of Christian love, violate the freedom of the human person and diminish trust in the Christian witness of the church" (Orthodox consultation on mission and proselytism, Moscow, 1995).
>
> Proselytism – which may be open or subtle – is always a wounding of koinonia at the centre of the life Christians are called to live amidst their differences (Phil. 2:2-5; Rom. 15:2-7). It discredits the work of the Holy Spirit in each person and church, and must always be distinguished from conversion in Christ that is biblical, free and genuine.
>
> Proselytism is a destabilizing factor, especially for mainline churches and even, in some countries, for society. The WCC New Delhi assembly described it as "a corruption of Christian witness"... [It also] emphasized that the difference between authentic witness and proselytism is a matter of "purpose, motive and spirit as well as of means"...
>
> There are a variety of manifestations of proselytism. One form, of which many churches complain, is the offer of interchurch aid in human, material and other forms (for example, kilos of rice for conversion, clothing for baptism, language classes as a bridge to the future) as inducement to join another church. Yet such assistance could have been a sign of Christian love and solidarity and an expression of common Christian witness...
>
> The churches need to assess their own internal life to see whether some of the reasons people change church allegiance may lie with the churches themselves ("Gathering into Unity", paras 32-34,36,43).

We decry the practice of those who carry out their endeavours in mission and evangelism in ways which destroy the unity of the body of Christ, human dignity and the very lives and cultures of those being "evangelized"; we call on them to confess their participation in and to renounce proselytism. We also decry expressions of Christian triumphalism in religiously plural contexts.

At the same time, however, we rejoice in the religious liberty now available in many parts of the world, especially within Eastern Europe. This freedom opens up new opportunity to work for the renewal of the church, the rebuilding of the body of Christ and the spiritual re-enlightenment of believers. It also provides opportunity for the world church to support and strengthen the historic churches in Eastern Europe as they seek new guidelines for mission and renewal of ministry.

Local churches in other contexts around the world are faced with other crises. Some have to deal with socio-political conflicts and large numbers of displaced persons, while others (in minority situations) have to cope with persecution from fundamentalist systems. These may also be opportunities for the world church to support, strengthen and engage in common witness.

It is important for all who feel called to mission and evangelism to engage in such with sensitivity and concern for the churches already in that place. Discipline for mutuality in mission should always be respected.

Specific actions that could be taken include:
– that the central committee of the WCC be requested to commend to the churches for study and action the "Gathering into Unity" document following its adoption;
– that a dialogue be initiated among those involved in mission within as well as outside ecumenical circles to address proselytism and others issues related to mutuality in mission.

CONCLUSION

Called to one hope in Christ, we commit ourselves to take seriously our common call to mission and to work towards mission in unity. We actively seek a new era of "mission in Christ's way" at the dawn of the third millennium, enriched by one another's gifts and bound together in the Holy Spirit, to the glory of the triune God.

NOTE

[1] A revised version of the "Gathering into Unity" document, entitled "Towards Common Witness: A Call to Adopt Responsible Relationships in Mission and to Renounce Proselytism", was received by the WCC central committee in September 1997 and commended to the churches for reflection and action. The extracts which appear in this report do not necessarily correspond to the final text.

Gospel and Culture

Metropolitan Kirill of Smolensk and Kaliningrad

The first part of the theme of this last world mission conference of the second millennium – "Called to One Hope" – is profoundly symbolic. We have come close to the juncture between two centuries, summing up the one about to end and looking with anxiety and hope to the one to come. We look with anxiety because we cannot help seeing how many unresolved problems humanity faces today, and in what a hopeless situation – both spiritual and material – millions of people live. The world is confronted, on the one hand, with an aggressive globalizing monoculture which tries to impose itself everywhere, dominating and assimilating other cultural and national identities, and, on the other hand, with nationalistic upheavals, tribalization and disintegration of the human family. Yet in the midst of contemporary hopelessness and despair, we live as Christians with hope in the eschatological expectation of *parousia* – the coming of Christ – and Christ's ultimate triumph over the forces of evil. In our journey towards the future we are strengthened, encouraged and led by the vision that all things in heaven and earth will be gathered and reconciled in Christ "who fills all in all" (Eph. 1:22-23). For this reason it is important to address the "one hope" to which Christians are called, in the light and from the perspective of the one gospel as it is expressed through and lived in diverse cultures.

Two thousand years ago, our Lord Jesus Christ gave this commandment to his disciples and all succeeding generations of Christians: "Go therefore and make disciples of all nations, baptizing them in the name of the Father and of the Son and of the Holy Spirit, and teaching them to obey everything that I have commanded you" (Matt. 28:19-20). Has this mission been fulfilled today? Has the

---

This paper was presented in Russian.

gospel been proclaimed throughout the world as a testimony to all the nations (Matt. 24:14)? Has the world lived out the commandments of Christ? Is there any hope at all for Christian mission to be fulfilled on earth and for the longed-for parousia, for the presence of Christ to become a reality, for God to find a place "on earth as it is in heaven" (Matt. 6:10)? This conference is an opportunity for us to reflect on these questions, to assess the missionary situation at the end of the 20th century and to look forward towards a renewed mission in the 21st century.

The second facet of the theme of this conference – "The Gospel in Diverse Cultures" – poses another set of questions, which primarily concern the need for dialogue so strongly felt by Christian churches in the 20th century. To what extent should Christian mission be a dialogue with non-Christian traditions? How can the proclamation of the gospel interact with various cultures? What is inculturation of the gospel? What is culture at all? Is it alien and dangerous to the mission of the church? Is it an altogether external reality that should be radically transformed, or can culture itself become a bearer of the gospel where the voice of church missionaries has grown weak?

The mission of the church in today's world

Before sharing with you my ideas on these issues, I would like to say a few words about the situation in which humanity finds itself today. For long decades the world was divided into two zones of confrontation, with two hostile camps, and human civilization developed wholly within the context of this rivalry between the two military and political giants. During the cold war a billion dollars was spent daily on armaments, and the accumulated arsenal of weapons was large enough to destroy the whole world many times over. Many people in the West believed that once the "Soviet threat" ended, evil itself would perish from the face of the earth and an age of universal prosperity, peace and harmony would come. They thought that stopping the arms race would solve all problems.

Then the "iron curtain" collapsed before our very eyes and the "Soviet threat" perished, together with the need to spend the billion dollars a day on armaments. And what happened? Have people become happier? Has the longed-for peace come? No, it has not! On the contrary, we are horrified to see the chaos into which Europe has been plunged and the fratricidal wars being waged in the former

Yugoslavia, Chechnya and the republics of the former Soviet Union. Mothers are losing their sons on battlefields, civilians are killed in air-strikes, children and adults are blown up by land-mines.

The military and political crisis has been accompanied by economic collapse as whole regions have found themselves below the poverty line, on the edge of survival. In this situation we are not surprised to see that people in the former Soviet Union feel a growing nostalgia for the socialist past. They may have lived a miserable life, isolated from the outside world and deprived of many civil rights and liberties. But they did have their bread, a roof over their heads and a certain social security, a certain confidence in the future. Nowadays many are starving. Thousands of refugees are wandering the cities and villages of the once-powerful Soviet empire. People have literally nothing to live on. Workers and civil servants have not been paid their yet-more-miserable salaries for months. The unemployed have stopped receiving their social allowances, while old people's pensions are so meagre that they cannot afford decent food, let alone medical treatment. Criminality is growing at a disastrous pace. In the large cities people are afraid to go out at night, freezing with fear at every ring of their doorbell. Many feel powerless and defenceless in the face of the evil that has fallen upon them so suddenly and forcefully.

Moreover, severe political and economic problems have affected many regions in the world. It is enough to mention the recent atrocious massacres in Rwanda, the open hostilities between Zaïre and Rwanda, the never-ending war in Afghanistan, continued tension in the Middle East – all this despite the diplomatic efforts made and the political consultations held to resolve the crises. For more than forty years now, humanity has been struggling to improve the military, political and economic situation in the world, but paradoxically the situation has not improved. The disparity between North and South continues to increase, as does the gap between rich and poor. No redistribution of resources, no social programme has been able to deliver humanity from poverty, disease and hunger. The infant mortality rate in Asia, Africa and Latin America remains high. Millions of people have become infected with HIV/AIDS. Millions are dying of starvation. Hunger in the 20th century is a challenge to all humanity, and a disgrace to the entire human race!

The ideal of a super-consumer society characteristic of Western civilization has led to global devastation. Christian churches are deeply concerned about the pollution of the environment that has reached a catastrophic level, the contamination of water and air by chemical wastes, the deforestation and depletion of other natural resources, the exploitation of flora and fauna – resulting in global climatic changes with unpredictable consequences. All this cannot but disturb Christians, who see in it a spiritual problem involving the basic relations between humanity and nature entrusted to it by God to "till" and "keep" (Gen. 2:15), not to ravage. Humanity has failed to hear the voice of God calling it to cherish its home, the earth. As a result it finds itself on the brink of a global catastrophe. The flood about which the Bible tells us (Gen. 7) was a punishment for the sins humanity had committed. It was also a warning to subsequent generations: "Unless you repent, you will all perish as they did" (Luke 13:3).

What then has caused the present crisis of human civilization? It is my profound conviction that the crisis has been caused primarily by a global crisis of personality. Human survival today depends not so much on military-political changes, economic reforms, efforts to overthrow totalitarian regimes (as almost none of them still remain) or improvements of the existing social system, as on the spiritual and moral state of the human person.

Underlying the crisis of any system is a crisis of personality. Any reform of that system or structure or society should therefore begin with a change in people themselves. The classic argument about what comes first – system or person – becomes meaningless if the gospel's standards are applied. Jesus Christ as revealed to us in the gospels was not primarily a social reformer, but rather a great reformer of the human spirit. That is why his preaching did not address "systems" or "structures" but always the living human person. That is why he did not call his contemporaries to overthrow Roman rule, to eliminate slavery, to redistribute material resources, but spoke of a spiritual transformation and moral rebirth of every person and all humanity. Then "you will know the truth, and the truth will make you free" (John 8:32). St Paul echoed Jesus: "For you were called to freedom, brothers and sisters" (Gal. 5:13). It was not social freedom that came first, nor the "freedom and brotherhood" which were to become the slogans of the French revolution. Rather, it was the liberation of human beings from slavery to sin and their union in the millions-strong fellowship which is the church, in which "there is no longer Greek and Jew,... slave and free; but Christ is all and in all!" (Col. 3:11).

I do not want at all to say that Christian churches should reconcile themselves to social injustices or refuse to struggle for civil rights and liberties. But I would like to stress that *the spiritual and moral rebirth of humanity* will be a priority for the churches if they remain faithful to the spirit of the gospel of Christ. A renewed humanity will then be able to create and sustain a society in which justice, peace, love and understanding will live together.

There are many people of good will in the world who are eager to devote themselves to the struggle against totalitarian regimes, exploitation and various forms of discrimination. We highly appreciate the efforts of these people and honour their effort. I should think, however, that the mission of the church is somewhat different. The church should address the heart of each individual person, influencing and transforming his or her mind and will. "Save yourself, and millions around you will be saved," said Seraphim of Sarov, a Russian saint of the 19th century. These words contain the profound truth that the salvation of the world begins with the salvation of the individual. For Christianity there are no impersonal "popular masses" but a living person standing before God, other people and himself or herself. And the fate of the entire humanity will ultimately depend on how each particular person will relate to God, neighbour and self.

Therefore, mission as a witness to the spiritual and ethical heritage of Christianity becomes the number one task for the churches. For almost fifty years the World Council of Churches has spoken about concrete matters such as overcoming the consequences of the second world war, disarmament, liberation from social oppression and the elimination of racial discrimination and sexism. We have to acknowledge that it is vital for Christians to address these issues, as they are common concerns for the whole human community. But in addressing them what should be the specific and unique contribution of the churches in the light of the gospel? Are these not the effects of certain more profound causes of a spiritual and ethical nature? And has the time not come to clarify the causes instead of being fixated on their consequences? Has the time not come to address a human person, to return to the gospel's message, "Repent, for the kingdom of heaven has come near" (Matt. 3:2, 4:17)? Expressed in these words of John the Baptist and Christ is the quintessence of Christian morality. Repentance/metanoia is a change of mind, thoughts and heart, and a spiritual transformation. Is it not the fundamental moral message of the gospel? Does it not offer a way out of the impasse in which the human civilization has been caught? Is it not what we should "proclaim from the housetops" (Matt. 10:27) for everybody to hear?

We are living at a time when humankind is suffering profound moral decay. Human vocabulary seems to have lost the notion of personal sin and personal responsibility before God. "If there is no God, then everything is permissible," says one of Dostoyevsky's characters. We seem to have reached the climax of moral permissiveness. Sin has not merely been legalized, it has even been encouraged and propagated. In Russia, as in many countries in the West, the mass media are involved in widespread propagation of lust, debauchery and violence. The Christian ideals of purity and virtue have been systematically ridiculed and blasphemed. Alcoholism and drug addiction have become chronic diseases for entire generations. Who will raise a voice against this moral decay if not the church? If we are to speak about mission, is it not our primary mission to raise this voice?

The present crisis of the missionary and ecumenical movement is largely the result of having lost the personal dimension. Ecumenical documents on ethics tend to pass over in silence the burning problems of human personality. But is it not our mission to listen carefully to the word of Christ and learn to apply it to the present situation? Perhaps the old contradiction between mission and dialogue can be resolved by common efforts of churches to save the person. I am strongly convinced that it is morality that will save human civilization today. This is what our mission should be aimed at. The churches should by no means be under the thumb of "this world". They should not abandon the gospel's norms of morality to please the times. On the contrary, they should join their efforts to win and transform the human heart and to witness in common to the Christian moral ideal. Only then will our mission succeed, only then will our voice be strong and prophetic, and only then will the world hear our voice.

Culture as a bearer of the gospel of Christ

Let us move on to the second part of the conference theme: the interaction between the gospel and culture.

Since the middle of this century, especially since the Second Vatican Council, it has increasingly been heard in the churches that

Christians should use local culture so that Christianity may be understood by people in a given time and place. According to the 1973 world mission conference in Bangkok, "culture shapes the human voice that responds to the voice of Christ". A conclusion drawn from that statement is that Christianity everywhere should take on aspects of the local culture. By the end of the 20th century, a whole theology has been formed and a practice of inculturation developed on this basis.

Some participants in the ecumenical movement who support in principle the idea of interaction between Christian mission and local cultures have warned from the very beginning against the danger of theological syncretism and have reacted strongly to its manifestations.

The contemporary sporadic tendencies to identify inculturation with syncretism seem to be rooted in a particular theological understanding of culture. No doubt "the wind blows where it chooses" (John 3:8), meaning that the Spirit can speak the languages of various cultures. The message of the gospel is always embodied and conveyed to people in a certain cultural framework. Therefore culture can become a carrier of the gospel. On the other hand, when the gospel is preached to the people in their own language and within their own cultural patterns, they will be able to understand it better and to grasp new and deeper spiritual meanings. To reach that stage, however, cultures need to be deeply transformed and transfigured in their encounter with the gospel. Although the Holy Spirit blows and is present in all cultures, not all aspects of cultures are necessarily the voice of the Spirit. That is why the apostle warns us to "test the spirits to see whether they are from God" (1 John 4:1). Early Christian writings indicate how important this discerning of spirits was in the life of Christian communities. Already St Paul describes it as a gift (1 Cor. 12:10). It is significant that although the early Christians used the pre-Christian Greco-Roman culture for defining Christian doctrines and relating to their contemporaries, they did not accept altogether its religious and ethical content but rather tried to transform and transfigure it in the light of the gospel. One of the reasons for the persecution to which they were subjected was precisely that they refused to worship idols, that is, to accept a major religious aspect of the culture of that time.

Christian acceptance or non-acceptance of a particular culture should be based on certain criteria. For the Orthodox it is the living

Tradition of the universal church which guards the scriptural mystery of the incarnation against the invasion of "other gospels". If we reject this protection or ignore this criterion, do we not become vulnerable to "other gods", to "the spiritual forces of evil in the heavenly places" (Eph. 6:12)? These forces are lying dormant in many cultures of our contemporary world, ready to awaken and come into the ecumenical field.

Without entering into polemics regarding extreme practices of inculturation, I will try to offer a vision of the interaction between the gospel and culture from a slightly different perspective.

I recall my visit in 1975 to the old monastery of St Cyril of White Lake in the north of Russia. Founded by the monk and educator St Cyril in the late 14th century, the monastery was turned into a museum during the Soviet period – which saved it from the destruction and defilement that was the fate of most churches in our country. The magnificent cloister located on a lakeshore amidst the virgin beauty of the north was kept in good order by the state as a tourist attraction. Yet there was not a single soul within its walls. There was neither prayer nor eucharist nor sermon.

The only active church in the vicinity was far away, next to a cemetery near a small village on the opposite shore, lost in the woods and inaccessible by road. An old priest ministered there to elderly women. It was a typical, even symbolic, situation in our country at that time. The church was a ghetto isolated from the "mainstream" life and culture. Church charity was unthinkable, as were believers speaking to the press or on television, or the independent involvement of the church in social processes. True, the eucharist was celebrated and sermons were heard in a few active churches. But for the majority of our people these churches were a sort of "internal abroad", dangerous to enter and not so necessary.

Even outstanding monuments of church culture such as the monastery of St Cyril of White Lake were turned into centres of antireligious propaganda, or at least put at the service of purely Soviet culturological ideology. I joined an excursion group at the monastery's cathedral. As the guide explained the architecture and the icons, she tried to persuade the group that the magnificence of the church was created in spite of Christianity, which, she maintained, did not allow architects and icon painters to express themselves fully. But in speaking about the architecture and icons, she willy-nilly spoke about the gospel, and what she said and the icons and architecture themselves came out as a witness to Christ – a witness far more powerful than the scum of so-called scientific atheism!

By the 1970s the communists were no longer worried about the revival of religion in Russia because it had been systematically eradicated over nearly seventy years. Mass executions of the clergy in the 1920s and 1930s had decapitated the church. There were about 300 bishops before the 1917 revolution; by 1939 only five diocesan bishops remained. Most of the priests were executed and most of the churches destroyed. Some 8000 churches were closed in 1937 alone, and only 100 churches throughout Russia were still open at the end of 1939. After a brief respite in the last years of Stalin's regime, a new persecution fell upon the remnants of the church under Khrushchev in the 1960s, accompanied by a grand eloquence about democracy. It was at that time that the chief communist of the country promised the people that the last remaining priest would be exhibited at a museum twenty years hence. Finally, in the "stagnation" period in the 1980s the mass persecution stopped, but the church remained a ghetto completely isolated from society.

Suddenly in 1988, when the millennium of the baptism of Russia was celebrated, Christianity broke out of its confinement in the churches and moved into the streets and squares. The celebrations united the intelligentsia and the church and showed that Christian faith was still alive among the people. All this overwhelmed and frightened the civil authorities. They had done everything possible to eliminate Christianity. They had had three generations of people brought up on communist ideology making a caricature of the church. Now suddenly it was apparent that Christian faith was still very much alive.

When I asked the mayor of the small Russian town of Vyazma to make the stadium available for the millennium celebrations, he replied, "Why do you want the stadium if you will not be able to gather even a thousand believers?" But when *forty thousand* – two-thirds of the town's population – took part in the festive procession, it became a spiritual rebirth for many, including the mayor himself. Shocked, he came to me and said that he could not even imagine how religious the people under his governance were. It is from that year, 1988, that we Orthodox Russians count the perestroika period. It has been marked by a gradual democratization of society, a collapse of atheist ideology, and "velvet revolutions" in the countries of the former socialist camp. A period of spiritual recovery in our country has begun which we describe as the "second baptism of Russia".

Why did the totalitarian authorities fail? Why did state godlessness, imposed on three generations over seventy years and almost completely eradicating traditional religious education in families, suffer such a shattering defeat? True, an important part was played by social processes, including international processes, which brought pressure to bear on the authorities. But the crucial factor lay elsewhere. When scientists, public figures and millions of ordinary people took part – at great risk – in the millennium celebrations, the leaders of the country realized that faith was truly alive among the people. Russians who may have never gone to church or read anything about religion and who almost certainly received no religious education at home, proved to be inwardly Christian.

A unique situation developed in Russia. At a time when the voice of the church itself was barely heard, the gospel was preached not through priests or missionaries or ecclesiastical literature, but through culture, which became a bearer of the gospel's message. This is hardly surprising, since Russian culture was shaped under the influence of Christianity. The pre-Christian culture absorbed the spiritual power of the gospel through the church, its worldview and moral message, to give it back to the people when the church was subjected to persecution. Literally everything that was created during centuries of cultural development – literature, poetry, architecture, art, music – bears witness to Christ. Religious tradition and religious searching continued explicitly or implicitly, even in the Russian culture of the Soviet period, oppressed as it was by totalitarianism. A Christian worldview, church wisdom and biblical quotations lived on in the people's consciousness, preserved in songs, proverbs and sayings, even though their origins had been completely forgotten.

Soviet power could not prevent people from reading Dostoyevsky, even though he was not studied at school. This great writer was a profoundly religious man, and his works are imbued with Christian ideas. The instructions of Starets Zosima, a character in *The Brothers Karamazov*, were largely borrowed from the writings of early church fathers, in particular from the 7th-century Christian mystic St Isaac the Syrian. So while works by the holy fathers were not published and the writings of St Isaac the Syrian were impossible to obtain, Dostoyevsky was widely read and appreciated. The same is true of the works of other writers, composers and artists. Through the Russian cultural tradition our people were introduced to the great patristic heritage.

The Soviet regime tried to create its own version of pre-revolutionary Russian culture. Everything in it that was associated with the church was either eliminated, distorted or given an atheistic interpretation. Thus Pushkin's poem "A Prophet", a poetic rendering of the biblical story of the calling of Isaiah, was interpreted as a reference to the calling of a revolutionary to class struggle. The choral music composed by Bortnyansky on liturgical texts was performed by Soviet choirs without words. New "neutral" texts about spring or nature or birds were often written for such music.

Nothing, however, could remove the Christian core from Russian culture. Even in Soviet times religious motifs were strongly present in the works of poets, writers, composers, film directors. Many of these works did not fit into the framework of "socialist realism" imposed by the Soviet party ideology. Paradoxically, the Soviet state had an anti-Soviet culture, and this culture was essentially religious. Even censured books by Russian authors and short films of the Soviet period were strikingly charged with authentic humanness and anti-totalitarianism, in search of the ultimate truth.

People were drawn to Christianity through Western European culture as well, which is also imbued with religious motifs. It is impossible to overlook Christ or to fail to come into contact, even indirectly, with the gospel's message when listening to Bach's *St Matthew Passion* or Händel's *Messiah*, or when contemplating Raphael's *Sistine Madonna* or Michelangelo's *Pietà*.

That culture, transformed by the Christian content with which it was imbued, has proved to be more powerful than all the efforts to destroy religion. This is our answer to the theory and practice of inculturation. Inculturation does not mean that Christianity has to change its content and message according to the standards and expectations of different cultures, but rather that cultures are affirmed in the process of their transformation and transfiguration in encountering the one gospel. Culture cannot be used for tactical purposes; culture should become a bearer of the message of Christ.

A culture can be transformed by the gospel even when non-Christian principles dominate the public realm. This is characteristic not only of Soviet and post-Soviet Russia. In societies where non-religion has been asserted as an indisputable vanguard, religion is still there in the innermost cultural consciousness – and the entire culture, both past and present, protests and opposes secularization, materialism and anti-culture, thus bearing witness to Christ.

But what do we mean by culture? The Latin term *cultura* is derived from the Latin *cultus*, meaning both "worship"/"service" and "cultivation"/"tillage". These meanings point both to the religious roots of culture and to its educational function in human life. God created male and female and established a living relation with them based on worship and service. He put them in the garden of Eden to work it and take care of it (Gen. 2:15). This means that human beings are called to cultivate the world around them, of which they are caretakers, and to cultivate their personality through God's constant living presence in their life. Culture should be a co-creation of God and people, their cooperation, their actions together to educate the human person and to preserve and cultivate the environment.

Thus we affirm culture as a means of human spiritual and moral growth. Those forms of culture and art which promote not spiritual growth but passions, instincts and the decay of human personality represent an anti-culture; and anti-art cannot be the church's ally. Authentic culture, from a Christian perspective, should not release the Dionysian element in human beings to which the philosophers of antiquity referred, but should rather elevate, inspire and bring people closer to God. Violent passions and rebellion against peace, harmony, life and God generate not only anti-culture but also anti-Christianity. Is this not the way in which the devil works? Is it not the devil's presence that is felt in some forms of today's culture, plunging people into the dark depths of passion?

Any anti-culture, wherever or whenever it is generated, is anti-Christian, since it has and promotes life-denying elements. I say this not out of nostalgia for the culture of the past, nor out of any anti-modernist opposition to new cultural forms and developments as such. What is important is not form but content (though to a degree the former cannot but reflect the latter). The church should neither blindly and uncritically try to be in tune with new cultural trends nor indiscriminately pronounce them as evil and renounce them.

The mission of the church today is a struggle for humanity "against the rulers, against the authorities, against the cosmic powers of this present darkness, against the spiritual forces of evil in the heavenly places" (Eph. 6:12). To help human persons out of the embrace of anti-culture and anti-Christianity, to bring them back to God – this is the urgent task we face today.

Mission and proselytism

I would like to touch upon yet another problem which has become especially acute owing to the changes that have taken place and continue to take place in Eastern European countries. This is the problem of proselytism, which, in my opinion, belongs to and must be dealt with in the framework of the conference theme. It is more than a purely theological issue or a mere matter of church relationships. It is primarily an expression of cultural and ideological clashes, as newcomers try to impose their own culturally conditioned form of Christianity on other Christians. In my reflections I will again proceed from the context which is closest to me, namely, the reality in Russia yesterday and today.

For the last three decades of its existence under Soviet rule, the Russian Orthodox Church, despite the severe restrictions on religious freedom, maintained a living link with Christians of other confessions. Ecumenical contacts developed first of all within the USSR itself, where Christians of various confessions lived peacefully side by side. Solidarity in the face of a common adversary united Orthodox, Roman Catholics, Protestants. It was the only way to survive under a totalitarian regime. Ecumenical contacts were consolidated on the international level as well. The Soviet government in the 1960s, 1970s and 1980s was afraid of the church's influence on the people and of extensive ecumenical activity. Nevertheless, they began to allow us to go abroad and participate in ecumenical meetings when they realized that the absence of the Russian church from those meetings would only serve to intensify what was being said in the West about religious oppression in the USSR.

One of the wise achievements of our church was to manage to secure the permission of the authorities to join the World Council of Churches. The atheistic state leaders could not help realizing that the role and influence of the Russian Orthodox Church in the world would only grow if it joined the WCC, but they took the risk. They also permitted the church to organize international ecumenical and interfaith peace conferences, with the participation of Christians from other countries. All this helped to make the condition of the Russian church known in the world, even though its representatives were forced to keep silent when asked about the real state of affairs.

The religious and ecclesiastical situation in the USSR became an ever more constant item on the agenda of international Christian organizations as the Helsinki process drew world public attention to it. The external activity of the Russian Orthodox Church and its cooperation with the Christian world were among the factors that contributed to the growing authority of the church and, indirectly, to the collapse of the atheistic system.

International Christian solidarity was not the least factor in the failure to destroy the church in the Soviet Union. The support other Christians proffered during our hardest times helped the church in its struggle for survival. We are profoundly grateful to those Christians who showed solidarity with us and did not allow the godless authorities to crush the church. We thank those who took the risk of sending or bringing copies of the Bible and other religious books into our country. These books were then reprinted by *samizdat* (self-publishing), a powerful underground network. We thank Christians of other confessions and the ecumenical movement for the support we felt throughout those long and difficult years.

We expected that with the coming of religious freedom these relations would develop further and that other Christians would support us in the new, no less difficult, situation as the Russian Orthodox Church suddenly found itself before a door wide open to the broadest possible religious freedom and a huge field for missionary work. We sincerely hoped that we would be supported in this task.

Our hopes, however, were not fulfilled. As soon as freedom for missionary work was allowed, a crusade began against the Russian church even as it began recovering from prolonged disease, standing on its feet with weakened muscles. Hordes of missionaries rushed in, believing the former Soviet Union to be a vast missionary territory. They behaved as though no local churches existed, no gospel was being proclaimed. They began preaching without even making an effort to familiarize themselves with the Russian cultural heritage or to learn the Russian language. In most cases the intention was not to preach Christ and the gospel, but to tear our faithful away from their traditional churches and recruit them into their own communities. Perhaps these missionaries sincerely believed that they were dealing with non-Christian or atheistic communist people, having no idea that our culture was formed by Christianity and that our Christianity survived through the blood of martyrs and confessors, through the courage of bishops, theologians and laypeople asserting their faith.

Whereas we expected that our fellow Christians would support and help us in our own missionary service, in reality they have started fighting with our church. They have come with their dollars, buying people with so-called humanitarian aid and promises to send them abroad for study or rest. The annual budget of some of the invading missionary organizations amounts to dozens of millions of dollars. They have bought time on radio and television and have used their financial resources to the utmost.

All this has led to an almost complete rupture of the ecumenical relations developed during the previous decades. An overwhelming majority of the population has refused to accept this so-called missionary activity, which offends people's national and religious sentiments by ignoring their spiritual and cultural tradition. Indeed, given the lack of religious education, people tend to make no distinction between the militant missionaries we are speaking about and ordinary people of other faiths or confessions. For many in Russia today, "non-Orthodox" means those who have come to destroy the spiritual unity of the people and the Orthodox faith – spiritual colonizers who by fair means or foul try to tear the people away from the church.

What is happening in Russia and other countries of the former "Eastern bloc" can be described as an ecumenical disaster, as it has cancelled out the incredible achievements of the last forty years in the ecumenical field. At the same time, among those who have been involved in proselytism in our territory are not only sects but even our partners in the ecumenical movement, including some WCC member churches.

I would like to state with all clarity: ecumenism and proselytism are incompatible. Incompatible also are mission and spiritual enslavement, the preaching of Christ and violence to people's conscience, the proclamation of the gospel and bribery.

In general, any competitive or parallel mission is fraught with threats to the unity of the church and fraternal relations among Christian churches. We are grieved to see these zealous missionaries from abroad creating their own church structures at our expense, thus bearing witness to anything but ecumenical solidarity. At the same time, not only is damage being done to the Orthodox Church, but also the tremendous ecumenical efforts towards Christian unity are coming to naught. It can be said that joint ecumenical efforts have now become blocked by the unrestrained "assault from the West". What is even more frightening is that the credibility of Christian witness is declining in the secular world as it watches the competition, enmity and mutual attacks raging among various Christian communities.

Proselytism is not some narrow religious activity generated by a wrong understanding of missionary tasks. Proselytism is the fact of invasion by another culture, even if Christian, but developing according to its own laws and having its own history and tradition. This invasion is taking place according to the old missionary patterns of colonial times. It is not merely a desire to reveal Christ to people – people who have confessed Christianity for over a thousand years at that – but also to refashion their culture in the Western mode.

Clearly, it is impossible to bear common Christian witness in a situation where each other's religious traditions and cultures are not respected. We call upon the WCC to take up the problem of proselytism with all seriousness to help avoid new divisions, so painful and difficult to heal. Such divisions within the Christian community are inadmissible, especially in an age of rapid secularization of the world community and globalization of its culture through global communications, computer networks, telecommunications and, eventually, the common market. If the churches do not make special efforts to transform this community by the power of the gospel, they risk marginalizing themselves and becoming foreigners in their own countries. This is even more probable as the technological society becomes increasingly engaged in searching for ways of meeting its spiritual needs. Unfortunately it is apt to find them not in faith in our Lord Jesus Christ but in such fields as psychoanalysis, social psychology and sexology, on the one hand, and in "new religious movements" and sects which consciously want to replace Christianity, on the other. In this situation we as Christians should find strength first to consolidate our own energies and resources and then bring the word of reconciliation to the world.

The missionary situation as it has developed in Russia and the other republics of the former Soviet Union appears to have reached a deadlock. Yet there is a way out. It lies in basing mission on the fundamental principle of early Christian ecclesiology: the principle of the local church. This stipulates that the church in a given place is fully responsible for its people before God. This principle can be applied not only to the Russian situation but to Christian mission in the world in general, on the understanding that nobody anywhere shall ignore a local church. To ignore a local church means to break a whole into pieces, to tear the seamless robe of Christ. Missionary efforts from abroad should be made in each place as a support and assistance to the local church(es). The same principle should be included in the basis of missionary work in the 21st century. Indeed, even where a Christian church was founded by foreign missionaries, it has long since become part of that place and culture. Everyone who, armed with the Bible, sets off to enlighten peoples should remember that by the end of the 20th century there are local Christian churches virtually everywhere. Independent actions taken by missionary groups at the expense of these churches represent an attempt to redraw the map of the world, and inevitably result in tension, alienation, bitterness.

The holy martyr Cyprian of Carthage wrote about the church schisms of his time: "Who is so impious and perfidious and so infected with the passion for strife that he believes that he can or dare break the unity of God, the robe of the Lord, the church of Christ?" This question can well be addressed in our day to those who act to the detriment of local churches, tearing the faithful away from the church and thus excommunicating themselves from the world Christian community. St Cyprian made it clear that these people are enemies of the church and Christian faith: "What unity is respected, what love is cherished or what love is contemplated by him who, indulging in strife, cuts the church, ruins faith, disturbs peace, eradicates love, defiles unity...? Indeed, he arms himself against the church and impedes divine construction; he is an enemy of the sanctuary, an agitator against the sacrifice of Christ, a betrayer of the faith and devotion; he is an apostate..."

These words uttered in the 3rd century are still relevant today. At the end of the 20th century we can state that the work of sectarians and schismatics to destroy the unity of churches continues. And this work is not Christian mission, it is spiritual colonialism. Our urgent task therefore is to get rid of colonial practices and develop a new attitude to mission – or rather, to return to the apostolic and early church understanding of mission not as enslaving or bribing people but rather as liberating and bringing them into the light of Christ's truth. The 20th century has been the time of a mass collapse of colonial regimes and the liberation of peoples, nations and regions from foreign domination, from the yoke of foreign cultures. The colonial ideology should be overcome in the realm of church and mission as well. Indeed, for many peoples in the southern hemisphere, Christianization meant above all Europeanization and destruction of their traditional culture, which the Europeans believed to be low and pagan.

* * *

Dear brothers and sisters, the reality described above as being relevant to both national and global contexts presents a considerable challenge to individual churches, to the world Christian community and to the entire human civilization. We can see how sinful and demonic elements acting in the world and in what is called the cultural sphere have led to a personal moral crisis which leads, in turn, to a global crisis of civilization. If we save the person we will save the culture, civilization and our common future.

We are witnessing today the fulfilment of apocalyptic prophecies, the decay of human personality and the mass rejection of fundamental norms of morality. A triumph of the forces of evil may lead to the spiritual death of humanity. In the human community, however, there are those who "now restrain" such forces (2 Thess. 2:7). These are the good elements expressed through a Christianized culture, transformed by the gospel. We can see fruits of this good everywhere in the world, including Russia, where by God's grace thousands of churches and hundreds of monasteries have been restored and millions of people have recovered their Christianized culture, making it not only the form but also the content of their lives.

Responding to this reality, the entire world Christian community needs to become conscious of its mission in a broader and bolder way. We should discern the apostolic sources of the uncompromising desire to transform the world around us. Some fifteen years ago one of my brother Russian bishops was summoned to a local official in charge of atheistic work who said to him: "Why do you gather children for a Christmas-tree party? It is not your function. You should meet *religious* needs." Obviously he meant conducting worship services for pensioners. The bishop answered: "My religious need is to change the world." We should come to the same understanding of our missionary service, even if humanly we have no chance, just as the apostles of Christ humanly had no chance. But their mission succeeded and transformed the world, because they walked together, uniting – not separating – people. And a miracle occurred, because where people act in unity Christ is there acting together with them.

Our mission, dear brothers and sisters, is a mission of "one hope", a mission for salvation, for a spiritual transformation of humanity and each individual person, for the kingdom of God in people's hearts. If we follow in Christ's steps without turning back, if we join one another in common witness to the world – supporting one another, not competing – then the Lord will support us and give us new strength and breathe a new spirit into world Christian mission. Only in this way will we be able to restore the spirit of Christ in those who have fallen away from the church, those who are lukewarm and searching. Only in this way will we be able to enter a new millennium as a spiritually strong civilization knowing the meaning of its existence.

Called to One Hope:
The Gospel in Diverse Cultures

Musimbi R.A. Kanyoro

The theme of this conference is "Called to One Hope – The Gospel in Diverse Cultures". The theme chosen for this year's World AIDS Day is "One Hope, One World". Even though the offices of the World Council of Churches and World Health Organization are close to each other in Geneva, I am quite sure that there was no consultation on this matter. Yet this coincidence can remind us of the inclusive nature of hope. The longing for "one hope" is not just a religious matter within the Christian community, but something with significant implications for all people everywhere. "Called to one hope" reminds us that, whatever our agenda, we cannot pursue it apart from the values that make common life possible.

This conference is set within the broader context of dialogue and discussion which has popularly come to be termed "gospel and culture". Culture is not a marginal issue appended to gospel, but touches the core of the church's identity and mission. Culture calls us to accept diversity, while gospel calls us to affirm unity – and both of these are essential for dialogue. "One hope" and "diverse cultures" is a natural combination of two realities that cannot be separated, for indeed people can express or live out their hope only within the context of the culture that shapes them.

Yet this theme with its two attractive parts puts me in the position of the proverbial African hyena, who was following the enticing and mouth-watering aroma[1] of barbecuing meat when suddenly he came to a fork in the path. Unsure which direction would lead him to the meat, he put his legs astride the two paths and tried to walk along both. Alas! the poor hyena split in the middle and died. I will let myself be educated by this proverbial wisdom from my roots and will walk on one path at a time: I shall look at the two parts of the theme separately, and then, begging permission from the wisdom of my community, invert the fork and look at the meeting-point of the paths. In that section, I will map out what I see as the challenges for mission in the coming millennium.

Called to one hope

The word "hope" is ambiguous. In many languages it refers both to *the activity of hoping* and *that which is hoped for*. Thus, hope is a word which on the one hand sets off the flashing amber lights warning us, "Beware, barriers ahead!", but on the other hand encourages us with assurance not to give up. In hoping, we have permission to keep going on, and to insist and persist despite all odds. The Old Testament scholar Walter Brueggemann clearly captures this journey of hope when he says, "Hope is the refusal to accept the reading of reality which is the majority opinion, and one does that only at great political and existential risk."[2]

I came to this conference to ask you to risk disbelieving what you see, to be defiant and rebellious, because hope calls for resistance – active resistance to the void of hopelessness that is defining our world. Thus hope is not merely an intellectual frame of mind. Hope is to be lived out. To hope for justice and peace is to work for the elimination of injustice and to be a peacemaker. To hope for democracy means to practise being democratic in our personal relationships. To hope for wholeness means to face our own lack of wholeness with courage and to be prepared to go through the pain of self-examination which leads to change. Change is, more often than not, a painful metamorphosis.

Hope is a central theme of the Bible and a major tenet of the Christian faith. For Christians, hope is *an expectation linked to faith.* We do not hope for what we have, but rather what we long for. Paul writing to the assembly in Rome says: "Now hope that is seen is not hope. For who hopes for what is seen? But if we hope for what we do not see, we wait for it with patience" (Rom. 8:24).

Christian hope is *radical* in nature, for it is grounded in God's act of raising Jesus from the dead and thus "making all things new" (Rev. 21:5). Resurrection for Christians is victory over any death-dealing possibility. It is a victory of the cross. In his *Theology of Hope*, German theologian Jürgen Moltmann states: "Hope is the distinctive contribution of Christian faith to our world in the midst of the ambiguous and even hopeless circumstances that plague human existence."[3] I really like this statement, but I cannot fail to ask what exactly it means. Can Christians claim to be the only vendors of hope?

I am raised in Lutheran theology and therefore sincerely proclaim again and again that Christian hope is linked to *grace.* It is by grace that we have this privilege to proclaim Christ incarnate as the hope of all creation and of the church. In this sense none may claim that they and only they deserve to hope.

Christian hope moves us to *a new order of priorities.* There is no greater witness to hope than Jesus of Nazareth. He was not silent about his mission to preach the good news to the poor, to release those who were captives and to give health to those who were ill (Luke 4:18-19). As he visited the towns and villages and saw with his own eyes the poverty, the inequality, the religious and economic oppression, the unemployment, the depression, the mental and physical illness and the cultural uncleanness facing the people (Matt. 9:35-38), his heart was filled with pity. In his witness Jesus told the people, "The time is fulfilled, and the kingdom of God has come near; repent, and believe in the good news" (Mark 1:15).

Christian hope invites *praxis.* Through his message about the reign of God, Jesus challenged his followers to be his witnesses, to have a new vision of what life is about, to live by new values and to enter into new relationships with each other as brothers and sisters in Christ, thus helping to transform the world through acts of love and service. The church, as the community of faith entrusted with communicating the gospel, is called to be a sign of the promised reign of God which is present wherever the liberating, saving and transforming power of Christ is incarnate. This is the hope that gathers us here as people from different cultures, yet committed to the gospel of Jesus Christ incarnate. In this conference we must dream God's dream that all people may have life and have it abundantly. It is not enough that some die and others just survive. It is our thoughts, actions and attitudes that make the difference.

From a faith perspective, this means engaging hour by hour with life in such a way that our deeds express that for which we hope, even while acknowledging the reality of disappointment, frustration, anger, brokenness and even despair. The challenge before us is *to dare to hope* as we dialogue together and find so much that is contradictory to hope. In daring we must wrestle with that which seeks to deny us hope and to disempower us. As we meet in Brazil, we would do well to listen to the words of the former Roman Catholic bishop of Recife, Dom Helder Câmara:

We must have no illusions. We must not be naive. If we listen to the voice of God, we make our choice, get out of ourselves and fight non-violently for a better world. We must not expect to find it easy; we shall not walk on roses, people will not throng to hear us and applaud, and we shall not always be aware of divine protection. If we are to be pilgrims of justice and peace, we must expect the desert.

Hope in a world of hopelessness

Our times are ripe for flirting with hopelessness. Cast your mind's eye over the news of the world or of your own community during the past few weeks. Think and explore with me for just one second! Our collective memory by now will have gathered a world of enormous problems. There is a kind of pessimism in the air which can afflict anyone concerned about hope. For the masses, traumatized by war, violence, poverty, insecurity, hunger or disease, the very mention of "hope" is ominous and deadly.

I embody some of the contradictions and dilemmas that speak the language of hopelessness. For I stand here not just as an individual but as one connected to a people. I embody a continent whose cultural and spiritual history in regard to mission and evangelization has left its people insecure and unsure. Yet we are also a continent that has been hospitable to all kinds of religions and religious beliefs. We have welcomed all our guests, to the point where the song of the guest has become the household song. For all these centuries of embracing Christianity, whatever has come out of Africa has not been seen to be appropriate in the missiological discussions about God.

As I prepared this presentation, war was looming in central Africa. Pictures of weeping women and children with small bundles on their heads, moving to unknown destinations, flooded the media as I struggled with "one hope... in diverse cultures". Reality seems to mock conversations about hope. It is not easy to grasp the full range of problems of faith that this kind of destabilization inflicts on the church and society. I bring the vulnerability of my continent to this gathering. According to our cultures and traditions, we are living with the curse of the blood of our massacred brothers and sisters, the children of the land of Africa. Our rivers and lakes are marked with that blood. The mass graves and the roaming spirits of the unburied dead have polluted the land, pointing to sins of omission and commission. What can we do to capture and celebrate a unity of purpose in the linguistic, ethnic, spiritual and cultural diversity that is our heritage, when in fact all our energy is spent on senseless wars that have left us hopelessly uprooted in a continent which has the largest population of refugees and displaced people in the world.

And so I ask, where shall we turn for hope? To African cultures? No, we have erred so much that we would never have enough animals to sacrifice for our atonement. In the face of all this humiliation, we must try to hear and face God's question to Cain: "What have you done? Listen; your brother's blood is crying out to me from the ground!" (Gen. 4:10). But "the neighbour" is also called to wear sackcloth and to lament. Where were you when all this was happening? What did you do? What is happening where *you* are? The neighbour too is guilty. What is happening today on our continent is rooted in histories which were exacerbated by our Western neighbours. The ethnic wars and violence in Africa are in a way present to a fair degree in all parts of the world. The current language of globalization should also be addressing the globalization of injustice and disrespect to life and to creation. It is at this moment of facing our own death in a world cluttered with death that we come face to face with the question of Christ crucified; it is through him alone that we are enabled to be free and to regain our dignity, and through him that we are made a people called to the ministry of reconciliation (2 Cor. 5:18-20).

This context prompts the question of whether the church offers *something new, different, helpful and hopeful* to lead people to rediscover the God-experience in lives which are governed by the question, "My God, my God, why have you forsaken me?" The question of what it means to be church in societies experiencing crisis looms large in any discussion of mission and evangelism today. An experience of faith that holds itself aloof from people seeking to escape marginalization poses a serious risk to the future of the church and the church of the future. The witness of the church will not be credible unless we who claim to be church take into account the traumatic situation of millions of people living in perilous conditions in many parts of the world. What meaning can mission have in churches that seek to witness to Christ without sharing the people's battles with the forces of oppression which assault their dignity? Is this not the time for the church to reclaim the language and practice of being a conscience of society? If the church does not, who will speak in God's name against the injustice, hatred, oppression, discrimination and greed of our time? Who will bring God back to the people? We cannot avoid seeking answers to the question, "Does the church make a difference?"

Over these past months as I read and prayerfully considered what I might say at this conference, what kept me awake was not the big debates regarding the major issues confronting our world, but rather people for whom Christ died. I was kept awake by the pain in families as marriages break up, jobs become harder to come by and food and shelter – once thought to be a basic need – become in reality luxuries affordable only to some people. I was kept awake by children. Children crying out for love, reaching out in vain, and turning to the streets, to crime, to prostitution, to death. Children in hospitals, in prisons, on the front line of wars – children who have never been given the chance to be children. Children orphaned by AIDS and wars. Children abused by adults and turned into commodities by society. Children whom we would rather not see because they upset our neat, comfortable lives. And I pondered, what does mission have to say about these little ones whom Christ welcomed: "Let the little children come to me...; for it is to such as these that the kingdom of God belongs" (Mark 10:14)?

For several years now the media have been drawing attention to the plight of children in our host country, Brazil. We have heard of children killed in the streets on "clean-up" missions, children who have become commodities for the trade in human organs. Just a few days after an international conference on children was held in Sweden (August 1996), we read of the horrendous rape and killing of two Belgian girls in the prime of their youth, and of the many other Belgian children who are still missing. The reaction of some people in Europe made it clear that this was the first time that crimes against children had become real to them.

Why have the thousands of Brazilian street children, Liberian child-soldiers or Filipino child prostitutes not elicited an equal reaction of shock? The international trafficking in women and children, from Asia in particular but now from Eastern Europe as well, has not been high on the agenda of the churches, even though activist groups have been speaking against it for more than two decades. Does the world react differently to the sufferings of people of different cultures and different economic possibilities? Is *one hope* possible for people of diverse cultures?

I table these issues because I am convinced that our times call us to maturity and honesty in dialogue. Dialogue is a conversation that entails two-way communication. Only when there is mutuality in our relating will we be able to wrestle with the realities of our diversity and still hold onto hope.

Brazil is a fitting venue for this world mission conference on the gospel-cultures dialogue because it enables us to learn something about mission from the realities of people in this country of so much diversity. To speak of children makes Bahia and Brazil a relevant place to meet. Yet it is also here that we might begin to raise our voices on culture and difference. This is the place to table the agenda of race relations. What does it mean to be black in this country? What does it mean to be a descendant of a continent so far away and to live here with a history of slave trade? This is a place that presents the meeting of cultures and religions. Expectantly, we must be curious about what we will learn from the Afro-Brazilian religious expression called Candomblé. In what ways does it inspire hope? What can we take home with us from Brazil?

And so I turn to my next path in the forked road of the proverbial African hyena.

The gospel in diverse cultures

Gospel and culture has been an issue of concern for the church since the beginning. Already in the book of Acts we read about conflicts in the early church over worship, table fellowship, circumcision, the Holy Spirit, gospel and government.

Yet in missiological discussion a kind of dualistic thinking developed in which culture was for a long time simply seen as a concern of the South. Discussions about inculturation, indigenization and contextualization, wherever they took place, were aimed mainly at addressing issues and theologies of the former missionized churches. It is interesting for those of us who come from these churches to see the issues of culture now being brought to the forefront of global church discussion. Not only are we reminded of the various condemnations of our cultures throughout history which stripped us of our very identity, but we vividly remember the WCC seventh assembly in Canberra (1991), where the keynote address[4] of Prof. Chung Hyun Kyung of Korea sparked controversy. Truly speaking, how do we define syncretism today? Is this perhaps a word that has served its purpose and is no longer useful for the

Christian church? Is there any confession that can claim to be free from syncretism?

Neither gospel nor culture is good news until it liberates. That is to say, there is no gospel or culture that is automatically liberating. All hearing of the gospel in any culture is situation-variable. Gospel always comes with culture. We must always ask, is it good news for others? For whom is the gospel good news? For whom is this culture good news? My putting of gospel and culture on the same level could be provocative and will surely make many uneasy. In reality I am appealing to missiologists and evangelists to consider the intercultural dimension of evangelization. We must exercise the hermeneutical function of theology when we are invited to speak about gospel and culture.

"Gospel" and "culture" are not abstract terms but are descriptions of realities. Within these words are people with faces, people who bleed when pricked and laugh when tickled. Participation in culture is so natural and ubiquitous that most people take culture for granted and do not reflect critically on it. To me, mission means giving gospel and culture a human face. Mission is unwrapping the gospel packaged in theological words and concepts and making it relevant to human beings for whom Christ gave his life on the cross. The communication of the gospel happens only through culture – language, structures, art, music, dance and other expressions which influence the relationships between people and with God. If that culture is not liberating neither will the gospel that it interprets be liberating.

I grew up in a village in Africa. When I think of culture I think of a little animal we call the *ekogongolo*, which is often found in fresh moist soil. When touched, it coils into a harmless small spiral. Under normal conditions it can move either way without turning itself. Culture has this kind of double mobility. In some instances culture is the badge, or even the "creed", for community identity – for culture defines who we are and gives us security as a community. In other instances culture is used to make distinctions between different people in the community and to assign roles, functions and practices (some of which can be oppressive).

When we speak of dialogue in cultural matters, the issue is not just to become accepting of the diversity of cultures, but rather to find ways by which we can work creatively with cultures and traditions so that they can be liberating. For nearly ten years I have been involved in reading the Bible with groups of rural women in Africa.

I began to write about my accumulated experiences about three years ago in an analysis which I have come to call "cultural hermeneutics".[5] I came into that work after realizing that under the rubric of accepting cultures – our own and that of others – we risk tolerating unjust behaviour.

For generations, African women have unquestioningly obeyed all that society prescribes for them in the name of culture. Child marriages, female circumcision and the rites of passage from birth to death, whether useful or harmful, are imposed on African women simply because it is "our culture". This might be taken to mean that what is culture is natural, good and unavoidable. Culture has silenced many women in Africa. It has hindered them from experiencing Jesus' liberating promise of abundant life for all (John 10:10). Cultural hermeneutics seeks to demystify the abstractness of "culture" by calling for analysis of and reflection on culture and its effects on people.[6]

African women (whose voices are only now beginning to surface) are calling the churches to go beyond a theology of inculturation and place cultures themselves under scrutiny, in order to determine whether they promote justice, life, peace and liberation or whether they diminish and dehumanize people. Cultural hermeneutics is therefore the analysis and interpretation of cultural practices with a view to discerning their liberative and oppressive aspects. African women do cultural hermeneutics by telling stories of our own experience and explaining how we read and understand the scriptures within our cultural setting. By telling our stories and reviving those of our foremothers, we will be able to unearth those elements of our culture that were holistic and bring them back into the church. We will be able to unmask those aspects of our culture that are harmful and bring them to the public as collective sins for which the society, the church and especially we as women must make confession and receive forgiveness. For me, that is renewal in the power of the Holy Spirit, renewal for the whole church in Africa. Women in other parts of the world[7] have also identified cultural hermeneutics as an urgent need in their own contexts.

Doing cultural hermeneutics is not easy. It requires, on the one hand, questioning and examining age-old beliefs and practices and, on the other, finding possibilities to affirm and reclaim those aspects of culture that are good but have been discarded. The missionary, anthropological and colonial era condemned the cultures of many of their subjects. The formerly colonized world has responded by glorifying culture, and the skin of both colonizer and colonized is still too raw to accommodate criticism. Critiquing other people's cultures is a very sensitive matter at this point in history. The former colonizers have shifted their attitudes, so that they too either over-glorify the cultures they once criticized, or stand aloof even in the face of injustice because "it is their culture". The tension is now how to take part in analyzing cultures – our own and other people's – objectively. Can people cross boundaries and speak about the ills in other people's cultures without being seen as neo-colonialists? How can dialogue take place in our world today when we have become so "sensitive" to each other that we can no longer draw a line between the needed and the unjust critique? I consider this the most difficult issue facing intercultural hermeneutics. We are trapped in emotions and subjectivity and sometimes this is counterproductive.

Mission challenges for the 21st century

Let me return now to the meeting-point of our two paths – "one hope" and "diverse cultures" – and suggest six areas of mission which I consider urgent for the 21st century:
– mission involves helping people to read the Bible for themselves;
– mission involves celebrating difference and diversity;
– mission involves developing new models of partnership;
– mission involves listening to the new voices from struggling communities;
– mission involves addressing new issues of our time and age;
– mission involves listening to the small voices of hope from the seemingly weak.

Reading the Bible

Reading the Bible on one's own creates the possibility of a sincere response to the message of the Bible. Many people, even churchgoers, are biblically illiterate, because the tradition of reading the Bible in the family and in one's private life has greatly diminished. The Bible as a book of faith has become distant, and while many people know about it, few *know* it. It is urgent that the Bible be returned to its central place in the lives of Christians. Churches must work together with ecumenical bodies for this mission. The Bible societies, which seem to be almost marginalized in the ecumenical movement, should be given their rightful place of leadership because they publish the most important resource for churches, for mission and for all Christians' spiritual growth. Here we have lessons to learn from the Bible itself. Recall the Ethiopian finance minister who upon reading the scriptures for himself asked Philip for baptism (Acts 8:26-40). I also would like to lift up the work of the so-called evangelical churches or the base communities in Latin America where people have been transformed by gathering and reading the Bible together. Women's prayer groups and Bible study groups have from time immemorial been witnesses to the importance of the Bible in the daily lives of Christians.

Celebrating difference and diversity

Our times compel us to accommodate contradictions and diversities on the one hand, and uniformity and globalization on the other. In this context the question posed by African American womanist theologian Katie Cannon is appropriate: "Can we be different, but not alienated?"[8] Mission today requires a painful and heart-searching effort to walk with people in "difference". If we want to build strong and faithful relationships throughout the world we must deepen our trust of one another and develop a healthy approach to diversity reflected in styles of worship and relationships of race, gender, generation. Healthy diversity builds upon trust and a common vision for the good of the whole community.

Mission today must face the challenge of being hospitable to those who question the exclusive jargon and way of presenting what appears to Christians as the ultimate truth. The institutional church must come to terms with the challenge of what to do with our faith that is built on the "foundation" (or is it the *myth*?) of certainty. How will the mission and evangelism of the church of today and the next millennium appropriate the knowledge gained by working with other faiths? The San Antonio world mission conference humbly stated, "Since God's mystery in Christ surpasses our understanding and since our knowledge of God's saving power is imperfect, we Christians are called to be witnesses to others, not judges of them."[9]

While we carry this affirmation into the 21st century, we cannot say that it ends the daunting questions of how to be faithful in presenting the message of Christ in a pluralist society and in a world of cultural diversity. We have to be clear that our certainty is not to be equated with security, but rather is dependent on the faithfulness of God. It is a spiritual certainty which we can express only through an attitude of love towards other people as enjoined by the Christian faith. Our worship and actions of faith must reflect that we are at every moment in the presence of the living God.

Developing new models of partnership

In our globalized world, mission too must be seen as a global phenomenon. The mission of the church today begs for new models of partnership that promote mutual and reciprocal learning among people globally. Missiological reflection still takes place mostly in the North, and the persons who teach in these institutions are rather homogeneous. The decision-making boards of church mission departments and missionary societies are still predominantly male. Whenever I visit missiology departments and mission boards in connection with my responsibilities with the Lutheran World Federation, I am delighted to meet the "experts" (who are mostly former missionaries to the South), but wonder whether this does not have the unintended consequence of maintaining Western intellectual dominance (or possibly intellectual myopia). Churches in the North and South have to work together to find forms of theological and ministerial formation that promote and encourage mutual learning and healthy partnership.

To foster sustainable new models of partnership, the former missionizing countries need to rethink their superiority complex, and the former missionalized countries must squarely face and overcome their inferiority complex. Only then can the present monologue be turned into a dialogue on what it would take to be partners in mission. Let me speak to the inferiority of the South and challenge my brothers and sisters from the North equally to make yourselves vulnerable by addressing your superiority complex. We have been and are still angry about being dominated by the North. It would be naive simply to dismiss the past, but it would do us no good to continue this litany until doomsday. Having awakened from the slumber of considering Europe and North America as the cradle of world civilization, we must now ask ourselves what we are to do with this knowledge. How do we assist former missionaries and colonial masters to look at the world with different eyes? I am convinced that mission today calls people of the former mission fields into more responsibility than we seem to understand. We have gone through a period of justified resistance. In the Bangkok world mission conference in 1973 we said: "We refuse to serve simply as raw material which others use for their salvation."[10] At one time this frankness was shocking to traditional missionary agencies and churches in Europe and North America, who were not prepared for the new consciousness of the South and its articulate voicing of this rejection. I believe there is more openness to change now. I see signs of willingness on both sides – but also regret that the inferiority complex of the South is fuelled by poverty in terms of material goods, money and power.

Listening to new voices from struggling communities
For many years the ecumenical agenda has been influenced by the desire to promote the unity of the church, to such an extent that it sometimes sacrifices the integrity of the groups within it. Today these groups question an ecumenical agenda that does not take a decisive option for their needs. The voices of the marginalized, seeking to move their concerns to the centre of ecumenical debate, will increasingly define ecumenical formation. The solidarity groups, bound together by race, ethnicity, gender, various orientations of opinions and practices on (for example) environmental concerns, indigenous issues and human rights interests, require fundamental changes in the powers, procedures and forms of being "ecumenical" as well as being "church". Do these voices not mirror the signs of the reign of God?

To take but one illustration: women in many parts of the world are calling the churches to be accountable with regard to the attitudes to women reflected in their theology, liturgy and worship, structures, history and access to ministry and leadership. The struggle for the acceptance of women is at the same time a struggle for the trustworthiness of the church's proclamation (Gal. 3:28). Can the church take an issue like violence against women and develop programmes around it to help the society to change? Can the church give hope without first being renewed itself?

Addressing new issues of our time and age
One of the most visible challenges to Christianity today is posed by urbanization and the secularization of societies. People in the cities of the South and North alike are adopting similar globalized cultural behaviour conditioned by the constraints of their context. They are striving to make sense out of their lives amidst so many contemporary struggles. The majority have no church background and are unfamiliar with the message of the gospel, and so will not listen to the message of the church unless the church itself is signif-

icantly different and has something particular to offer. If Christianity is to make sense to them, it will have to be what Paul described as "all things to all people".[11] In the church we speak the language of Hallelujah and Amen, but we must remember that today our world also speaks of Coca-Cola and Toyota.

Another urgent issue of our time is how to do mission in a divided world among divided people. How will the church of today and the next millennium package and market the gospel of one hope in the face of globalization and rapid transformation of a world catalyzed by information technology, the never-ending gap between rich and poor, urban and rural, those advocating ethnic unity and those seeking national unity, men and women, youth and adults?

Drawing hope from the "weak"

I believe that people from the South, through their experience of suffering and longing for God, have a chance to share their hope with the world. It is Africa which prompts me in this belief. In Africa we know death, humiliation, what it means to be down. Yet it is precisely at such times, when we search for God in the midst of the rubble, that we are called by the Christian faith to embrace *hope*. Economic and political issues challenge the self-understanding of Christians as an ecclesial community and have consequences for their understanding of the role of the church in the wider human community. However, the church's mission comprises more than ecclesial and social issues. The church is about God and the love of God, which is not limited to those who do good and live rightly but which invites and begs us daily to turn to God who first loved us (1 John 4:19) and to rejoice in hope. There is some of that rejoicing among the people of Africa. The churches are full and people sing and dance to the message of the gospel. Let the picture of Archbishop Tutu dancing during the days of apartheid tell the story of African hope.

The hope of the church is a *spiritual* hope based on God's love. The certainty of the Christian faith is grounded not in religion but in the everlasting God of love. Those who are at their weakest depend upon this God of hope, who loves and forgives.

The hunger for faith and for spirituality in Africa never ceases to surprise both the guests and the hosts on that continent, whether in times of death or in times of celebration. It is precisely this search for God, even now when things are bleak, that makes my region a continent of great hope. For us in Africa, this is *a time to hope*. In our diverse cultures, we hope because God promises liberation from all that oppresses us. Hope with us, by embracing the theme of this conference, "Called to One Hope – The Gospel in Diverse Cultures".

NOTES

[1] In the past few months, I have been thoroughly enticed by the aromas of what has been written and spoken in preparation for this conference. The WCC-stimulated gospel and cultures studies which have been published in (to date) 15 pamphlets, together with the numerous reflections that have appeared since January 1995 in the *International Review of Mission*, have been the major source of that enticing sweet aroma, pulling me in different directions. Knowingly or unknowingly I certainly draw from these materials, and therefore I offer public acknowledgment of and gratitude to the authors of the various pamphlets and articles, and to the WCC's Programme Unit II for having made these resources available to me.
[2] Walter Brueggemann, *The Prophetic Imagination*, Philadelphia, Fortress, 1978, p.67.
[3] *Hope for the Church: Moltmann in Dialogue with Theology*, Nashville, Abingdon, 1979, p.10.
[4] Chung Hyun Kyung, "Come Holy Spirit – Renew the Whole Creation", in *Signs of the Spirit: Official Report, Seventh Assembly*, ed. Michael Kinnamon, Geneva, WCC Publications, 1991, pp.34-37.
[5] See, for example, Musimbi Kanyoro, "Cultural Hermeneutics: An African Contribution", in *Women's Visions: Theological Reflection, Celebration, Action*, ed. Ofelia Ortega, Geneva, WCC Publications, 1995, pp.18-25.
[6] In 1989, a group of women theologians met in Accra, Ghana, to create the Circle of Concerned African Women Theologians. The theme of the convocation was "Arise, daughter". There we arose and began writing our first continental volume, *The Will to Arise: Women, Culture and Tradition in Africa* (Mercy Amba Oduyoye and Musimbi R.A. Kanyoro, eds, Maryknoll, NY, Orbis, 1992). We have never returned to slumber. We are writing, speaking, preaching, meeting to reject dehumanization. We have now produced more than ten books, most of which focus on the need to liberate women from oppressive aspects of culture.
[7] Mercy Amba Oduyoye has done perhaps the most extensive work on cultural hermeneutics, although she has never named it such. Her *Daughters of Anowa* (Maryknoll, NY, Orbis, 1995) is the most complete work produced to date. Elsa Támez, Letty Russell and Mary John Mananzan all speak to the need for cultural hermeneutics in *Women Resisting Violence: Spirituality for Life*, Mary John Mananzan et al., eds, Maryknoll, NY, Orbis, 1996.
[8] This is the title of an exchange of letters between Katie Cannon (African American womanist theologian) and Carter Heyward (white American feminist theologian) published in *Feminist Theological Ethics*, Lois K. Daly, ed., Louisville, KY, Westminster John Knox, 1994.
[9] *The San Antonio Report*, Frederick R. Wilson, ed., Geneva, WCC Publications, 1990, p.32.
[10] Bangkok world mission conference, 1972-73. Many third-world forums and writings are even more outspoken today than they were in the 1970s.
[11] See 1 Corinthians 9:19-23, where Paul argues that he became like every other person in order to be able to be a blessing to them. Jesus was accused of eating with tax collectors and sinners. He neither avoided nor condemned those who were different from him. What better model for Christians could there be than Jesus the Christ!

THEME PANEL I

A German Perspective

Cornelia Füllkrug-Weitzel

It is not easy for a Christian from Germany to talk about gospel and culture with the same emphasis as do Christians from other cultures, for two reasons – one historical, the other contemporary.

The misuse of gospel and culture by the National Socialists
National Socialism has made it difficult for us to have a straightforward, unbroken relationship to "German culture". The National Socialists created a national identity and a Germanic culture to shore up their antisemitic, racist tyranny. Not only did they revive ancient Germanic rites and symbols, but they also created identity models for their own immediate purposes and projected them into the past. Many elements of popular culture were incorporated into this image of a master race and were absorbed by it. This hypostatization – almost idolization – of the Aryan race (blood), the German nation and national character and Germanic culture was sometimes held up in place of the Christian tradition as the original pre-Christian formative element in Germany,[1] sometimes portrayed as the decisive component of the Christian tradition.[2] In the latter case, the Christian faith was then subjected to a process of re-Germanization, which considered race, people and nation to be absolute, God-given life-principles which had to be protected and preserved in all social and church activities.[3] "Racial definition", "our own race", "the mission of our people" were seen as orders of creation and set above all Christian ethical values. In practice they were used to justify the eradication from the culture of all things "un-German" and the subjugation and annihilation of "non-Aryan races" in Europe.[4]

From this widespread esteem for nationalism in the church and theology it was but a short step to subordinating the gospel to the

---

This paper was presented in German.

imperatives of a nationalistic culture and the dictates of a nationalistic interpretation of history.[5] Many German theologians became involved in what was known as the *Glaubensbewegung Deutscher Christen* (German Christian movement) – a collection of national-conservative, nationalist and cultural Protestant theologians who came together for the religious development of National Socialism and the renewal of the church in the National Socialist spirit. Some of these "German Christians" saw the coming of National Socialism as a call from God and justified swimming with this tide of "national awakening" on the grounds of mission to the German people. The "rebirth of the church" was part of the "rebirth of the German people" and the revival of German consciousness. But the content of the renewal of faith among "German Christians" was National Socialist ideology, to which the gospel was subordinate, and not the other way round.[6] The influence and political power they managed to gain within the church came only through massive support from the National Socialist government. Their aim was to reshape the church into a kind of "storm troops of Jesus Christ" – an effective factor in the life of the nation and an instrument in the hands of the political authorities of the Third Reich. This form of "national church" and "national mission" was based on the exclusion of essential parts of the biblical witness and of the people of God. It closed the good news of salvation to all those among the German people – and all peoples – who did not fit the political definition of the German people and nation.

In opposition to this synthesis of the gospel with an exclusive authoritarian culture, the Confessing Church was formed, stating in the famous Barmen Declaration: "We reject the false doctrine, as though the church could and would have to acknowledge as a source of its proclamation, apart from and besides this one word of God, still other events and powers, figures and truths, as God's revelation." Those who drafted the Barmen Declaration pointed out that the theology of the "German Christians" was no accident, but the result of a weakness in German theology, specifically the post-Enlightenment theological current known as "cultural Protestantism", with its quest for the "reconciliation of religion and culture" (Richard Rothe). This was accused of not only sharing but also reinforcing theologically the German bourgeoisie's sense of cultural superiority and nationalism, and of having lost sight of the distinct sovereignty of the word of God spoken in Jesus Christ.

Life in the "post-modern world"[7]

Germany can no longer claim to be a country with a uniform culture.

- Since the 1960s rapid processes of modernization[8] have been undermining industrial society and traditional institutions like the family, churches and political parties, encouraging individualization and the fragmentation of society into different cultures. An array of cultures has emerged, each specific to its milieu, existing side by side but not in contact with one another – a self-service supermarket of cultures.
- The division of Germany into the German Democratic Republic and the Federal Republic of Germany gave rise to completely different cultures.
- With the arrival of migrant workers, asylum-seekers and ethnic Germans from central and eastern Europe, Germany has become a country where people of different cultures and religions live side by side. In Berlin, for example, there are more than 60 congregations of Christians from different cultural backgrounds.

At the same time, a process of uniformization is taking place. In Germany as in the rest of the world, all cultural expressions are ever more clearly and ruthlessly dominated by economics. The demands of the global market and the needs which it creates are moulding the country like a meta-culture. The foundations of traditional cultures and the distinctions among them are being destroyed, and enduring new cultures cannot emerge, since the call for constant progress and ever more rapid change is altering every culture at a breathtaking rate. The advertising slogan "Accept no limits" aptly illustrates the boundlessness of the ideology of growth and competition.

New and artificial demands for all sorts of superfluous goods and services are being created all the time, with no respect for anything whatever. Cultural expressions and social relations are commercialized and subjected to market pressures. Art, spirituality, education, communication, along with kindness, helpfulness, love and the like are reduced to the level of marketable goods. Human relations, the natural environment and social standards are sacrificed in the name of the market. The image of "the good life" dangled before people by the advertising world is tied up with unreflecting consumer thinking and unfettered materialism. Hedonism, loss of solidarity and egocentrism are the consequences.

The flip-side of this market culture based on domination and permanent economic growth is a "culture of exclusion" for entire nations and ever broader sectors of the population. For them, it is effectively a "culture of death". As non-consumers, they cease to exist in terms of political and public planning and responsibility.

A second feature of the contemporary context in Germany has to do with the cultural influence of the church. Even though European culture has largely emancipated itself from the church, in central Europe the churches and their theological traditions have remained significant components of the secular culture on into the post-war period. In the western part of Germany one can still speak of a "cultural representation"[9] of the church in society. Collective everyday life to some extent has retained ties with the Christian tradition, even though the influence of Christianity on individuals has steadily dwindled.

But although this was true for western Germany, it cannot be said to be true for Germany as a whole since reunification. Studies by sociologists of religion in the eastern part of Germany[10] have shown that the forced break with the Christian cultural tradition under the Socialist Unity Party of Germany (SED) led to an almost total lack of Christian knowledge among the unchurched population (around 80 percent) which is without parallel in Europe.[11] Forty years of anti-Christian, atheistic propaganda and deliberate destruction of the Christian cultural foundations of the society mean that in eastern Germany the church can no longer work and carry out its mission against the background of a Christian culture.[12] (This experience highlights how much harm was done to the church and its proclamation by the destruction of the supporting culture – in other words, how much the church, at least in Germany, depended upon it.)

Third, while it is true in both parts of Germany that "religion has again become socially acceptable as a topic of polite discussion"[13] and that we are now living in an era of religious awakening, religious needs are no longer being channelled through the Christian churches, and the churches are unable to harness and guide the potential of religious feeling in society. The churches in the land of the Reformation, though still thinking of themselves as a national church, are on the way to becoming a minority interest group among many other communities based on various faiths and worldviews.

The logic of the market which says that the customer rules prevails in the sphere of religion as well. The Enlightenment principle of freedom of religion is construed in today's post-modern society as the freedom of individuals to shop according to their fancy in the religious supermarket, for elements from any religion or philosophy (including what is on offer from the different Christian confessions) and to paste them all together. At the same time the freedom of the consumer, post-modern pluralism, has itself become the content of faith, taking on a pseudo-religious character as a kind of ersatz religion. The quest for truth has become taboo, and the possibility that a meta-truth exists is aggressively denied. In the area of worldviews, the logic of the market has taken on totalitarian features.

Proclaiming the gospel for such a time as this

It is more important than ever before to emphasize that neither God nor any of God's creatures is ours to control, and thus to counter the destructive, rationalistic and capitalistic claim to dispose freely of God, humanity and nature. The divine cannot be realized in any culture, nor by any individual, people or church by its own strength, and what is achieved can never be divine. That is why no one – no ethnic group, no nation or group of nations, no market, no church – can claim universal validity and hence superiority for its norms. The resurrection of the Crucified One is the only realization of the divine on earth which does not represent some individual interest, which excludes no one and which does not have a destructive reverse side. On the contrary, it represents a counter-reality, offering encouragement and guidance for the commitment to genuine universal justice and peace.

The task for Christians, within their own situation and culture, is to look for and to foster appropriate analogies, practical demonstrations and parables of reconciled reality in the world, signs of hope of the reign of God, always bearing in mind their own inadequacy and need of grace. This can be done by joining constructively in shaping the world and culture. But it can also take the form – as it did with the Confessing Church – of challenging the dominant power by a radical "no without any yes" to a self-deifying tyrannical culture when this is the only possible form of obedience to God's word which the situation will allow. In the history of the ecumenical movement, one such refusal came about over the issue of apartheid.

We have only begun to consider the implications of all this for the church, and there are more questions than answers. I mention only three broad points.

1. We must remind ourselves again that we as individuals or as churches belonging to a culture depend on the Spirit of God, who also comes to meet us in other people of different skin colours, different cultures, different confessions. This means that we must bear our witness in society in ecumenical openness and fellowship, not in a spirit of rivalry and opposition in which every person and every group claim that they alone possess the true faith. That obscures the gospel and the proclamation of the gospel. It must be made clear that the churches of different confessions represent different attempts to be true witnesses to the gospel in their own culture. A credible act of witness and an important contribution to peaceful coexistence in our country would be to demonstrate to society by the way we live that our identity is not threatened but enriched by the diversity of cultures, and that all agree that we are equally dependent on God. This could also encourage Christians to look for their own ways of expressing their Christian faith. In other words, the gospel cannot be proclaimed in a spirit of aggressive exclusiveness, competing for a share of the religious market, but only in the awareness of our own relativity and in cooperation with Christians of different confessions.

As a consequence of our history and in response to our present reality, Christian life in Germany must be ecumenically open and ready for intercultural dialogue. This means that we must accept the questioning of our country's theology and politics by our ecumenical partners, and must take the experiences of other Christians and churches into consideration as we develop our theological and ethical opinions. This applies both in our external contacts, as part of world Christianity, and in our sharing with Christian communities of other confessions and cultures within our own country. We can learn to recognize with gratitude the wondrous variety of God's creation in other cultures, and we can find in theologies shaped by other cultures new possibilities for interpreting our own tradition as well as the gospel.

2. The question of inculturation in Germany can no longer be framed in terms of "gospel and culture"; even within our own context it must be described as a question of "gospel and *cultures*". The rapid tempo of cultural change and the resulting variety of cultures and distinctions are more than the church can cope with, as a large institution with pretensions to giving oversight and instruction, and with its parish principle of covering the needs of an area by means of a local pastor. The church itself – at least in the eastern part of our

country – has become a sub-culture of sorts, appealing to only a very limited circle of people of a specific social background. We need therefore to be open to the different sub-cultures in our country and migrate actively towards them. Like the disciples and apostles, who had the courage not to stay put in Jerusalem, where the religious establishment was based and where the religious authorities held the believers together through dogmas and rules, we must have the courage to tread new paths which will bring us into contact with people of other cultures, who have been excluded from the community of the faithful.

We need therefore to recognize that the gospel is differently inculturated in different sub-cultures[14] – whether among women or men, the younger generation or the middle-aged, the homeless or members of the middle classes. The churches would do well to be open to various forces of inculturation and to enable new access to the church for groups, communities and people who represent the different cultures outside the middle-class, official church. This calls for a variety of entry-points into the Christian message and Christian fellowship. It also means encouraging and enabling people of different generations, different gender, different cultural origins and different group allegiances to discover the meaning of the gospel for their own experience and to translate it into their own symbols, so that they can testify as living witnesses in their own place. The authorized office-bearers of the church should not be seen as the only ones who proclaim the gospel. Laypeople, especially women and young people, whose understanding of faith and forms of piety have often been disparaged and underestimated, need to be taken seriously and need encouragement to witness to the faith in their own words and their own cultural forms of expression in their own setting and place of activity. Such a "migration" by the churches into the diversity of cultures in our country should not be bewailed as a loss of control and unity, but gratefully welcomed as expressing God's sovereign will to raise up new witnesses in every part of society.

The problem for the church is whether it can manage to organize and maintain community during this process. It will have to find forms of cohesiveness which do not depend on claims to domination and monopoly. Such cohesiveness will be found in discovering and celebrating connections and commonalities, in relating to one another in mutual accountability, and in together seeking a new and practical solution to each dispute over truth.

3. In response to the sovereignty of God's word, the churches in all cultures must rise up together to contradict the totalitarian pretensions of the logic of the market. Any synthesis of gospel with the interests of capital and the logic and culture of the market – as manifested in an extreme form in the "prosperity gospel", but in a less obvious form also in many references to the market economy as "Christian" – is by definition not reconcilable with the gospel. While the churches may differ in their ethical assessment of and attitude towards the various forms of market economy, they are bound, on the basis of the gospel, to oppose any idolization or absolutization of the market, together with any absolute claims of pluralism, its philosophical variant. By proclaiming the only real liberation story and by setting the example of an alternative counter-culture of simplicity, they must free people from the slavery of the consumer society and the fiction that consumption will make them happy. They must help the people of the rich nations to learn that "enough is enough" and to turn away from the ideology of unlimited economic growth at the expense of others, and the life-style that goes with it. They can help to restore the Christian vision of a more fulfilled life – the vision of a life in which quality counts more than quantity, a life of giving and taking, of communal values rather than individual self-realization; a vision that opens new perspectives and hope to the millions of excluded people as well. "Starting from here we can wade into the human struggle with our gospel of hope, side with the victims, find ways to confront influence, modify and make responsible the powers around us, suggest structures of great justice and human compassion, and above all, let others know who the Lord of the struggle is. This, too, is a form of mission to our culture."[15]

NOTES

[1] Cf. for example the theoretician of the master race, the editor-in-chief of the newspaper *Der Völkische Beobachter*, Alfred Rosenberg, and his "Alliance for German Culture".
[2] There were rival currents within the National Socialist movement which took these different positions. In 1930 the National Socialist German Workers' Party (NSDAP) did a strategic turnabout in its religious policy, moving away from new paganism to positive Christianity.
[3] "The God-given basis of all human life includes, not only among other things, but first of all and above all in importance, the *nation (Volk)* and *national character (Volkstum)*, to which each of us is bound. The nation grows from family, custom and tribe, and thus deci-

sively is a community of *blood* and *race*. National character is therefore the type of mind which is common to a people, its 'soul' which is revealed in its language and all its cultural activity, and which holds it together in 'elemental love'... Each nation's particular nature is the particular idea God had in creating it... The nation has moral primacy as the full, natural moral community... It calls for respect and obedience towards the Creator's law in nature and the Creator's guidance in history. Therefore the church, too, must be the '*national* church' in this sense: it must, through its mission and structure, proclaim the gospel to *this* people in *its* language... etc., and again and again... has proved itself to be a creative force for national identity" (H. Weinel, "Nation", in *Religion in Geschichte und Gegenwart*, vol. V, 1926).

4 "The practical life of the church should go hand in hand with, and dignify, the national tradition in its celebrations; it must support, as far as possible, all efforts to keep our national tradition healthy" (H. Weinel, "Nation", *ibid.*, quoted by K. Barth, *Kirchliche Dogmatik*, III/4, pp.348f.). After the "German Christians" seized power the German Evangelical Church justified this policy in certain provincial churches by excluding Jewish Christians from among its members (in the so-called "Aryan paragraph").

5 "We confess an affirmative faith in Christ in keeping with the character of our race, in the German spirit of Luther and the piety of the heroes" (Guidelines of the "German Christian" movement, 26 May 1932, in *Church Yearbook 1933-1944*, p.14).

6 "We expect our national church, as a German people's church, to free itself of everything un-German in its worship and confession, especially the Old Testament and its Jewish morality of earned rewards. We demand that a German people's church should take seriously the proclamation of the simple good news, purified from every oriental distortion, and of the heroic figure of Jesus as the foundation of a Christianity in keeping with the character of our race" (resolution of the Greater Berlin Region of the "German Christians" movement, meeting in the Berlin Sports Palace, 13 November 1933, in *Church Yearbook 1933-1944*, p.38).

7 David Bosch described the post-modern society as a totalitarian society whose totalitarianism is scarcely recognized, since it is experienced as benevolent. "Its prerequisites and by-products include centralization, bureaucratization, damage to the environment, manipulation and exploitation of human beings, relentless consumer thinking and chronic unemployment... It is a permissive society, without standards, role models or traditions, a society that lives for the moment, without a past and also without a future. People live completely in the present and seek instant gratification" (Bosch, "An die Zukunft glauben: Auf dem Wege zu einer Missionstheologie für die westliche Kultur", in *Weltmission Heute*, no. 24, Hamburg, 1996, p.12).

8 "Modernization means the technological steps towards rationalization and the changes in work and organization. But it includes much more besides: the alteration of the character of society, of the course of normal life histories, styles and ways of life, structures of power and influence, of political oppression and participation, perceptions of reality and the norms of human knowledge" (Ulrich Beck, *Risikogesellschaft: Auf dem Weg in eine andere Moderne*, Frankfurt, 1986, p.25).

9 E. Neubert, *Volkskirche – Minderheitskirche – was sonst?* East-West conversations on the identity and public role of the church, *Encounters* 9, Berlin, 1994, p.29.

10 Cf. for example, Ehrhart Neubert, "Gründlich ausgetrieben", a study on the profile and the psycho-social, cultural and religious situation of churchlessness in eastern Germany and the preconditions for church work (mission), *Encounters* 13, Berlin, 1996.

11 This extends even to loss of language and the inability to recognize Christian symbols, let alone decipher them. This abolition of the Christian social and cultural milieu, making it no longer the tradition, took place as a violent destructuring, a forcible severing of the population from the church tradition, linked to the (SED) party's illusion that it could cre-

ate a socialist culture and way of life. The party tried to replace the traditional tie to the Christian religion and the churches with a quasi-religious tie to state and party as the carriers of religion.

[12] Church art and historical church buildings – their symbolism often scarcely understood – are the only relics that remain of a once-Christian country.

[13] Manfred Josuttis, "Religion – Gefahr der Postmoderne", in *Evangelische Kommentare*, 21, 1988, p.16.

[14] We must keep on asking: "Who is inculturating what? Is it up to a person or to a church to inculturate the gospel personified in Jesus? Does not such an intention mask the secret Christian pretension to have jurisdiction over both gospel and culture as elements accessible to our analysis and useful to our strategy? This is why the subject and object of the cultural link-up must be indicated very precisely" (Klauspeter Blaser, "Kultur und Christentum", in *Evangelisches Kirchenlexikon,* an international theological encyclopedia, E. Fahlbusch, J.M. Lochmann, J. Mbiti, J. Pelikan and L. Vischer, eds, vol. 2, Göttingen, 1989, col. 1518).

[15] Charles C. West, "Gospel for American Culture: Variations on a Theme by Newbigin", in *Missiology: An International Review*, no. 19, 1991, p.441.

THEME PANEL I

An Australian Aboriginal Perspective

Wali Fejo

The relationship between evangelism and culture

I want first to emphasize the togetherness of gospel and culture, for within culture is where the gospel – which also transforms – is revealed.

Let me step back a little and view what Australia was before 1788. It is our homeland – a great land, a land flowing with milk and honey (I use the biblical expression). But then came the invaders. In 1788 began the destruction of this wonderful land. Relationships disintegrated. My indigenous people started to dwindle away.

Djiniyini Gondarra, George Rosendale and other Aboriginal and Islander theologians say together, "God gave us the dreaming". From that perspective the land is the mask of God, warning us not to conceal but to reveal, "because the land is all living things, not just earth or ground to walk on". Every person's history is the history that is lived against the beauty of the land.

Our creator spirit, of whom our history teachers teach, gave to us our ceremonies, our songs, our dances, our stories and our languages. This is where we learn to walk and talk, laugh and cry, sleep and make love. He is our breath, he is life. He is seen in flesh and blood in each of his living creatures.

My first story comes from a woman from a Roman Catholic background, telling about her father:

> The old man Mowinjin was a kidney fat man, a killer, a tribal warrior who was feared. One day he was out hunting with three other men. The others went on ahead and he stayed sitting by a tree. As he sat there he received a vision. (This was before the missionaries came.)
>
> He saw a man of God and he was given a song. He did not know what the words meant. A great peace came over him. When he "woke up" he took his fighting spear and broke it in half. He began to play the music. The others heard it in the distance and as they returned and drew

closer to Mowinjin, they were amazed at the change in him. He seemed to be different, although he was still Mowinjin. He had become a man of peace; he told them – and later all the people – about his vision. He never killed again. He was no longer an angry man, feared by the people; he became a man of peace. When the missionaries came, he said: "I have already seen Jesus, the one you are telling us about." When Mowinjin was very old, before he died he asked to become a Christian and was baptized.

Jesus said..., "I am the way, and the truth, and the life. No one comes to the Father except through me. If you know me, you will know my Father also. From now on you do know him and have seen him" (John 14:6-7).

The second story comes from Central Australia. This too is told by an old man (who is still alive) about a vision he received before the missionaries came.

Arunya was with some of the Central Australian Arrernte people as they walked through the desert. Night came and the people rested. Their water, stored in a *coolamon*, was put in a safe place. Arunya stayed awake, thinking how thirsty he was. He was pulled this way and that in his mind, wanting to take some water for himself, but not wanting to deprive his family either. Finally, as everyone else was sleeping, he moved aside and reached out for the water. To his amazement he saw in the water a mass of glimmering stars. He lifted up his eyes, and there he saw a man from *alira* (the sky) – a man shining with light all around him. Arunya was filled with joy; he didn't want any water, he felt refreshed. The vision disappeared, but he stayed awake, longing to tell the others when they awoke in the morning. He told them about his vision, how he had seen a man from God.

When the missionaries came and spoke of Jesus, Arunya said: "Yes, we already know Jesus. He has come to us."

"Those who drink of the water that I will give them will never be thirsty. The water that I will give will become in them a spring of water gushing up to eternal life" (John 4:14).

The Aboriginal cultural context

This part of my presentation brings us into the context of seeing, feeling, hearing and believing.

Life is sacred, therefore seeing, feeling, hearing and believing are imperative. This seeing is both eyes and heart and understanding.

An Australian Aboriginal Perspective

Feeling is both comfortable and unpleasant: the gentle breeze on your face is comfortable enjoyment; tripping and falling brings gravel and ash to the hands, painful and unpleasant. Laughter, silence, surprise, anger – all are parts of living. Life is sacred and must be cared for.

Work and leisure need each other. Around our campfires at night our thoughts are for the centre circle of our community life at evening meal times, sharing the food and the day's experiences, songs and dancing, laughter and tears. The fire becomes the centre of all our human living, its joys and friendships. This affects our spirituality. The fire is the centre of the land, and within the darkness of the night as we see the light reflected in each other's eyes, we accept this flame as a symbol of sacredness and the deep centre of all life; and as we come closer to the fire we come closer to each other. For one needs to realize that the world outside is the land, and the world inside is the spirit, and both are centred in the sacred. The sacred ceremony of the spirit burns in the centre, relating all persons to the other and to the land.

(Very interesting is the WCC statement on uprooted people: "A Moment to Choose: Risking to be with Uprooted People". But why? For the very same reason that a church looks at what happens to uprooted people, we in Australia look at our lost generation, exemplified by the death of so many blacks in custody.)

We value greatly the stories of our history, our teachers and our people, and we love to share this sacredness with others.

Believing is so simple, like breathing gently yet deeply the oneness of the land, the respect for all creation. The land was given to us by our ancestors to care for and protect, never to abuse or misuse. It is sacred. Upon it and within it is the breath of the spirit.

A traditional story about a peacemaker:

> A long time ago, Brolga and Jabiru were sisters; they lived on the mud flats and near lagoons. Emu, their cousin, lived over the hills, in the high country.
>
> One day, Emu decided to visit her cousins. When she came to the top of the ridge, she saw dust on the plains below. Realizing her cousins were fighting, she ran down as fast as she could and got between them to stop them. Just then, one of the sisters swung her yam stick and accidentally hit Emu across the back. Emu's blood got on the neck of Brolga and on the legs of Jabiru. To this day, indeed, Brolga has a red neck, Jabiru has red legs and Emu has a hump on her back.

Jesus, our peacemaker, carries our scars in his hands, his feet and his side.[1]

A second story:

Come with me to Uluru. Come and sit quietly and hear the didgeridoo and the singing stick.

Uluru[2]

You will marvel at Uluru's greatness, its beauty and its grandeur. It is the Rock. "*... And drank from the rock which was in the centre of the land.*" Uluru. It calls our people to special ceremonies, it stands for solidarity, for protection and assurance of strength.

I waited patiently for the Lord's help.
Then he listened to me and heard my cry.
He helped me out of the desert bog, out of its quicksand,
and lifted me up onto the big rock
and now I am safe and can see all around me.
(paraphrase of Psalm 40:1-2)

Hear my cry, O God; listen to my prayer.
From the end of the earth I call to you, when my heart is faint.
Lead me to the rock that is higher than I;
for you are my refuge, a strong tower against the enemy.
(Psalm 61:1-3)

Marlu
Marlu the kangaroo. Spirit creature, timeless, quick, distance no problem. Sensitive to danger, caring, friendly. He leads others to better feeding grounds, to water and shade. We love dancing with him.

Didgeridoo
Now our didgeridoo, the music of the land, keeping time and rhythm. Nature's instrument bringing the songs of nature, the land, its people, spirituality together.

Evangelism and the indigenous church

I start with the question: was the mission policy of the churches to separate peoples within the mainstream churches, or to develop by self-determination and self-government a healthy indigenous church?

After this question I come with a plea: please, please come with us on our journey of sharing and walking with our great creator spirit; for if Noah and Enoch enjoyed their walk with God, nothing should prevent us from experiencing the same.

One of our major concerns is the importance placed on *money* for mission and evangelism. This is a very big obstacle. In the development of ministry it seems that we have moved from being Spirit-filled, Spirit-led people to simply placing people if we have the means to put them there. If this is the work of God, should it not be for the glory of God? I would hope so, but where is the Spirit?

Another concern is that the missionaries stay too long, and this hampers the local leadership of indigenous people and their self-development in ministry. And some of those who want to work with indigenous peoples, who learn our language and our culture, do so for their own fulfilment and advancement. We do not ask for the world, rather to be appreciated as being part of the world.

In our kind of evangelism we love to tell stories, not merely because someone can get up and preach and be heard if their voice is louder than somebody else's. What we have learned from the message of the evangelists who came has not been very helpful. We like to do evangelism in story fashion, because if the story is good, people will just naturally come because of instinct and because they want to see and hear what is happening.

The evangelist needs to see Christ in our culture. We are trying very hard to see him in your culture (the culture of non-indigenous peoples).

The story of the spear, the cross and the *coolamon:*

> Whenever any kind of law is broken, whether cultural or non-cultural, it imposes a penalty. Our spear is used in a cultural way to demonstrate what happens when a law is broken. The leg is speared to allow blood to flow, life-blood.
>
> Once the penalty of the law is fulfilled, the *coolamon* containing water is given to the offender and some water washes the wound. The identified area is in the camp so that all may see the spearing of the offender – in the same way that the cross on which Jesus was killed was in a designated place.

We need to recognize the gospel in each of our cultures, to experience the calling to the one hope and gracefully to accept indigenous contributions to mission and evangelism as we share our dream.

NOTES

[1] This story comes to us from George Rosendale, Lutheran elder and visiting lecturer at Nungalinya College in Darwin, Australia.
[2] Uluru is one of the great wonders of the world, in the centre of our homeland, Australia.

THEME PANEL I

A Brazilian Perspective

Robinson Cavalcanti

As evangelical Christians we believe in the gospel as a divine *revelation*, a communication on God's initiative concerning an historical fact – God's incarnation in Jesus of Nazareth – with cosmic, social and eschatological implications. Reconciliation with God by faith on the part of those who repent in response to grace produces new creatures, new relationships, new systems and fresh hopes. This tremendous mystery is universal, for all times and all places. Evangelism is the church, the community of faith and vanguard of the kingdom, constantly proclaiming the gospel in word and deed.

As evangelical Christians enlightened by the human sciences (which are themselves systematic presentations of God's revelation in nature), we acknowledge that human beings are essentially cultural beings. The language of holy scripture, the mentality of its actors and authors, the life of Jesus, and the understanding and expression of the gospel through the centuries have been marked and conditioned by cultural factors.

These cultural factors are not generic or uniform, but diverse and often conflicting due to differences of race, gender, region, religion, generation, level of education and – particularly – social stratum (caste, class or estate).

Our experience of history, maturity and common sense should lead us to a balanced position which avoids polarization between a vision of an evangelism floating in the clouds above history and culture and claiming to be neutral, and a vision of the gospel so conditioned by culture that it either loses its dimension of revelation and universality or sacralizes culture or views it in such a static and idealized way that it is prevented from confronting it morally on the basis of revelation.

This paper was presented in Portuguese.

The cultures of those who evangelize and those who are evangelized should be respected and at the same time changed by the liberating presence of the good news, which is salt and light to all sinners. In the case of Brazil, the dominant culture is Portuguese: European and Roman Catholic, with Roman, Iberian, Arab and Jewish elements, marked by the warlike spirit of the Reconquest against the Muslims, of the Inquisition and of the Counter-Reformation. This dominance was strengthened by the use of force against the indigenous peoples and the slaves of African origin. This met with cultural resistance, which ultimately affected the culture of those in power, giving it a new colouration which could be described as "Luso-Afro-Amerindian". This culture is open to incorporating elements from other cultures, provided its predominance is not threatened. The other cultures are destined to be assimilated, with vestiges surviving in elements of folklore, such as food and music.

The gospel in Brazil in the early centuries was linked with the Roman Catholic Portuguese culture of the colonizers, and evangelism went hand in hand with the colonial enterprise. The gospel was often heard as "bad news" or at best ambiguous news, simultaneously containing liberating elements and oppressive and alienating elements. It was used to justify genocide, slavery and patriarchy, authoritarian political rule by monarchs, oligarchies and dictators, and the exploitation of workers by capitalists.

The ecumenical movement and liberation theology have brought radical change in some sectors of the population as regards solidarity and justice in the content of the gospel message. But at the same time, the tenuousness of the relationship of ecumenical and liberation theologies to culture has become apparent. The prejudice, under-rating and lack of understanding of the mystical dimension manifested in both these movements have exposed them as Eurocentric, with an approach based on the European Enlightenment.

For its part, Protestant evangelism in the last 150 years has provided fresh openings and opportunities: in mainstream Protestantism for the emerging middle class (as opposed to the established Roman Catholic aristocracy); in Pentecostal Protestantism for migrants and workers, with its work ethic encouraging thrift and discipline and its more communal and less bureaucratic way of doing things. Mainstream Protestants have stressed grace over against the cultural tradition of law, whereas Pentecostal Protestants have ended up by adopting this tradition.

Protestantism in Brazil has never succeeded in completely disentangling itself from its Anglo-Saxon origins and has clashed with Brazilian culture in the areas of *play* and *eroticism*. It is an evangelism with ascetic and repressive implications, a point at which fundamentalists, evangelicals and liberals surprisingly converge.

Another example of cultural tension has occurred in Christian sectors of the feminist movement, again because of its Anglo-Saxon ethnocentric origin, which is often not sensitive to the distinctive features of the cultures of the periphery and is tempted to impose universal solutions from its viewpoint and experience.

We are a culture characterized – positively and negatively – by mysticism, eroticism and social inequality. A culturally sensitive and relevant evangelism cannot be pursued by heightening mysticism to an alienating degree, nor by denying it on grounds of reason. It cannot be pursued by indifference to prostitution or by denial of the erotic. It cannot be pursued by the promise of prosperity or by resignation in the face of poverty, or by a purely material assessment of social justice.

Would it be possible for evangelists sensitively to accept a culture rooted in belief in the supernatural, giving a liberating content to the miracle of faith and to faith in the miraculous? Would it be possible for evangelists sensitively to acknowledge that Anglo-Saxon asceticism is only Anglo-Saxon and not necessarily Christian, and that the Latin, African and Amerindian life of the senses can (and should?) be compatible with Christian belief, resulting in a Christianity which would be more joyful and healthy, less morbid and neurotic, because it listens to what our bodies are saying to us?

Would it be possible for those Christian women messengers of a new relationship between the sexes to have sufficient humility to recognize that their experiences do not have to be universally applicable and that the sexes in other cultures, in their diversity and creativity, can choose other ways of expressing relationships, which can include the mutuality of consenting sexual courtship as something artistic and playful and nonviolent?

Brazilian culture, with all its problems of being on the dependent periphery of the new international (dis)order and of its internal imbalances, is nevertheless rich and complex, at one and the same time permeated with gospel values and lacking them. The challenges of cross-cultural communication occur when people come among us, or when we send missionaries abroad, who may attempt to impose our culture, or (which is worse) who may simply be transmitters with dark faces of the Christian faith in its Anglo-Saxon clothing.

There are fears of evil spiritual forces which oppress and paralyze our fellow citizens, and which cannot be "respected" nor yet replaced by fresh fears, but which can be healed by the love of God in Jesus Christ. There are doubts, misunderstandings and violence which are calling out for conversion, which is given by the power of the Holy Spirit. There are individual, social and structural signs in our culture which indicate how lost people are and how much they need conversion to the gospel of liberation.

The relation between the gospel and culture must not be an occasion for xenophobia but for open, respectful dialogue among those who share the same Lord, the same faith and the same baptism, and with all the peoples to whom the word of God is addressed. Our culture has much to receive, but it also has much to give, and it can do that only if it can be itself.

If post-modern civilization is tending towards a recovery of the human person in all its multifaceted richness (holism), then Brazilian culture, because of its distinctive features, will be able to be a laboratory of this new age, to which the church is called to minister – a laboratory which is producing an erotic neo-Pentecostalism of the left, the synthesis and precursor of a right relationship between the gospel and culture and our humble contribution to the pilgrimage of the people of God in history.

Opening worship

1. Entrance procession led by the drums of former street children of Salvador
2. Sharing coconuts as a sign of giving and receiving the gifts of each other's culture
3. Edinburgh to Salvador: lighting a candle during the litany of remembrance for past world mission conferences
4. Worship enriched by music from many cultures

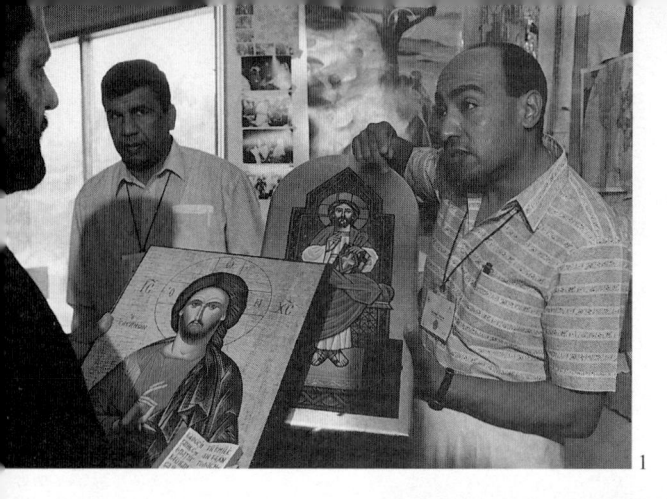

Rainbow – Festival of Gospel in Cultures

1. Coptic Orthodox (Egypt)
2. Pacific
3. Caribbean
4. Norway

Plenaries

1. Left to right: Ana Langerak, Sigrun Mogedal, Erme Camba
2. Metropolitan Kirill   3. Musimbi Kanyoro
4. Theme panel on "The Bible in Context", with Konrad Raiser moderating

Bible studies and worship

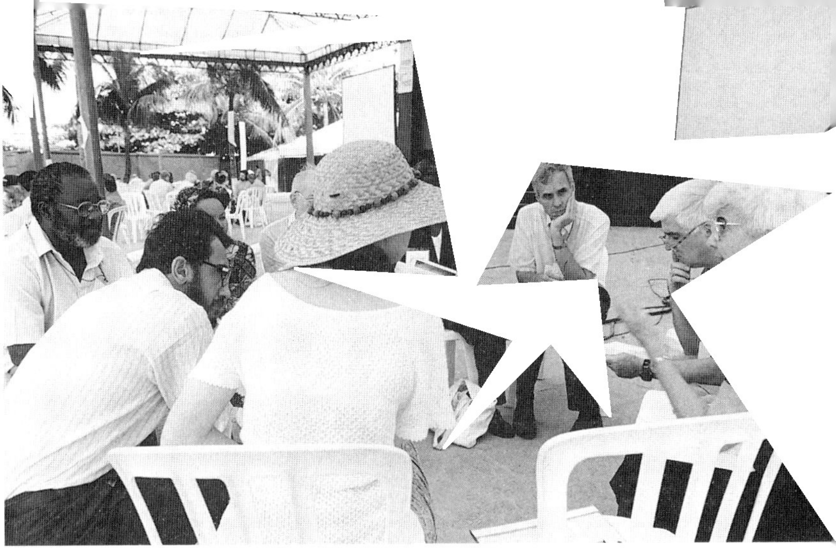

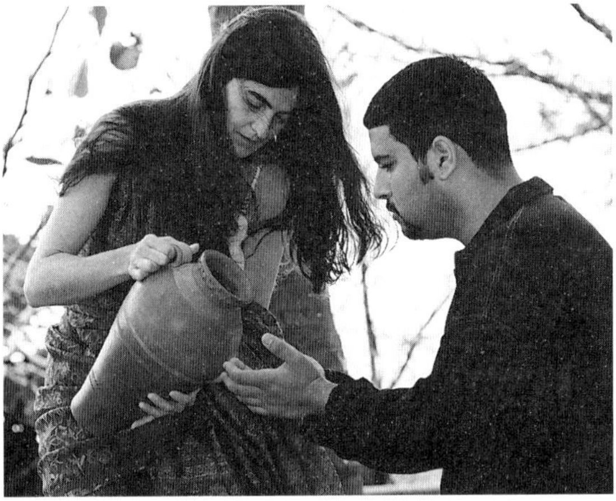

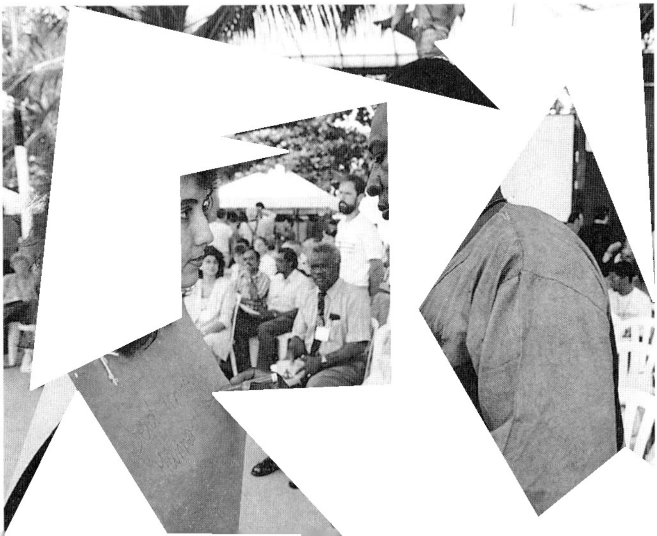

Theme panel on "Evangelism and Culture", with Emilio Castro moderating

Left to right: Christopher Duraisingh, Guillermo Cook

Below: Part of the youth leadership

Afro-Brazilian presentation

Indigenous people leading worship

Indigenous Encontro

Salvador slave dock

Below left: Cleansing rite.
Below right: Recalling with p⟨⟩ the millions brought into slavery from across the sea

Solar do Unhão

Aaron Tolen leading the African prayer of confession

THEME PANEL I

A Jamaican Perspective

Marjorie Lewis-Cooper

To many people living outside Jamaica, two dominant images inform their perspective of the Jamaican people. The first is that of a tourist paradise where Caucasians frolic on white sandy beaches under a blazing tropical sun or stare romantically at their mates over a candlelight dinner with a calm sea and a setting orange sun on the horizon. Along with this promise of luxury and love for the Caucasians is an army of smiling Jamaicans with African features who make beds, manicure lawns beautifully, serve exotic meals and drinks and babysit troublesome Caucasian children. The tourist hype can be summed up in a popular slogan seen on T-shirts sold mainly to tourists: "Jamaica NO Problem".

The second image is that of Bob Marley, a dreadlocked Rastaman, belting out lyrics of Blackman Redemption, liberation for all Africans and a stinging critique of "Babylon", the evil conspiracy of the Christian church and the state colluding to "downpress" black people – all to the pulsating beat of indigenous Jamaican reggae rhythms. Marley, the icon that has inspired protest and resistance by the poor and marginalized in Jamaica and by freedom fighters in Mozambique, Angola and South Africa, among other countries.

These two images, in a country reputed by the *Guinness Book of World Records* to have more Christian churches per square mile than any other in the world, highlight one of the recurring challenges to the church as it seeks to evangelize in the Jamaican culture: the question of identity and of how evangelism has sought to affirm or deny the *imago Dei* in the psyche of the Jamaican people. It is the complex issue of the gospel spoken, preached and lived by officials in the church and the gospel read, experienced and interpreted by the Afro-Jamaican majority.

The Christian church came to Jamaica with the Roman Catholic Spanish colonizers. The church affirmed the right of Europeans to conquer other peoples, provided theological justification for colonialism and watched with scant protest as the indigenous Amerindians were annihilated.

The subsequent introduction of African slaves, which continued after the British – in the name of the monarch and the Church of England – succeeded the Spanish in 1665, continued the dominance of European Christianity. Christianity was used to justify European colonialism, and the doctrine of the innate inferiority of non-European peoples, cultures and religions was widely accepted by the white planter class in Jamaica. Africans were thought to be of inferior intellectual capacity and moral behaviour, cursed children of Ham and destined to be "hewers of wood and drawers of water".

The liturgy supported and sustained these images. "Black" represented evil and sin and "white" represented goodness and purity. Africa was portrayed as a savage and heathen country, sentiments immortalized in the verse of Lewis Hensley's well-known hymn:

O'er heathen lands afar
Thick darkness broodeth yet:
Arise, O morning Star,
Arise, and never set!

A deeper analysis of the encounter of European Christianity and colonialism reveals that the gospel-culture dynamic in Jamaica was much more complex than appears on the surface. Certainly not all white missionaries supported the doctrine of the inferiority of Africans and other non-white people, and certainly not all Africans accepted uncritically the notion of a liberation attainable only after death in the "sweet by-and-by". The temptation to demonize persons or to romanticize is often an over-simplification of the reality of the human condition.

Some important perspectives on this issue come from Mary Turner in *Slaves and Missionaries: The Disintegration of Jamaican Slave Society, 1787-1834*:

- In the 18th century, Jamaica was England's most important asset in the Caribbean. The industrial revolution, however, altered Britain's economic base, and the power of the Caribbean sugar planters and their lobbyists in the British government came under serious attack from manufacturing interests and new social and economic ideas.

- The work of non-conformist missionaries such as Quakers, Baptists, Moravians and Wesleyans assumed great importance for the African slaves. Whereas the Church of England had been largely indifferent to the African population, the non-conformist missionaries engaged in rigorous evangelism and literacy programmes for the slaves and offered them leadership opportunities (for example, as church deacons). In addition, the parent bodies of these non-conformist churches were active in the abolition movement in England.
- The approach of the missionaries was not without its limitations and contradictions. In the words of Turner:

  The missionaries went to Jamaica to improve life for the slaves within the parameters defined by the slave system, and on these terms they won the cooperation of a small liberal element among the slave owners. For the missionaries, as for their patrons, religious instruction for the slaves was entirely directed to the rescue of their souls from sin and preparation for life eternal. To achieve this end, however, the missionaries had to attack the slaves' established cultures, to root out their religious ideas, to divorce them from the social traditions and normal assumptions of plantation life, to replace Anansi, the supreme Ginal, with Christian the Pilgrim, who fought his way through life. In doing so they appealed to the intellectual and moral capacities that the slave system, in principle, denied its chattels and introduced them, in the mission churches, to new activities and organizational forms based on the assumption that all men were equal before God. Mission work among slaves, in short, was an innovation with a disruptive potential (p.65).

- As a result of this encounter between Christianity and Afro-Jamaican culture, new ideas and choices were opened up to the slaves and a new dynamic was set in motion which was outside of the control of both the missionaries and the planters. In the process of missionary evangelism the Africans appropriated to themselves the birthright of the *imago Dei*, based principally on a biblical interpretation different from that of the missionaries.

Many missionaries held up the idea of faithful servants as a pattern of virtue to the slaves. The story of Onesimus (in the epistle to Philemon) was a favourite text. Turner records the following questions put to a class of boys by a Wesleyan missionary:

Was [Onesimus] a good and dutiful slave?
No, he was a very bad one, for he was a thief and a runaway.

And how did the slave behave himself after his repentance and conversion to Jesus Christ?
He behaved himself well and was profitable to his master.

Does religion produce the same effect now on slaves that have it?
Yes, they neither rob nor run away, but are good servants (p.77).

Many slaves – exemplified by Sam Shape, a domestic slave, Baptist deacon and leader of a famous slave rebellion in 1831 – had a different approach to biblical interpretation. "Christianity became a positive justification for action. Shape and his aides proclaimed the natural equality of men and denied, on the authority of the Bible, the right of the white man to hold the black man in bondage. The text 'No man can serve two masters', persistently quoted by Shape, became a slogan among the slaves. To protest against slavery was a matter of 'assisting their brethren in the work of the Lord'... This was not the work of man alone, but they had assistance from God" (Turner, p.155).

In the appropriation of the *imago Dei* the slaves became involved in activities such as the following:
– monetary contribution to the churches;
– attendance at literacy classes conducted by the missionaries;
– setting up of independent churches, under the sole leadership of Africans and with distinctly African features in the liturgy;
– corporate action by the slaves to protest injustice and to seize their freedom.

It is impossible in a presentation of this length to do justice to the complexity of the experience of slavery and the role of the gospel in the fight against oppression of every kind. The struggle for the assertion of the *imago Dei* has, however, continued to be a source of challenge to the church in Jamaica.

The dynamics of economic and social domination of a white minority over a black majority still obtain. The power of external control by economic "principalities and powers" has succeeded the arguably more visible colonial control. There are still elements in some liturgical expressions which suggest that white is "good" and black is "bad" and which advocate submission of workers and women to a patriarchal system justified in the name of God.

Alongside this reality is, however, a persistent and recurring appropriation of the *imago Dei* by the poor and oppressed – sometimes visible in religious expressions such as Rastafari and the Afro-

Christian revivalist churches, and sometimes with the reluctant and inconsistent support of clergy and church leaders. Visible signs of the promotion of the *imago Dei* by the church include:
- the development of Caribbean church music, using indigenous rhythms alongside the continued use of European tunes;
- the formation of clergy in the Caribbean by Caribbean theologians, which has generated a vigorous challenge to European Christianity and encouraged a culture-sensitive approach to mission and evangelism;
- the design and development by the Caribbean Conference of Churches of "Fashion Me a People", an ecumenical church school curriculum which provides a link between the Bible and Caribbean culture through its audiovisual material and the stories of Caribbean people;
- the use of the Jamaican language in preaching mainly by Pentecostals and "evangelicals", and the current project of the Bible Society of the West Indies to translate the Bible into the Jamaican language.

The future

And what of the future? "For such a time as this" the church in Jamaica has to "forth tell" the word of the Lord based on a reading of the signs of the times. Certainly globalization, advances in technology, violence, abject poverty and sexism are some of the challenges to the *imago Dei*. From past experiences perhaps three lessons will serve us for the future:
- The need for humility even as we proclaim the good news without apology – a humility that makes it possible for us to listen to what God is saying and how God is expressing God's self in the culture and life of the people. We need to be careful lest we become allies of the forces which seek to mar and destroy the *imago Dei* in humankind.
- The need to affirm and build up the solidarity of the people, especially in light of the rabid individualism of the current market theology. It is impossible to comprehend the *imago Dei* in oneself and not recognize it also in others. God's covenant, after all, is with people.
- The need for hope in a world becoming cynical in the face of human failure and the inability of science to deliver justice. Those non-conformist missionaries, flawed, human, tentative and

vacillating, struggling with the limitations of their cultural conditioning and the demands of their Christian convictions, and those slaves, subjected to dehumanizing conditions that sought to deny their identity as persons made in the image of God – these are living proof that the word does not return void.

THEME PANEL II

The Bible in Context: An Indian Story

K.M. George

The annual month-long chanting of scriptures is in progress in the small Hindu shrine on the bank of a beautiful river in Kerala, South India. It is a 24-hour, non-stop recital, using audio cassettes and loudspeakers turned up to a deafening volume.

Just across the river is a Christian theological seminary where the community of staff and students worships in the chapel four times a day. They read the Bible and sing hymns to the accompaniment of the loud incoming waves of Hindu scriptures.

The theological students are in the bizarre situation of being forced to listen to two different scriptures at the same time. Never mind that some students think the blaring of sacred music drowning out every other sound in the neighbourhood comes from an aggressive fundamentalist group. Christians, Muslims and Hindus in India do it whenever they can. In fact there are places in India where you can simultaneously listen to the ancient scriptures of four or five religions, all using the favourite Indian technology of Infinite Sound Amplification. Behind the facade of sacred verses stand different communities of faith, some far older than Christianity and probably more sophisticated in spiritual techniques and psychological insights.

If the whole body were hearing...

In general the different faith communities respect the rule not to offend each other's sensibilities. But my country is always afraid of what we call "communal" conflict: the conflict between communities under the guise of fundamentalist religious sentiments whipped up by political opportunism to a high degree of violence and hatred. The country is still bleeding from some such recent eruptions. Religio-political *arrivistes* are constantly looking for the slightest provocation. In some places the blaring of scripture can constitute such a volatile situation.

In the Indian tradition all scripture is called *sruti*, "hearing" or "that which is heard". In Christianity too, *hearing* the word of God assumes central significance. In Judaism and Islam also scripture is to be heard.

The difficulty is that the faculty of hearing is often vitiated by propagandist preaching. The too-loud sound of scripture offends and hurts deeply. Mahatma Gandhi, a lover of Christ and a fervent reader of the gospels, could not stand the aggressivity of evangelistic preaching. He believed that it cut at the root of the gospel of love. As a sensitive and enlightened Hindu, he could discern the growling of a greedy beast beneath the benign rhetoric of the gospel preacher. In his conversations with missionaries he repeatedly used the metaphor of the rose, which does not preach, but exudes its fragrance in peace and makes its presence known in silence.[1]

Gandhi regularly read the Bible as well as Hindu and Muslim scriptures. He pioneered inter-religious prayer meetings, at which all these scriptures would be read with appropriate reverence. He acknowledged his indebtedness to the gospel of Christ in his life-long "experiments with truth" and in his unique spiritual-political adventure to disarm the mighty colonial empire through the practice of *ahimsa* (non-violence). In fact, Gandhi was instrumental in *effectively* communicating the gospel of Christ to millions in the Indian subcontinent and elsewhere. His witness to Christ was far more credible than that of many missionaries, for whom the effectiveness of the gospel could be measured only by the headcount of the converts and their total subservience to the cultural and spiritual paradigms of the West.

Gandhi stands in the best tradition of Hinduism, in which genuine openness to other scriptures is possible. So as far as the Bible is concerned, the religiously pluralistic context is nothing new in India.

The *Advaita Vedanta*, the celebrated non-dualist school of philosophy which held sway over many brilliant spiritual-intellectual figures like Sankara (8th century CE), resolved the polarity between the one and the many in favour of the one. It relegated the diversity in creation to the level of illusion *(maya)* or, at best, to the level of day-to-day phenomenal reality *(Vyavaharika sattha)*. Any description of the ultimate one, however, is apophatically negated. Any conceptual, iconic or linguistic representation of the ultimate reality is immediately negated by applying the principle "not this, not this" *(neti, neti)*. Ancient Indian religious philosophy, however, witnessed competition and conflict of interests between different schools. There was active opposition and even persecution against Buddhism and Jainism (6th century BCE offshoots of Hindu tradition) from the side of conservative Brahmanism. But the general Hindu attitude has been one of toleration and openness to other religious traditions.

The Bible and cultures

The Bible from beginning to end reflects cultural processes inspired and guided by the Spirit and word of God. The very word "Bible" shows Phoenician and Greek heritage and the interpenetration of different cultural elements.

The gospel cannot be considered as a finished product. The cultural and spiritual processes behind the formation of the text involve nations and cultures, confessions and confrontations, tears and prayers, faith and fellowship, self-denial and martyrdom. "The agony and the ecstasy" behind such a dynamic gospel is created by the total experience of communities of faith across time and space.

Rooted in the cultural matrix of its world, the Bible can stimulate as well as receive stimuli from cultures which are not part of its formative process. For instance, the Johannine "word" *(logos)* brought up to the level of Christian scriptures from pre-Christian Greek philosophy, will find a ready resonance in India in the theological/philosophical meditations on divine *sabda* or *nada* ("sound") and *sruti* ("hearing" or "that which is heard", the Indian synonym for scripture).

This requires interpretation, and interpretation is obviously a kind of cultural activity. Good translations of the Bible accomplish to a certain degree this interpretative act, since all translation is interpretation.

Let me make three remarks.

The interpreter's role: The tradition of the church has esteemed the interpreter's role very highly. The patristic writings are for the most part theological expositions of the Bible. The East Syrian Church, which flourished in Mesopotamia (present-day Iraq) and developed an extensive non-colonial mission in Asia as far as China some 800 years before the Western colonial missions, gave such critical importance to interpretation of the scriptures and biblical studies that the director of its theological school in Nisibis had the title *mepasquana*, "interpreter" or "exegete".[2]

Some remarkable attempts to interpret the Bible in particular religious and social contexts have been made in the Indian subcontinent. But these "inculturation" efforts are becoming increasingly suspect in the eyes of some of the fundamentalist Hindu movements, who still have the bad memory of massive proselytism of the poor, cultural alienation and political domination as the concomitant of gospel preaching. They view any attempt to contextualize the gospel or theology with suspicion as part of a new strategy by Western Christians and their Indian allies to proselytize and to recapture political and cultural control. It is hard to erase this stigma, since the allegation of proselytism is not entirely groundless. The only way out is to be consistently genuine and transparent.

Some Indian theologians have attempted to follow a new method of biblical interpretation which they call *dhvani*, the Sanskrit word for the resonance or evocation of numerous levels of meaning.[3] It is a well-known literary theory in India. Instead of reductionist criticism of the text, this method hopes to derive new insights and enrichment of meaning from the biblical text in response to the challenges of every context. While such attempts are not without benefit, culturally speaking they cannot make much headway, since the Euro-American cultural presuppositions in biblical study form the main text, so to say, and all the efforts of the rest of the world become a rather insignificant footnote. As everyone knows, footnotes are supposed to support and confirm the main text.

The context of myth and mystery: The mythical and the historical are intertwined in the Asian religious heritage. Historical criticism as developed in Europe with regard to the Bible has no appeal to the Indian religious mind. In India the grand *Ramayana* and *Mahabharata* epics, which are second-order scripture telling the human story of gods like Rama and Krishna, have recently been rendered into films and television serials. Men and women who act in the roles of gods and goddesses become divinized in the eyes of many common people. Heroes leap out of the silver screen and walk among people as new incarnations of gods. Some of them stand for political elections in the largest democracy in the world and win landslide victories!

Despite the apparent disregard for history, violent religious conflicts may also erupt in the name of the historicity of the epic characters, as happened recently in the conflict in Ayodhya around *Ramjanmabhumi* (the birthplace of Rama) and the Babri mosque.

An amazing wealth of art and poetry, dance and drama, spiritual techniques and systems of education has been created around these mythico-scriptural epics in southern Asia.

But what do our poor Indian students of the Bible do today? They waste the best creative years of their life miserably nibbling at unpronounceable (for Indians) names like Schleiermacher and Schlegel, Dilthey and Heidegger, Bultmann and Cullmann, Gadamer and Wittgenstein, Rahner and Schillebeeckx. And yet, most of them barely get to anything beyond a reasonably correct spelling of these names. They add to it some words like hermeneutics and *Heilsgeschichte*, paradigm shift and patriarchy, oppression and option for the poor... and "complete" their education. They are poor victims of a monstrous system, sustained by a certain known model of mission, theological education and culture. It is hard to break the system since the power of mind and money in our unjust world today is determined to prop it up. Christians shaped by such an alien and alienating system cannot hope to enter a culture informed by myth, mystery and meditative mediation.

It is, however, interesting to hear from the West calls for remythologization after the high tide of demythologization: "Finally it is time to stop telling the Bible what it may mean and to let its mythological language restore imagination to our faith and thought."[4] In the Western academy itself voices of protest are being heard against manipulating the Bible and mustering up power in the name of scientific objectivity and ideological neutrality. Increasingly these voices affirm that with the general breakdown of scientific positivism "our modes of theological interpretations from the recent past are less and less pertinent".[5] If the Bible is the unique testimony to God's love, healing and salvation for all humanity, it should not be an instrument to wield power – spiritual or material – over others.

In India people are particularly sensitive to this. We have enough gurus, yogis and swamis who can cleverly deploy spiritual power to access the world of wealth and pleasure. These are original Indian brands – why go for the expensive foreign missionary brands? If the gospel of Christ has played a significant role, through a faithful Hindu, in the liberation of my country from the clutches of colonial slavery, I am sure it will continue in unpredictable ways to ferment the ongoing struggles of the people for greater justice and human dignity.

One of the regular questions in Christian student and youth conferences in post-colonial India was whether Mahatma Gandhi would be saved. The Christian theologians who answered almost always fumbled. The question was similar to Jesus' question to the Jewish religious leaders whether John's baptism was from heaven or of human origin (Matt. 21:23-27). If the Christian theologians said an unequivocal Yes to Gandhi's salvation, they would have trouble with the biblical doctrine and leadership of their churches, because Gandhi was not baptized nor did he confess Jesus as Lord and Saviour. If they said a plain No, they would be contradicting the obvious testimony of the people to the deeply Christian character of the Mahatma. So sometimes the clever theologians simply answered that they would not be too much bothered if they happened to see Gandhiji in heaven (as if they were sure they themselves would be there!).

Young people in our part of the world are no longer worried about Gandhi's salvation. They are being brought up on post-Gandhian political promiscuity. Like young people in other poor countries, they are deeply anxious about their future and the future shape of the world.

Civilization and self-consciousness: One of the most significant contributions of Western civilization and its missionary enterprise to the rest of the world was to make other cultures and religions self-conscious. This self-consciousness, which has been brewing for the last 500 years, carries explosive power. While Alvin Toffler's book *Powershift* does not recognize this kind of power of the Spirit, it does acknowledge that the power of "knowledge, wealth and violence at the edge of the 21st century" could be overturned by the power of the religious spirit.[6] The theme of this conference is necessitated by the potential of this self-consciousness to lash back as well as to draw the contours of a new world.

In the reassertion of new cultural contexts for interpreting the Bible and doing theology, one can sense the search for a new time and a new space. The present time and space have been shaped by a conquering, possessing civilization. With clocks and calendars this civilization has measured time for all cultures. It has mapped out space and decided its configuration all around the globe, reaching to outer space. Peoples of different cultures have been denied their own time and space, so essential for genuine growth and freedom. Since modern Christian missions occurred in the trail of this phenomenal civilizational blaze, they were mostly blind to the peoples' profound need to conceive and organize time and space in their own way. Facing up to this need is the missionary challenge of the new century. The emerging self-consciousness of cultures and religions, however, may take surprising turns in the re-definition of time and space. The old clock-makers and map-drawers may not be able to predict or control it.

Metaphor for mission

John R. Mott, the celebrated champion of the missionary movement, had two remarkable conversations with Mahatma Gandhi. On the first day Mott tried to defend politely the conventional concept and method of European missionary work. At the end of the conversations on the second day, he said to Gandhi: "The greatest thing you have ever done is the observance of your Monday silence. You illustrate thereby the storing up and releasing of power when needed..."[7]

It seems that Mott, by using the word "silence", was unknowingly providing a metaphor for mission. Silence here is not mutism or passivity. It is the storing up of energy by stopping the violence of words, thoughts and actions. Gandhiji effectively used this silence against the spectre of violence engendered by British colonial rule. If Christianity has used its mission to violate the will of God for the creation, if the Bible has been used as a weapon to violate the word of God's love for all nations, then it is time for depoisoning time and space.

Christian tradition celebrates the role of saints and martyrs – women and men, ordained and lay, adults and children – as the epitome of Christian witness. They sanctified time by the intensity of their prayers and good words and by constantly pointing to the transcendent and the trans-temporal. They perfumed space by becoming "the aroma of Christ" and by dispossessing space by their martyrdom on the model of the self-emptying Christ. They became live Bibles, something millions of people like Gandhi deeply desire.

NOTES

[1] M.K. Gandhi, *Christian Missions: Their Place in India*, Ahmedabad, Navajivan, 1941, p.226.
[2] Samuel H. Moffett, *A History of Christianity in Asia*, vol. I, San Francisco, Harper & Row, 1992, p.201.

3. Joseph Pathrapankal, *Text and Context in Biblical Interpretation*, Bangalore, Dharmaram Publications, 1993, p.9f.; also several articles in *Biblebhashyam*, vol. 5, 1979.
4. Leander E. Keck, "The Premodern Bible in the Postmodern World", in *Interpretation*, vol. 50, no. 2, April 1996, pp.130-41.
5. Walter Brueggemann, *The Bible and Postmodern Imagination*, London, SCM, 1993, p.2.
6. Alvin Toffler, *Powershift*, New York, Bantam, 1991. The subtitle reads: "Knowledge, Wealth and Violence at the Edge of the 21st Century".
7. M.K. Gandhi, *op. cit.*, p.246.

THEME PANEL II

The UK: A Post-Christian, Post-Modern Context

Kristin Ofstad

The Bible in popular British culture

In Britain we live in confusing times. We have lost our roots of faith both in Christianity, which shaped our history, our culture, our art and our view of the world for 1900 years, and in the modern era, which replaced the Christian faith with its supremely confident faith in human reason and autonomy and the assumption that scientific knowledge, technology and economic growth would provide the necessary solutions to all the problems facing the world. Instead of having two coherent ways of perceiving reality struggling to live with each other (as they have for the last two hundred years), Christianity and modernity have now been torn apart and shredded into fragments that swirl around us like millions of snowflakes in a snowstorm.

Our human identity has moved from the richness of the biblical concept of "being made in God's image" and modernity's liberated rational individual, to that of "consumer". The world is to be seen as a huge supermarket where we are free to make up our own identity, our own worldview, our own god. Imagine the world as a shop that sells jigsaw puzzles – but instead of selling boxes of pieces that make up particular pictures, the shop has emptied all the pieces from all the boxes into a huge pile in the middle of the shop. You get a bag and scoop up a random mix of pieces to take with you. If you buy more than the minimum, you are given little scissors so that when you find that the pieces do not fit together, it does not matter: you can just snip away until you have shaped them to make a picture that suits you. When you get bored with the picture you have made, you simply go back to the shop and get another mix of pieces, having no idea which jigsaw pictures they originally came from.

The Bible also has been broken up into bits and pieces and added to the great pile of pieces from which the consumer chooses his or her "truth" for today. You can wear the cross and your star sign on the same chain around your neck. You can call yourself "Madonna" and make millions on a film about Madonna's promiscuous sex life. You can be an atheist and use the Bible to describe the rule by which you live – as does a well-known British writer, who says:

> Basically I am a liberal humanist. As a rule of thumb to live by, I would say, "Do unto others as you would hope they would do unto you." I would also agree with the biblical sentiment, "Judge not, and you shall not be judged." I haven't the faintest notion why we are here, and I doubt if anyone else has either. But I am full of wonder and awe at the mystery of creation... I look at the natural wonders of the world, and that line from the Psalms, "I will lift up mine eyes to the hills, from whence cometh my help", seems very true to me.[1]

A post-modern culture is one in which everyone can pick, choose and make up the picture or story that suits him or her at the moment. *The important thing to understand is that all the pictures and stories are equally valid. No one can claim that his or her picture or story is more "true" or "valid" than anyone else's.*

A post-Christian culture is one where the fragments of story, art and symbol that once belonged in the box of pieces labelled "Christian faith" now belong to everybody, and you may use the pieces you like without any reference to the rest of the original picture. You can get your scissors out and cut the pieces to fit with other pieces from other pictures and stories. So, for example, the story of Christmas is remade into pictures that include snow and Santa Claus and robins and Christmas puddings, all gloriously mixed up together. And for Easter we get cards with bunny rabbits and little yellow chickens together with the sun rising over Golgotha.

The way the Bible has been used throughout church history shows how easily we select the bits of the Bible that suit us and what damage has been done in the name of the church by such selective reading. The issue now, however, is that it is perfectly legitimate to pick out the bits you like and abandon the rest, just as you do with a box of chocolates. I always leave the ones with banana or strawberry fillings, and pick nougat and caramel. How about you?

The consumer can say, "I don't like Good Friday, so I will attend church only on Easter Sunday." Of course this is nothing new in practice, but in the post-modern, post-Christian culture of today's Britain, it is perfectly acceptable to say so without embarrassment. It is considered a perfectly valid point of view.

In this culture, where the residue of a religious culture long gone lingers in people's subconscious memory, the church claims ownership of the Bible at its peril. The Bible belongs equally in faculties of English literature (as great classical literature in the same league as Shakespeare), in university courses on cultural studies (how this book has shaped our language and culture), in advertising agencies (there is an advertisement on British television in which a father gives his three sons money to invest; the two sons who invest in Lloyds Bank are called "good and faithful", and the son who keeps his money in a piggy-bank at home is scolded!). The Bible even belongs to football clubs. Go to a football match and hear the fans sing:

The Lord's my shepherd, I'll not want...
Come on, you buggers, come on, you buggers!!!

Phrases like "good Samaritan" and "prodigal son" have entered everyday usage in the language used in Britain – that is, they have taken on a meaning and life of their own with some link to the parables they came from, but there is no need to know that they are biblical in origin. This happens to language all the time. In Britain we have several turns of phrase that come from advertising, but which now are loosed from their original moorings. The same has happened with our heritage of biblical metaphors.

Using the Bible in the church

I heard the following example of a story put together from a random selection of fragments from the Bible:

There was a good Samaritan going down from Jerusalem to Jericho and he fell among thorns and they sprang up and they choked him and left him half dead.

He said, "I will arise," and he arose and came to a tree and he got hung on the limb and he hung there for forty days and forty nights, and the ravens fed him.

Delilah came along with a pair of long shears and cut off his hair and he fell on rocky ground.

He said, "I will arise," and he came to a wall and Jezebel was sitting on the wall and he said, "Throw her down," and they threw her down. And great was the fall thereof, and of the fragments that remained they gathered twelve baskets full. And whose wife will she be in the resurrection?

I would argue that very often how we use the Bible in church reflects the pick-and-mix-and-snip way it is generally used in our culture.

We need to use the Bible properly, in ways that show the sham of making up "little" stories and "little" pictures that are one-dimensional and do not carry within them the echo of God's voice or the reflection of God's face. We need to be brave enough to admit that our Bible is made up of fragments which have been assembled together. But then we need to take another brave step of saying that our access to truth is precisely an "assembled" thing. Fragments in themselves cannot carry the whole truth; they can only be particles of truth – that is why they have to be assembled, collated, to get at the greater thing itself. All too often the church has offered particles, claiming to possess the whole truth.[2]

The church, that is *us*, has in its sacred text a sacred story that is assembled to tell us, in its flawed, human, imperfect way, *who God is* and *how God works*. It is not accurate down to every detail, because we cannot pretend ever to have anything but a glimpse, an echo, of this God who is Truth. The Bible itself admits that it is a narrative of inaccuracies by giving us the four gospels. There is no single perfectly accurate narrative about Jesus. Assembling four gospels gives us a better picture, a multi-dimensional narrative that opens up for us the possibility of recognizing God when God meets us, of hearing God's voice when God speaks.[3]

I suggest that we need to rediscover the whole Bible – its many echoes, its harmonies, its disharmonies, its internal debates and arguments and tensions.[4]

The small congregation that I serve in Cardiff, Wales, finds itself on the margins of the working-class housing estate where we live and worship. As a group, we are convinced that God has called us to be God's presence here. On a good Sunday there are twenty at worship. Our building was so badly vandalized that it had to be demolished, and our meeting-place is in the local school. But this small group of people has decided that we will build again and through us God will make wonderful, beautiful things happen in an area of material and spiritual poverty. How has the Bible helped us?

First, we looked at the world around us, both locally and globally. We agreed it was a frightening place. With so much against us, how could we imagine that we could be or do anything significant?

Second, we looked at the broad canvas of the biblical story. If you like, we put all the Bible's jigsaw pieces back into a box and began to assemble the picture.

- We discovered that God's people have *always* been small, insignificant groups who have lived in frightening times, certainly in the thousand or so years of history covered by the Bible.
- We discovered that in the face of humanity's capacity to destroy everything, the Bible tells us of one who will not be pushed by the created order into a corner. This God is sovereign over history, never on the defensive.
- When the Bible speaks of the end of history, of *that time*, it means the moment when God will *choose* to put an end to evil and pain and suffering and cruelty and violence and sorrow.
- We discovered that the future belongs to God, who intervenes in history to shape that future. We know how God intervenes, because we have seen it happen in the birth, life, death, resurrection and ascension of Jesus Christ.
- In Jesus, we see that God's intervention comes on God's terms, in God's own way, and that God's own way of working is not predictable or obvious. God destroys human power by refusing to be its victim. God turns seeming defeat into a world-saving victory. In Jesus Christ God spoke God's final word. We wait with longing to hear God speak that final word again.

From this exploration of *who God is*, we asked *how does God work?*

Here is the corner of the jigsaw put together by a tiny group who have embarked on an impossible journey, believing that they are a part of the great unfinished jigsaw that one day will be complete so the whole picture can be seen.[5]

God's way of working is to call powerless and insignificant people to share in "making the kingdom come on earth as it is in heaven", just when everything seems to be falling apart.

We are called to live God's victory...
> Throughout the history of the church, and present in all sorts of ways in the world today, we find the true makers of history – namely, those "little people" who live in confidence that they know the future. It belongs to God.[6]

... through the faithful telling of God's story...
In worship, we perform the truth of God's story through word, prophetic act, symbol, music. By performing the story in worship, we are shaped by it. We live to serve as witnesses to this story.[7]

... with all who affirm life as God's gift to us...
God's people must be partners with all who affirm life, because God's Spirit works not only through the church. As Christians join with others, they become the "yeast" of life.[8]

... challenging the powers and principalities...
God asks for fearless speaking of the truth in the public square.[9]

... with integrity and honesty...
If those who affirm life have nothing to hide and their integrity is obvious, those who seek to destroy life are put to shame.[10]

... and openness to the Spirit.
In the presence of God's Spirit, all else is shown to be hollow.[11]

Assembling the truth from the text that we have has told us that God chooses to change the world through "little people" like us, and that our faithful obedience lies in not losing courage or hope. If we remain alert to the echo of God's voice and God's laughter, if we look around us for a glimpse of God's smile, we will hear God and we will see God.

Each year after Easter we hear that Jesus appeared to his small group of disciples and friends who were hiding behind closed doors in an upper room. They recognized his wounds and were no longer afraid. God is the one who bears the wounds of a suffering world and helps us bear our brokenness. That is who God is. How does God work? Through those who, despite their wounds, are alight with joy and hope.

NOTES

[1] Ludovic Kennedy in *The Independent*, 23 December 1991.

[2] "So, good, you know the man, then, Heinrich Böll. Well, I once read an interview with Böll in which the interviewer asked him if he thought of written history as lies. He said, no, not lies perhaps, but it is more like a narrative of inaccuracies in as much as one can never precisely reconstruct it, and it therefore contains untruths. Böll said that, at bottom, truth was an 'assembled' thing. That it could not be found in one place, not in one book,

one man's perspective, not in one man's testimony, or one government's history. They had to be assembled, collated, to get at the greater thing itself. I thought about that a lot after I read it. It is such an obvious thing, yet until someone says it right out like that one seems not to be cognizant of it. It seems to me that all too often we go through life holding only the particles in our hands, thinking all along that we possess the whole thing itself" (David Lindsay, *Body of Truth*, London, Warner, 1993, p.313).

3 "'This Christianity,' I puffed and lisped through the tiny hole in the bandages, 'what does it really mean to you?'

"He took a good while to answer. His explanation was long and detailed. Greatly abridged, this is what he said: 'It's built up on an infinite number of ideas, each more crazy and absurd than the others, and if you examine them one by one you find nothing to believe in. But taken all together, those ideas give an absolutely true concept of life.'

"I think I understood what he meant. And for a thousandth of a second I too was a Christian" (Torgny Lindgren, *In Praise of Truth: The Personal Account of Theodore Marklund, Picture-Framer*, London, Harvill/Harper Collins, 1994, p.210).

4 "All things are cause and effect, supporting and dependent, mediate and immediate. And all are held together by a natural and impalpable link which joins the most distant and the most unlike; and so I maintain it is impossible to know the parts without knowing the whole, any more than it is possible to know the whole without knowing each part separately" (Blaise Pascal, *Pensées*, selections, London, SCM, 1959, pp.76-77).

5 "Wakening, peering through eye-windows, uncurious, not amazed,
Balance the day, know you lie there, think: I'm on earth.
Remember death walks in the daylight, and life still through filter seeps,
While you will remain unchanged, perhaps, throughout the day.
Time like an urgent finger moves across the chart,
But you are you, Time is not yours alone,
You are but one dot on the complex diagram.
Then are you a star, a nucleus, centre of moving points?
Are you a rock-crumb, broken from cliff, alone?
Or are you the point of a greater star, moving in unison?
If you are isolate, only a self, then petrify there where you stand;
Destinies crumble and bodies run down, the single sconces burn out,
*But you are complete if without you completion is lacking,
Then you burn with the perfect light* and are Time's bodyman."
David Gascoyne, "Morning Dissertation", in *Collected Poems*, London, Oxford UP, 1965; italics added.

6 Jim Wallis, *The Soul of Politics*, London, Fount, 1995. Also "Blessed are the History-Makers", in Walter Brueggemann, *Hope within History*, Atlanta, John Knox, 1987.

7 Psalm 73 and 2 Corinthians 4:1-2.

8 Matthew 13:31-33.

9 Walter Wink, *Engaging the Powers*, Minneapolis, Fortress, 1992. See Isaiah 58 and 59, especially 59:14: "Truth stumbles in the public square..."

10 The idea is juxtaposition – 1 Peter 3:15-18.

11 To illustrate: the Coca-Cola advertisement which claims that Coca-Cola is "The Real Thing" is shown to be a hollow sham when the true "Real Thing" is present.

THEME PANEL II

Interpreting the Bible in a Central African Context

Jean-Samuel Hendje Toya

The problem of culture in Africa today: a general overview
Culture may be defined briefly as the manner in which human beings think, express themselves, and behave according to particular scales of values in relation to self and others, to nature and, in our context, to the divine, in an historical process which constitutes and determines identity.

This is a tentative general definition. While it may have an epistemological ring to it, I would maintain that culture is primarily a phenomenological reality, for culture is not something one defines, but something one experiences in all the plurality of its expressions.

Black Africa, and especially Central Africa, despite its racial "homogeneity", is culturally plural and diverse. Yet amidst all its diversity and plurality, the expression of culture there is essentially marked by ambivalence, paradox and tension between traditional and modern values.

The traditional is often regarded as that which is inherent, endogenous, intrinsic, that which bestows identity. Its mode of expression is resurgent and regressive.

The modern, on the other hand, is regarded as exogenous, extrinsic, "alienating" in the true sense of the term, referring to that which comes from the outside, the foreign. Its mode of expression is "all-encompassing" and imperialistic – but, paradoxically, also regressive.

In speaking of the planet earth with reference, for example, to the inexorable spiral of globalization taking place today (thanks to phenomena such as the Internet, computerization, the ideology of democracy, English as the new "language of Canaan", McDonald's, CNN, etc.), we use an archaic terminology that likewise returns to

---

This paper was presented in French.

the past. Although our world today is covered with megacities brimming with electronic equipment, we still speak of it as a "global village".

This terminology is neither neutral nor innocuous. It reflects the implicit affirmation by the modern collective subconscious of an archaic prototype for which the frame of reference is the traditional village.

In Africa today, cultural life oscillates between these two poles of *tradition* and *modernity*, though it is not possible to draw the line of demarcation between them. Let me give a few examples to support my thesis.

Habitat: Cities in Africa are developing at dizzying speed – spontaneously, anarchically, without plan or control. In the enchantingly beautiful gardens of sumptuous futuristic villas also proudly stand the traditional huts known as *boukarous*. And often it is not in the gilded comfort of the villas but in these *boukarous* that difficult and delicate matters are discussed.

In Africa the shantytowns rub shoulders with the smart areas of town and are on familiar terms with them. This is not just a problem of urban planning or social economics, but a matter of existential and social equilibrium. In the morning people flood from the outlying districts and shantytowns to the smart areas; at night the opposite movement takes place.

Testifying to this search for social and existential balance are the large limousines that can be seen in the shantytowns after nightfall. All the luxury and comfort and extravagant artificial attractions of the cities take nothing away from the traditional essence of Africa.

Dress: In Africa today a marked resurgence of the traditional can be observed not only in the way people dress (*pagne, boubou*, etc.) but also in the use and management of textiles.

Fabrics produced in modern textile factories using local material bear the stamp "Afritude" or "negrotude" – an echo of the "negritude" proclaimed by Senghor in the 1940s or the "tigritude" of Soyinka in the 1970s. These cloths are printed with motifs inspired by local plants (such as palm trees, baobabs) or totems (such as caymans, panthers, lions).

Religion: The sphere of religion is increasingly syncretic. In the name of inculturation and incarnation of the gospel certain positive traditional practices (veneration of ancestors, libations, etc.) are being introduced into Christian worship.

The interpretation of the Bible in Africa: the problematic

Despite Africa's cultural effervescence, the Bible is recognized as theologically sacrosanct.

The Bible is intrinsically the word of God, that is, the collection of sacred writings relating and demonstrating the extraordinary love manifested towards humankind and all creation by God in Jesus Christ. Its unity springs from the diversity of the writings contained in it, each with its own author, time, context, culture, intention and ambition – social, political, religious, missionary, kerygmatic or even apologetic. The biblical text read and listened to is above all a cultural account, closed on the historical plane (past) but open on the existential (present) and anagogical (future) planes.

The problem of interpretation of the Bible arises in relation to this closed and open nature of the biblical account. Without going into technical details concerning the problems of historicism or fundamentalism or of literary, textual or other criticism, we may say that the interpretation of a text is not only an intuitive procedure, but also a demonstrative one using the theory of language and discourse. This requires the hermeneuticist to have the art of understanding, explicating and if possible transmitting meaning. That being so, biblical interpretation is the active process of constantly reconstructing fresh meaning from the expression of the word and will of God for human beings and all creation in Jesus Christ. God speaks to every living being in his or her space, time and culture. God's revelation to the world is never a-spatial or a-temporal, but always historically mediated. Consequently, our language concerning the Bible and our interpretation of it must always be open and plural, because they are never the perfect enunciation of the mind and will of God.

The interpreter is never the author of the biblical text, but simply a servant placing his or her skills at the service of the author.

The service rendered by the interpreter is referential in character, never normative, for the hermeneutical norm is the work of God in Jesus Christ.

In Africa today the problem of reading and understanding the Bible is posed in terms of:
- rejection of the exclusive hermeneutical claim of the West and the resulting confiscation of scripture;
- the incarnation of God's word and God's love in all the world's cultures, which biblical hermeneutics must take into account.

But this is possible only through the work of the Holy Spirit, who creates in us the capacity to listen, interpret, receive and recognize the primacy of God's word in our lives and over our words.

It is likewise the Spirit who, in the New Testament for example, grounds the actuality of the gospel in the unity of the discourse on the faith, flowing unbroken from the age of the apostles up to our own times, providing us with an unalterable frame of reference for formulating and expressing our faith (cf. Heb. 11).

The Holy Spirit thus offers us a tradition – one might even say an "anamnesis" – in the hermeneutic communion. This hermeneutic communion, inspired by the experience of the first Pentecost (Acts 2:7-8), summons the community of faith constantly to invoke the Holy Spirit *(epiclesis)* so that its life and witness may rest upon a constant Pentecost. This same communion strengthens the unity of the church in the tension between its two poles – in other words, the church which is at once local and catholic, synchronic and diachronic – and makes it the sacrament of the world's salvation and the visible sign of God's reign (eschatology).

A methodological proposal for an appropriate biblical hermeneutics

With the pioneers of the Reformation we say that "the word of God is its own interpreter".

- The biblical text which is read and subjected to interpretation lies at the meeting point of two contexts: the source context (or biblical context) and the target context, which is that of the reader/interpreter.
- Between these two contexts a distance of time and space separates the biblical account and the reader/interpreter.
- For the sake of the intimate underlying communion between the two contexts, the reader/interpreter must journey in mind and spirit in the Palestine of Jesus' time and if possible physically in that part of the world today.
- Having made these two journeys the reader/interpreter must don a pair of spectacles to help him or her read: the biblical languages and, if possible, the history of the Roman empire and especially of Palestine. If these spectacles are not available one can refer to different versions of the Bible.
- When this basic work has been done one can, in my view, interpret the Bible reasonably, rationally and spiritually, thanks to the

determining contribution of history, actuality, philology, exegesis and homiletics.

A brief hermeneutical reflection on Luke 3:1-17: African cultural contexts today

Without indulging in Afro-pessimism, I would say that the overall cultural context in Africa today makes our continent a jungle (the strong devour the weak), a dumping ground (the human and industrial wastes of the North are dumped in Africa) and a laboratory (Africa is a favourite testing ground for ideologies and weapons).

John the Baptist: The herald of Christ no longer has a place in Africa, even in remote areas, for modern communication structures (bells, radio, television, telephone) have replaced the village criers and the tam tams.

Baptism: Even though people show a marked fondness for being baptized, baptisms in the churches are more in the nature of a liturgical formality than an indication of the genuine acceptance of God's grace.

Of particular interest are the three questions asked by the crowd (v.10), the publicans (v.12) and the soldiers (v.14) involving the verb "do". Let us look simply at the soldiers' question: "And we, what should we do?"

In 1990, with Mikhail Gorbachev and his ideology, the wind from the East blew through Africa. Africa became infected by the perestroika virus. To save the continent, the International Monetary Fund, the World Bank and President Mitterand of France promised rewards for democracy. Especially in the French-speaking countries, national conferences sprang up and democratic regimes were installed almost everywhere, without any political culture or education at either the grassroots or leadership level. Institutional, administrative and constitutional entities in the Western mould were imposed on these regimes. And four or five years later, with a few exceptions, the result is a general fiasco.

What do we find in our continent? Let me simply list the facts:
– the return or attempted return to power of the military by force (Gambia, Guinea, São Tomé, Niger, Nigeria, Central African Republic, Burundi, etc.) or by free elections (Benin);
– aggression and intimidation of peaceful civilian populations by soldiers and armed police forces;

– in countries (like Cameroon) where the leaders are permanently haunted by fears of a military coup d'état, the military are pandered to and appeased: (1) their wages remain intact while those of civil servants have been cut by two-thirds; (2) they get petrol at special prices from military depots; (3) unlike the rest of the population, they enjoy the right to impunity and precedence; (4) they profess the creed of salvation through military power alone.

So here we have a text and a question which in other latitudes may say nothing, but which is both pertinent and telling when explicated and interpreted in Africa.

To conclude, interpreting the Bible in cultural contexts involves an historical and spiritual re-situating of the biblical texts in different contexts and cultures aiming, through the power of the Holy Spirit, to transform all forms of expression of the Christian faith into a set of propositions in which all individuals and groups may benefit from God's grace and work for God's reign in and in the light of their particular context and culture.

A few questions

In my culture and context people believe that:
– The Bible was written by God.
– For a church building to last you should bury a Bible in the foundations.
– The Egypt and Jerusalem of which the Bible speaks are in heaven.
– In case of serious illness or haunting by an evil spirit, you should sleep with a Bible under your pillow.
– A house key tied into the Bible at Psalm 90 confers certain police powers: detecting of thieves, criminals, etc.

What do you say?

THEME PANEL II

The Bible in the African American Cultural Context

Prathia Hall Wynn

Discussion of how the Christian gospel intersects with culture in the African American context requires some sharing of the historical experience which formed African American Christianity. We can then move to an exploration of the Bible in the contemporary African American context.

The pilgrimage of the daughters and sons of Africa on US soil has been long and tedious. The terrain has been more rough than smooth and the road more crooked than straight. The mountains have seemed so rugged as to make climbing them impossible, and according to a phrase from the African American prayer tradition the valleys have constituted a "low ground of sorrow". Yet, despite the gravity of the problems faced and the severity of the hardships, a complex African American community survives today with a population in excess of thirty million. It is true that the casualty count is large and that there are myriad threats to the survival of significant numbers of African Americans. These difficulties do not and cannot erase the rather amazing fact that predominant numbers of our people have found a strength which has enabled them to press forward even while the winds of adversity, deprivation and fear were driving them backwards.

How have African American people been able to endure the brutal "middle passage" through which they were transported from their African homeland to North and South America, the experience of slavery which literally tore apart their world, and the system of segregation, entrenched racism and economic deprivation which replaced slavery? The answer is complex. Central to it, however, is the gospel. But there is not a straight line running directly from the Christianity of the US slaveholders to the faith of African American Christians. There were many obstacles in the process of conversion and convergence through which African

Americans appropriated the Bible to the realities of their cultural context.

Slaveholders resisted the requests of missionaries to evangelize the slaves for many reasons. The English common-law tradition held that baptized Christians could not be kept as slaves. There was great fear that the gospel would cause slaves to become uncontrollable and seek their freedom. The most insidious form of resistance was the claim that blacks were inhuman beasts who did not have souls and therefore could not be evangelized. The most frequent rationale for missions to the slaves was also dubious: that Christianity would make them better slaves. A distorted version of the Bible was therefore preached by the plantation missionaries. They claimed that the best way to be a good Christian was to be a good slave. The primary text of this "gospel" was: "Servants, obey your masters as unto the Lord."

The critical question regarding the intersection of gospel and cultures in the African American context, however, is how the slaves responded to plantation Christianity. We can assume that some accepted the message as given. But significant numbers found secret "praying grounds" in the woods. They met far away from the eyes and ears of the slave-drivers in their own "hush arbours". They cried out their pain and anguish. They recalled their own African spirituality which they brought with them in their hearts and their heads. They subjected plantation Christianity to their own moral critique. They declared that it was impossible to be Christian and support slavery. They prayed, sang and danced all night. They heard what they called "real preachin'". They planned and plotted escape to freedom and secret and sometimes open rebellion. This was what sociologist E. Franklin Frazier describes as "the invisible institution", the place of authentic encounter between the African spiritual heritage and the Christian gospel.

The slaves forged an African American Christianity which was a blend of the Bible which they believed and their African worldview and spirituality mediated through the experience of slavery. The most critical biblical texts were those which spoke of God's concern for the poor, the captive, the oppressed. The slaves developed their own independent system of interpretation of the Bible which countered the distortions of the slavocracy. Some refused to believe that there was any such scripture as "servants, obey your masters". If there was such a text, it did not mean that God condoned slavery, they reasoned. Their understanding was that God did not and could not intend them to be slaves. Their interpretation affirmed their identity through the gospel. They were *not* the demeaning names they were called by racists – they were God's children. Their humanity was not only affirmed but celebrated. Their dignity was authenticated through the gospel.

The Exodus story was an important means of understanding God as liberator. They read that "the Israelites groaned under their slavery, and cried out. Out of the slavery their cry for help rose up to God" (Ex. 2:23). Their God was a God who heard bondage groans and, more importantly, acted on behalf of those who groaned. God understood their pain. God felt their pain. God acted to deliver them from the situation which inflicted that pain. Through the Exodus event, slaves *expected* deliverance from slavery. They further believed that every step they could take towards freedom, while they waited for freedom, was sanctioned and blessed by God. They were inspired by the gospel to take flight for freedom and to fight for freedom. Through the gospel they sought freedom from slavery and found a powerful freedom of spirit while enduring slavery.

Other biblical stories of deliverance such as Daniel in the lion's den and the Hebrew boys in the fiery furnace were embraced by the slaves for strength, endurance and courage. The prophetic messages of justice and the New Testament ministry of Jesus formed the context of their worship. Their spirituals tell the story of their appropriation of the Bible.

> Didn't my Lord deliver Daniel?
> Then why not every [hu]man?

"Steal away to Jesus" was a signal for religious meetings and plans for escape. The most powerful proclamation of the gospel was that of the inaugural sermon of Jesus:

> The Spirit of the Lord is upon me,
> because he has anointed me to bring good news to the poor.
> He has sent me to proclaim release to the captives
> and recovery of sight to the blind,
> to let the oppressed go free,
> to proclaim the year of the Lord's favour (Luke 4:18-19).

Throughout the African American religious experience, the community has continued to appropriate these texts through its independent hermeneutic to meet the needs of the people for strength, endurance, courage, insight, wisdom, identity, strategy and struggle for survival and liberation. The contemporary scene is one in which the struggle for survival, the struggle against racism, the struggle for human and community development are critical in the daily lives of African American people. We have passed out of the period of slavery, but we are not yet in the promised land of freedom and equality. We are yet a wilderness people. The primary struggle of the wilderness is for survival and forward movement. Historically African American women have led the wilderness ministries, trusting God to show them, as God showed Hagar, where there is water and sustenance for survival. The African American church is the institution whose task it is to promote these movements. The gospel is the primary means for struggle. It must still speak to the people in their socio-historical context with messages relevant to their critical needs.

The gospel transforms culture by speaking God's judgment against all forms of oppression. Hence just as the gospel empowered African American slaves and the African American churches to articulate their moral critique of racism and to develop as the foundation of their faith the prophetic principle of the equality of all human beings before God,[1] it critiques all other forms of oppression both inside and outside the church. Sexism, classism, ageism and other forms of bigotry are judged by the gospel as sin. The gospel transforms culture and the church by compelling struggles against oppression. Through the gospel, we hear the words of Paul: "For freedom Christ has set us free. Stand firm, therefore, and do not submit again to a yoke of slavery" (Gal. 5:1).

Today millions of our people are bound by racism, sexism, classism, poverty, drugs, domestic abuse and street violence, as well as governmental abuse and abandonment. And although many comfortable Christians do not wish to hear it, the gospel will not be silent. It requires those who will be obedient to the call of Christ to challenge all structures of bondage, "to break every yoke and let the oppressed go free". This persistent call compels us to work for the transformation of culture.

The gospel is transformed by culture because it meets people where they are. We hear the biblical message within the context of our historical and societal experience. We not only translate that message into our own languages, but also translate its meaning in relation to our own situations. Therefore the gospel lives only as it comes alive again and again and again as comfort and challenge, help and hope, healing to the sick, wholeness to the broken, peace to the troubled, freedom for the oppressed and living for the dying. The gospel reaches us where we are and we reach out for it as it meets our needs. We cannot imprison it for our own personal (mis)use. We cannot distort it and press it into the service of power for the privileged. It will not remain in those places. Rather it rises up in the lives of the marginalized, and as they are transformed by the gospel they are empowered to transform their contexts through the gospel. This is authentic Christian witness.

I shared with the recent WCC consultation on gospel and cultures in the African American context my struggle to understand a particular passage in Ephesians 4 in relation to the myriad images of captive humanity and especially youth in African American communities. The passage reads:

> But each of us was given grace according to the measure of Christ's gift. Therefore it is said,
> "When he ascended on high he made captivity itself a captive; he gave gifts to his people."
> (When it says, "He ascended", what does it mean but that he had also descended into the lower parts of the earth? He who descended is the same one who ascended far above all the heavens, so that he might fill all things) (Eph. 4:7-10).

The question of the text is also the question of the community. What does it mean that Christ has made captivity captive? What does it mean that the one who descended into the lower parts of the earth is the same one who ascended far above the heavens? And what does this mean in the context of young people who believe they have nothing worth living for, who are captive to street violence and other forms of self-destruction? What is the relationship between the text and our captive youth and the African American church which has historically been the institution which has led the freedom struggle? If Jesus Christ has taken captivity captive, why are there so many captives?

The answer did not come quickly or easily. There was a protracted struggle with questions of text and questions of community before I began to understand, as I worked with captive youth, that Jesus Christ has captured captivity but *he has left to the church the task of chain-removal.* That is our challenge: ministries which remove chains from hearts, minds, spirits and bodies so that the oppressed may go free and set others free. Engagement with the biblical message compels the church to do the work of chain-removal. And because of the Christ who has captured captivity and who descended and ascended in that process, there is now no unconquered space. Wherever captivity asserts itself, it is a fraud. It postures a power it does not possess. Jesus Christ has already been there. Captivity has been captured. Let us, the church, do our work of chain-removal.

NOTE

[1] Cf. Peter J. Paris, *The Social Teaching of the Black Churches*, Philadelphia, Fortress, 1985.

Part III

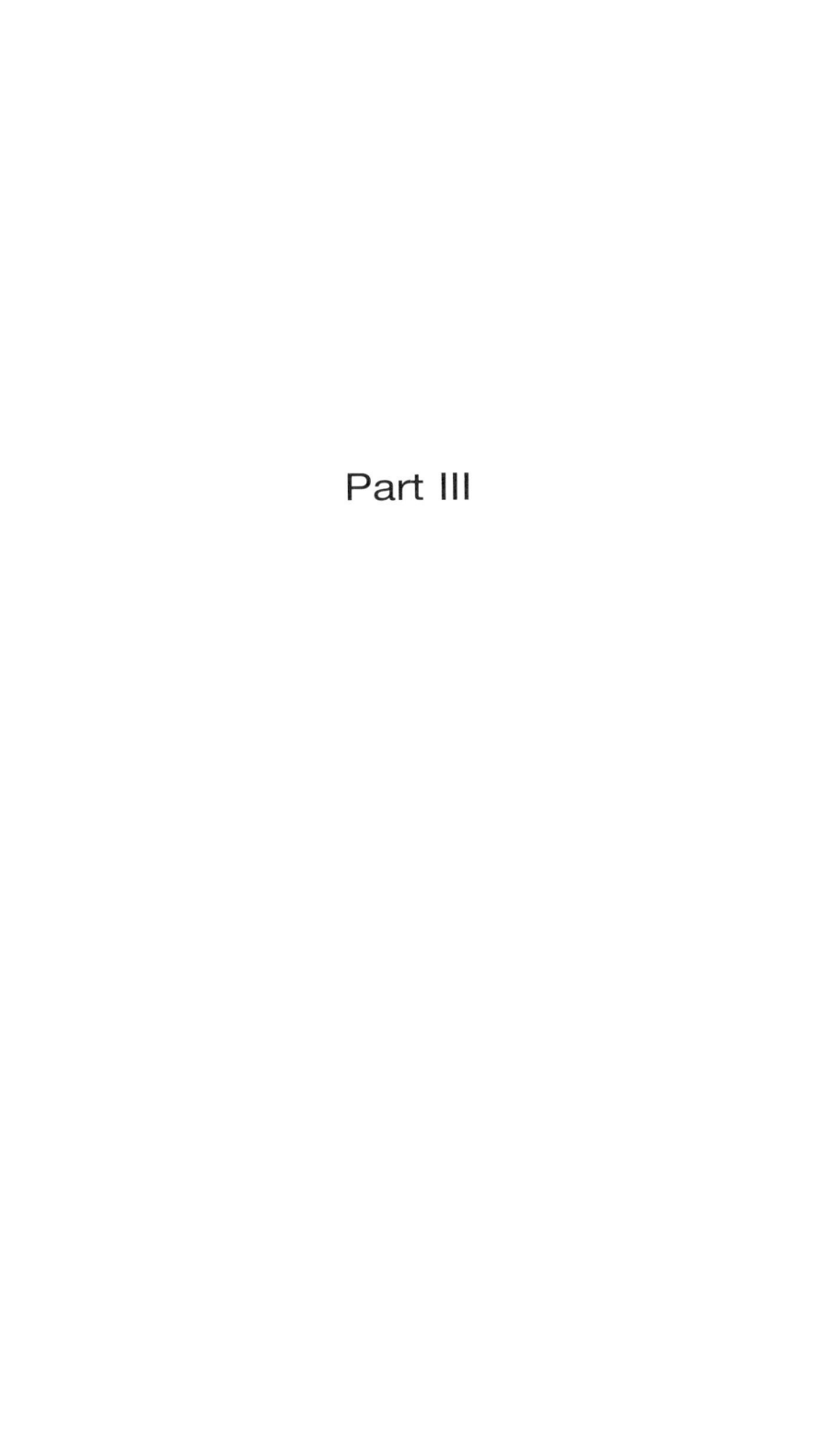

From Each Culture, with One Voice: Worship at Salvador

Jean S. Stromberg

The worship life at World Council of Churches' global gatherings has emerged over recent years as a significant and exciting contribution to the ecumenical movement.

Already at the Melbourne world mission conference in 1980 there were signs of a new understanding of the place of worship in ecumenical gatherings. The Vancouver assembly in 1983 broke new ground in giving such rich and full expression to worship within an assembly. Some 95 percent of the participants who filled out the evaluation forms named worship as the most significant part of the assembly for them; indeed, for many the abiding image of the Vancouver assembly is that of the brightly striped worship tent.

The 1989 San Antonio world mission conference, building on the experience of Vancouver, experienced a deepening of the theme "Your Will Be Done – Mission in Christ's Way" through the daily worship which focused on biblical images of mission, from the preparation of the soil through planting, watering, pruning, waiting and finally harvesting. An early morning "walking the way of the cross" was a high point of the conference for many participants. By the time of the seventh assembly in Canberra in 1991, there was an expectation that worship would be a significant part of the assembly experience and an eagerness on the part of the participants to participate fully in the worship life.

The worship at the Salvador conference takes its place in this growing ecumenical tradition. As is customary for WCC global gatherings, an international worship team worked over a period of two years to plan the worship life of the conference. The team had as resource the learnings of recent years: that worship is integral, not optional, to the total life of the conference; that ecumenical worship enables all participants to *worship* across cultural, linguistic and confessional lines; and that ecumenical worship affirms the importance of wide participation, shared leadership, careful preparation, and prayer for the presence of the Holy Spirit.

The planning team took as a significant part of its mandate for this conference the enabling of participants to experience the richness of cultural forms within the global Christian family. A prayer in the opening worship asked God to "nourish us with the gifts of many cultures". The team wanted the participants to feel invited, within the worship life of the conference, to live into the theme "Called to One Hope – The Gospel in Diverse Cultures".

In the opening words of the first worship service, participants heard the welcome to Salvador repeated in many languages of those who gathered from around the globe. The invitation which followed was a clear articulation of the expectation of the conference, which the worship life would seek to make a reality in the experience of the participants:

> At the start of this conference on world mission and evangelism we gather together from every corner of the earth to open our hearts and minds to God. From our diverse cultures we are "called to one hope". We have seen with our eyes, we have touched with our hands the word of life in our diverse cultures. But it is in our sharing within the community of the church that we shall discern the fullness of God that fills us all. Come then with joy to give and receive the word of hope in Christ and to be strengthened in our mission!

In these few words, participants were reminded of: their essential dependence upon God – "to open our hearts and minds to God" – suggesting the priority that would be given to worship and Bible study throughout the conference; the unity of their common faith in Christ – "called to one hope" – that transcends and transforms particular cultural experiences; the gift of culture which mediates the gospel to each of us – "we have seen with our eyes, we have touched with our hands the word of life" – in very diverse ways; the necessity to share the gifts of these diverse cultures in order to "discern the fullness of God that fills us all"; the purpose of the conference: "to give and receive the word of hope in Christ and to be strengthened in our mission".

The participants were reminded too that they had gathered in continuity with a long tradition of world mission conferences within the ecumenical movement. With a sense of being surrounded by a "cloud of witnesses" of those who had laid the foundations and gone before in the mission journey, the conference joined in a litany of thanksgiving for the earlier conferences, from Edinburgh 1910 to San Antonio 1989.

Sharing "within the community of the church in order to discern better the fullness of God" has been, of course, a regular concern of ecumenical worship. The necessity to share cultural gifts has been a more recent understanding, beginning with the concern to give voice to the experiences of all of the gathered worshippers. The use of short musical responses from various parts of the world and from many different traditions is one example of this sharing. It is not unusual today to find a Russian "Kyrie" or a Zimbabwean "Alleluia" as a natural part of a local congregation's order of service in many parts of the world. Ecumenical worship has also frequently crossed linguistic lines, especially in the reading of scriptural texts. Praying the Lord's prayer together, in the many languages in which persons in the gathered community first learned it, is a moving experience, reminding one of the sounds of Pentecost.

The Salvador worship services pushed these experiences of sharing across cultural lines even further and included other culturally specific elements as one way of enlarging the particular experiences of individuals. The greeting which opened the daily worship was observed in a different cultural style each day. After a word of explanation, participants were invited to greet each other in the specific way of the street children of Brazil; with a bow and the word "Namaste" ("the divine in me greets the divine in you") of some Indian Christians; with the Brazilian embrace of friendship; with clapping and African responsive singing to the question "On whom shall I call?"; or with a simple handshake, following a reminder that this tradition began as a way of saying, "I greet you unarmed; I am open to you".

Initial awkwardness at using another cultural style gave way to enthusiasm among many participants as they experienced not only the displacement of being outside their cultural forms, but also the freedom of enlarging the boundaries of their particular experience of Christian fellowship. One worship leader expressed it this way: "Some of us delight in the new and different. But others of us may be uncertain and question whether the Spirit of God is really present in such unfamiliar ways." All were challenged to lift the conference before God, offering thanks for what was revealed and understood as well as for the confusion and that which was not yet understood, with prayer for the Spirit's guidance.

Each participant might cite his or her own moments when the Spirit was felt to be present in the very crossing of boundaries and seemed to take the offered gift and use it to bless many. Among these moments would surely be the benediction chanted by the young Sámi from Norway who, in his native dress, used his own language to call a blessing upon all. The beauty of the sounds, the sincerity of the young seminarian hovered over everyone, through the action of the Spirit, for one of those suspended moments when the unity of those who confess Jesus Christ is truly felt as a precious gift. Another such moment occurred during the "blessing of bread and of other gifts of creation", when leadership of both Eastern and Oriental Orthodox families shared in the liturgy and the blessing of the bread. The bread seemed indeed blessed!

The actions which accompanied the biblical texts were also powerful moments in the worship. The following selections from the daily worship services attempt to convey the effective use of biblical texts to enlarge the understanding of mission as well as to challenge to personal faithfulness in witnessing.

Thanks for the woman, early missionary

The passage in John 4 concerning the Samaritan woman whom Jesus asked for water came alive as a mission text through the prayer litany, which follows, as well as the skilful dramatic interpretation as the scripture was being read.

Reading of John 4:5-9

> Thanks for Jesus, who broke oppressive cultural norms:
> he approached a woman, a Samaritan, a social reject in her own culture.
> *Thanks for the woman, who had audacity:*
> *she spoke with a Jew, a man, a stranger.*

Reading of John 4:10-15

> Thanks for Jesus, who respected genuineness:
> he took the woman seriously,
> credited her with spiritual desire,
> dialogued earnestly with her, neither preaching nor patronizing her,
> invited her to wholeness of life.
>
> *Thanks for the woman, who sought spiritual meaning:*
> *for her enquiring mind, her desire for life, her response to the invitation.*

Reading of John 4:16-26

> Thanks for Jesus, who revealed truth:
> he broke with the religious tradition of his time;
> he let the woman see that she was known and accepted
> and transformed her life.
> *Thanks for the woman, who had courage:*
> *to be humble, honest, open in spirit, to accept her own worth.*

After the reading of John 4:27,

> Just then his disciples came. They were astonished that he was speaking with a woman, but no one said, "What do you want?" or, "Why are you speaking with her?"

participants were invited to consider whether there were persons with whom they would not like Jesus to talk. Who are the persons – perhaps those seen as inferior or as outcasts in society – who, like the Samaritan woman, are not considered worthy of Jesus' attention, even by those who claim to be following Jesus today?

> Then the woman left her water-jar and went back to the city. She said to the people, "Come and see a man who told me everything I have ever done! He cannot be the Messiah, can he?" They left the city and were on their way to him (John 4:28-30).

> Thanks for Jesus, empowerer of people.
> *Thanks for the woman, early missionary.*

Water from large water jars was poured into the outstretched hands of the participants, as they reflected on the ways in which those considered to be "on the outside" are often springs of water, like the Samaritan woman who invited others: "Come and see!"

In the sharing of crumbs we are healed and included

Our world systems leave many people on the outside. Like the Canaanite woman in Matthew 15:21-28 they cry out, "Lord, help me." Churches may claim that their own communities ought to be the first recipients of resources, but the biblical texts suggest that no one is foreign to the mercy of God. The unnamed woman makes a claim on our resources: "Even the dogs eat the crumbs that fall from their masters' table." "Crumbs" became an image which tied together several biblical texts, including Ruth 2:1-12, and challenged participants to reflect on their role in the "gathering and sharing of crumbs".

A lament began with a verse from the Psalms:

Show me a sign of your favour, so that those who hate me may see it and be put to shame (Ps. 86:17).
Crumbs, some get only the crumbs, Lord, and some don't get even the crumbs. They are not allowed to sit at the table. They are kept outside the gate. They are kept on the other side of the border. How do we pray for those excluded even from the crumbs?
We are not worthy.

Be gracious to me, O Lord, for to you do I cry all day long (Ps. 86:3).
Why do they not make their life where they are? Why do they not use their own resources? How can we respect those whom we consider as cast-away crumbs?
We are not worthy.

Give ear, O Lord, to my prayer; listen to my cry of supplication (Ps. 86:6).
Why must they annoy us with their constant pleading? Do they not understand their place? How do we speak on behalf of those who are crumbs?
We are not worthy.

A prayer addressed to God as "God of gods and Lord of lords, the great God, mighty and awesome, who is not partial and takes no bribe, who executes justice for the orphan and the widow, and who loves the strangers, providing them food and clothing" (Deut. 10:17-18) inevitably led to the question: "Who is worthy to gather up the crumbs under your table?"

Some would be saved, God, if only they received crumbs. Some are saved when those who have only crumbs share with their neighbours.
Who is worthy to gather up the crumbs under your table?

Some are like Boaz to the Moabite woman, "Keep your eyes on the field that is being reaped; and follow behind them. I have ordered the young men not to bother you" (Ruth 2:9). Some extend their hand and welcome angels unaware (Heb. 13:2). Some speak love rather than fear.
Who is worthy to gather up the crumbs under your table?

Will you say to us, Jesus, "I was hungry and you gave me food"?
Will you say to us, Jesus, "I was naked and you gave me clothing"?
Will you say to us, Jesus, "I was a stranger and you welcomed me" (Matt 25:35)?
Who is worthy to gather up the crumbs under your table?

172 *Called to One Hope*

As baskets of crumbs were shared among the participants, they were invited to name a person or group of people who remain outside their church or community. It is in the "one whose property is always to have mercy", participants were assured, that those named and those who did the naming would be healed and included. All who seek the mercy of Christ, including Ruth and the Canaanite woman, are part of the body.

We are waiting...

The waiting of the Advent season was the entry point to a service which focused attention on the mission challenge presented by HIV/AIDS in nearly every part of the world in which churches give witness today. To each line of the Advent call to worship, participants responded in their own languages with the phrase "We are waiting."

> Someone is coming...
> *We are waiting.*
>
> Someone is coming to grant dignity to long-suffering bodies...
> *We are waiting.*
>
> Someone is coming to the breathless...
> *We are waiting.*
>
> Someone is coming to those who lack energy...
> *We are waiting.*
>
> Someone is coming to those who grow thinner day by day...
> *We are waiting.*
>
> Someone is coming to those who don't know if their hands will work tomorrow...
> *We are waiting.*

Singing the Advent hymn "O come, O come, Emmanuel" in this context was both prayer and challenge: Can the churches, as part of their witness to the God who is "with us", "close the path to misery" for those around us in despair?

The phrase from Isaiah 53 rang with perhaps unintended promise: "Who could have imagined his future?" This despised and rejected one becomes the very source of healing. The story of the unnamed woman in Luke 8 who in her desire for healing touches Jesus' garment was vividly portrayed through movement which accompanied the reading of the text. The woman had dared to touch Jesus' robe! A cloth became the focal point of that touch of faith. The cloth was then draped around a large cross and participants were invited to come forward to pray for their own healing, to touch Jesus in faith. They were then invited to pin on a red ribbon and to say the names of persons known to them who were infected or affected by the reality of AIDS. The low murmur of names, continuing for many long minutes, surrounded the participants and gave evidence of the desperate need for healing in our communities.

> Broken Healer, heal through us, who are also broken;
> And may this healing be our healing too.

What strength is this? What resistance is this?
For many people, the most memorable worship experience took place at Solar do Unhão, the infamous Salvador dock where kidnapped men and women from Africa landed in Brazil as slaves. Before Columbus's time, around 150,000 black persons had been captured by the Portuguese and taken to Spain and Portugal where they not only learned the language but also became Christians. From the 16th century, however, any concern for "Christianizing" and "educating" gave way to the needs of the colonial economic order. Cheap labour was needed for sugar-cane plantations; the crown of Portugal profited by collecting money from both sugar producers and slave traders. From 1550 onward, Solar do Unhão was kept busy with this evil trade.

The conference participants followed a guided meditation which took them first to the dock where the Africans disembarked. In a nearby white stucco shed, historians believe, men and women were classified by age, size and health as pieces of cargo; here participants were asked to remember the 40 percent who never reached this shed, but who died in the ships' hulls or chose to throw themselves overboard.

Moving in silence, the participants made their way to a small church behind the dock where, in the courtyard, water was thrown on the slaves and words said over them to increase their value as "baptized" slaves. Worshippers were invited to taste the salt water and to feel the salt dry upon their skin, thus recalling the grief of suffering and the sweat of forced labour of those carried over the ocean waters.

Following the singing of an African American spiritual there was a responsive prayer of confession, which began with repentance for "watching from afar when others are cast down, enslaved, made of no account except for the menial labour they produce for the benefit of their masters" and continued with other situations of injustice including children starved by indifference and church doors closed to those seeking refuge or asylum.

Then Aaron Tolen, a president of the WCC from Cameroon, reminded worshippers that the guilt in the years of the slave trade did not belong to Europeans alone:

> Dear African sisters and brothers, we have heard words of repentance. But those who brought us here were not alone in the making of this tragedy. We Africans share in the responsibility. We have degraded ourselves by selling our brothers and sisters as goods. Is it because we have never had the courage to recognize it and to repent that we continue to do the same today – hence the disgraceful situation of Africa? We want to repent and ask for forgiveness and God's mercy.

A brick from the outer wall of a now-ruined slave fort, Cape Coast Castle in Ghana, where slaves were loaded onto ships, was presented to the Afro-Brazilian community during the worship. A local chief in Ghana had gathered the bricks, calling them "stones of tears", and had sent one with a delegate from that country. In presenting the brick she said: "Words cannot express what this stone means to our very souls. Let it be a reminder that we will never do this to ourselves again."

The service not only brought tears in relation to the past, but also called to a vision of the future that is possible. The descendants of the slaves are now 60 percent of the population of Salvador. They are a reminder that the reasons behind their tragedy are with us still – the victims of unjust economic orders now number in the millions around the world. But their presence is also a sign of resistance and of hope for the future.

The image of water, powerfully present in the tasting of the salt water, returned as a prayer for blessing:

> Lord, God, with this water, cool our hands, our bodies from the heat of the sun;
> with this water, kindly remove the heat of the heart;
> with this water, soothe our injured feelings,
> remove the anger of yesterday.

> Cleanse us from true and false accusation;
> clean the stains left by our own wrongdoing;
> wash away the bloodstains of those who died unjustly;
> purify our hearts and minds;
> remove any trace of suspicion.
> With this water, give us a fresh start to build a new community;
> with this water, fill our hearts with a clean spirit;
> with this water, prepare us to be reconciled to yourself,
> through Christ and through one another and to one another.

Participants were then invited to wash their faces in the fresh water carried in large bowls among the participants as a sign of the healing, reconciliation and hope for which they had prayed.

In Salvador, ribbons are worn as a sign of enduring friendship; once a ribbon is tied on one's wrist it remains there until frayed. Participants were invited to take ribbons and, in acknowledgment of the need to be reconciled with each other, to tie another's ribbon and to invite another to tie one's ribbon. These ribbons, tied around participants' wrists, were a vivid reminder throughout the conference of the commitment to become a reconciled people, a people of hope.

The young drummers of Olodum, a troupe of former Brazilian street children who had led the participants in procession to the opening worship, now brought the service to a dramatic end. As the drums began quietly, the worship leader asked:

> What sound is this?
> What strength is this?
> What resistance, which overcomes years of oppression?

The drums grew ever louder, until the sound was all-consuming.

Participants experienced the reality that the past could not overcome all; they stood in the midst of living people who have resisted and who are moving on. It was the sound and rhythm of a community that would not die.

The leader continued:

> This is the sound of a culture that refused to die.
> It is the strength which comes from a dynamic people.
> It is the resistance of those building a new community.

The participants gathered around the troupe of drummers and, reluctant to leave behind the powerful impact of the experience, began to move to the beat of the drums, joining in the rhythm of the community that would not die.

Perhaps these young drummers of Olodum are the appropriate symbol of the worship experience at Salvador with which to conclude. At the opening worship the drummers had been something of a tourist attraction, the object of picture-taking. During the conference, however, the worship team had interacted with these former street children on several occasions and had begun to draw them into the experiences of the planning team. With so much work to do the team might well have used the gifts of these young drummers, but felt it did not have the time to take them seriously as persons because of their youth, their particularly difficult personal stories, the vast gap in cultural experiences with the international team. How could all those boundaries be crossed? One of the team took it as a personal concern and worked through the night to translate the texts of the Solar do Unhão service into Portuguese so that language would not be a barrier to the young drummers' full understanding and participation in that service. They were able to hear and understand that it was their history that was being lifted up; it was their story that moved Christians from around the world to tears of repentance; and it was their drumming that symbolized the resistant, living community with a future that the participants joined in celebrating.

The gifts of culture mediate the gospel to each of us. Only in the sharing of these gifts within the community of the church will we begin to discern the fullness of God. The worship experience at Salvador enabled the gathered ecumenical family to affirm the richness of that sharing in a desire to understand how great our God is and the necessity of such sharing for our faithful witness in mission.

Sharing the Riches of the Bible across Cultures
Bible Studies at Salvador

Sister Monica Cooney

The book of the Acts of Apostles seen through cultural lenses from around the world! The Bible study sessions at the Salvador conference became for many participants the highlight of the event. No report on the Bible studies could capture the richness and depth of the sharing that took place each day during the conference when participants from a great variety of theological, missiological and cultural backgrounds gathered in small groups to reflect, especially from missionary and cultural perspectives, on texts which had been selected from the Acts of the Apostles. In all there were 33 groups: 20 working in English, 3 in German, 3 in French, 4 in Spanish and 3 in Portuguese.

Group leaders chosen from different cultural, linguistic and confessional groups acted as companions and guides. Many participants paid tribute to the way the leaders enabled them to get to know one another at a deeper level and to engage positively with the text, their own experiences and one another in a mutually challenging and enriching exchange. The group leaders were prepared and the entire study process coordinated by a team of six persons led by Milton Schwantes from Brazil. The coordinating team also worked on daily reflection sheets as additional materials for the Bible studies.

Some groups met in hotel rooms. Most, however, met in the canopied Área Verde near the sea and had to contend with the noise of wind or rain or the heat of the sun. But this did not seem to dampen their joy and enthusiasm for studying the word of God together and sharing insights from their cultural vantage point.

Choice of Bible study texts

The planners of the conference had been convinced of the value of studying passages from a single book of the Bible rather than a few isolated passages from different books, selected to illustrate some of the points highlighted, for example, in the gospel and cultures study. The Acts of the Apostles was the logical choice. Even though Acts is not the only book of the Bible that speaks to the theme of gospel and cultures, it was considered to have a "more direct and greater relevance to the conference theme". The actual texts were selected from the first 17 chapters, in which a variety of issues arise from the ways the gospel interacts with different cultures and contexts. While each of the seven Bible studies focused on one or two particular passages, it was set within the larger context of the chapters selected – for example, study 2 on Acts 2:1-13 and 42-47 within the framework of chapters 2-4. These vivid glimpses of how the gospel was proclaimed and lived by early Christians in a diversity of cultures offered participants much food for reflection.

A small booklet, *Spirit, Gospel, Cultures: Bible Studies on the Acts of the Apostles*, had been designed by an international group who came together in Geneva 19 months prior to the conference, for use in local churches and groups as a preparation for Salvador. A number of the participants had already used the preparatory booklet in their own context.

Varying approaches

Groups and individuals had their own ways of approaching these texts: analysis, intellectual discernment, intuitive understanding and so on.

Many began with mission concerns from their personal and social experience – which was rich and varied, given that the group members came from such different cultural and denominational backgrounds. Questions were brought to the texts arising from the way people had culturally received the gospel themselves or the way they were trying to live and witness to it today.

Others began by letting the text address them: what was the word of God for them today? The texts raised questions and issues for churches in their particular cultural contexts. Stories were shared in response to the passages reflected on. Through listening, reflecting, interacting with the God who has revealed and continues to reveal, and creatively linking the texts and their own experience, many participants felt they were led to new insights and new levels of understanding. Only a few expressed disappointment with the level of sharing in their particular group.

The Bible studies provided the backdrop and orientation for the discussion of the theme of the conference, "Called to One Hope – The Gospel in Diverse Cultures", in the plenaries and sections. It was also intended that insights from the Bible studies would be shared in the deliberations in the sections. To that end the Bible study and section leadership met together part way through the conference. In addition, several had an opportunity to share their experiences and insights from the Bible studies in a conference plenary towards the end.

The book of Acts read cross-culturally: insights from the groups

STUDY 1: *Acts 1:6-14 – "You will be my witnesses"*
The first Bible study called forth deep reflection on "witnessing" to the risen Lord in a variety of contexts, for the good news is not restricted to any one nation or cultural group. The word "witness", of course, meant different things to different people: for some it was a problematic reminder of the aggressive evangelism to which their people have too often been subjected; for others it was the communication of new life, a sharing of the inner dynamism of the Spirit, a proclaiming of the good news in word and deed; for others again it meant working for justice, responding to the cries of people, especially the poor. There was also recognition that witness today can be costly; some shared stories of where it had brought betrayal, persecution, imprisonment, death threats and even death.

Several groups chose to reflect on Jesus' promise to the disciples that they would "receive the power of the Spirit", which led to discussion on power and powerlessness, including the misuse of power in evangelism (such as forcing "the truth" on others) and power struggles within the church.

The communal model of the church at prayer – men and women gathered in the upper room – spoke to many of what is important for the world church and what can bind Christian communities together beyond all cultures, namely prayer, fellowship, joy, listening to the word of God. It was noted that though names (which are always rich in meaning) are given for some of those gathered, only one woman is mentioned, and that in the city of Salvador where the conference gathered there had been a terrible denial of names – of African slaves.

180 *Called to One Hope*

STUDY 2: *Acts 2:1-13; 42-47* – *"They were all together in one place"*

For some groups, the powerful picture of Spirit-filled disciples gathered together was a major focal point for reflection. What could Pentecost mean for this multicultural group of disciples gathered in the "one place" of Salvador? To what extent would Salvador bind people together and unify a plurality of understandings from diverse languages and cultures? Would there be union of hearts as well as of place?

As participants reflected on the affirmation of cultural identities at Pentecost (none at the expense of the other) and how God's message and gifts are poured out into all nations, some asked: How is it that the churches have not yet learned this lesson? Why is their evangelism not more sensitive to people's cultures? Why do some continue to use language and culture in negative and exclusive ways? Others saw reason to rejoice that the Holy Spirit, present and active in the churches today, is helping them to rediscover and affirm cultural identities, to give value to crushed cultures or to excluded languages, to assist in recovering something of what was despised, rejected or lost.

At least one group felt that the churches need to explore further the marvellous diversity of ways of giving authentic witness. Certainly in the power of the Spirit, new expressions of living the gospel in diverse cultures are always possible. Pentecost remains a powerful symbol. Several asked how the transforming power of the Spirit in these human situations could be recognized. How could different identities and cultures be enabled to blossom and flourish in the one Christian family?

Acts 2:42-47 – *"They devoted themselves to the apostles' teaching and fellowship, to the breaking of bread and the prayers"*

There was much reflection on how the early Christian community embodied what Christian communities should be. Signs of a Spirit-filled community-in-mission where "all things [are] done for building up" (1 Cor. 14:26) were discussed. These included: active waiting for the Spirit's guidance; breaking bread together; common prayer; bold witness in the face of oppression and persecution; willingness to reconcile and forgive even when a church had been fire-bombed; sharing of material possessions with the unemployed; welcoming "strangers" into the local congregation; reaching out to minority groups, including "travellers"; caring for those living with HIV/AIDS; giving value to those without value in the eyes of others.

On the other hand, participants felt challenged by some of the factors causing the breakdown of communion within and among different churches, such as the scandal of denominational competition; a free-market approach to evangelism; too much emphasis on church growth; inability to use the riches which different cultural groups bring to the community; fear and distrust of the stranger; superiority and arrogance; racist and sexist attitudes.

STUDY 3: *Acts 5:27-32; 6:1-7 – "We should obey God rather than any human authority"*

Several groups raised the questions of how to know when they are obeying God rather than "human authority"; how to discern the nature of such obedience in contemporary situations of harassment by the authorities, persecution and even martyrdom. What does courageous witness in obedient response to the Spirit mean today? Some participants, on the basis of their experience of hiding asylum-seekers, felt that their churches were obeying God rather than the unjust laws which kept such people waiting for years only to be rejected in the end. Others asked how much intentionality there can be in confronting authorities, for example, in some Muslim countries where Christians are a minority.

Other issues included: What is the nature of prophetic challenge when the churches conform too much to societal structures or collaborate with the oppressors? What to do when Christians take these structures as normative, failing to heed the critique of the gospel? Does the church have "blood on its hands" in relation to indigenous peoples? To what extent may some churches be captive to cultural expressions not in keeping with the gospel, for example, in regard to child marriages or the status of women? Have some churches lost their prophetic voice?

Another focus of attention was the witness of resistance whereby church leaders/groups denounce injustices and proclaim Christian values. Examples from daily life situations included protest against: the state taking people's land for industry or commerce, with little or no compensation; structures that keep people poor; the cutting of state benefits for the poor; unjust taxation; nuclear testing and dumping in the Pacific; unjust dowry demands; corruption in government and church institutions.

Acts 6:1-7 – "The Hellenists complained against the Hebrews"

Most groups could identify with the breakdown in the life of the early Christian community that became focused on the sharing of goods between the Hellenists and the Hebrews. They were familiar with the many internal church tensions and divisions that exist today, leading to friction and pain that threaten Christian community and the danger of losing sight of the wider community to which they belong as followers of the risen Christ.

It was generally acknowledged that it is not always easy for groups in the church to come to terms with the plurality in which they live and work today. There were lessons to be drawn from the apostles' decision in this conflictual situation. After prayer and consultation with the community, they opted for cultural pluralism in unity, recognizing that a Christian community cannot be organized along ethnic or linguistic lines. For them, koinonia (communion) was more important than cultural and theological differences. Some groups felt that the church needed to learn this lesson again today, in order to live with differences in theological reflection and practice, as these are much less important than common faith in the risen Lord.

Church leadership was also challenged. Early leaders were seen as keeping pastoral concerns and cross-cultural issues in balance and being open to innovation in church structures. New ministries were opened up while safeguarding the central purpose of the apostles' own ministry. Changing painful human situations into occasions for community growth remains a challenge for leadership.

STUDY 4: *Acts 8:26-40 – "The Spirit said to Philip, 'Go over to this chariot and join it'"*

The groups generally found in Philip a missionary responsive to the Spirit – a model that can help churches today break down some of the prevailing cultural and religious barriers. His way of being in mission attracted much attention: his response to the prompting of the Spirit; his interest in the Ethiopian's salvation rather than in power or wealth; willingness to begin where the Ethiopian was; respect for the Ethiopian in his culture; "sitting with" the man and responding to his questions rather than forcing the good news on him; baptizing him when requested; accepting him into the new community (even though Deuteronomy would rule out such people); allowing him then to go on his way and express the gospel in his own life and culture.

Others focusing more on the Ethiopian noted in his "conversion" a movement towards ever-widening mission and a recognition of the universal significance and importance of all cultures in the church's mission. Reflection on the divine in-breaking into the Ethiopian's limited understanding brought to memory many examples of the Spirit's transforming action in the lives of people today who are awaiting a fuller understanding of the good news of Jesus Christ.

Acts 9:1-19 – "Saul, Saul, why do you persecute me?"
Some participants found parallels with their own situation, identifying harassment and persecution by the "Sauls" of today and the breathing of threats on Christians by people who may be blinded by their religious convictions, cultural preoccupations or prejudices – for example, the burning down of churches or centres for migrants and refugees. Putting faith into action was seen as a costly challenge for all true disciples today, in areas hostile to the Christian faith but also amid religious indifference and apathy.

The challenge of transformation offered to Ananias in going out to meet a former persecutor and enemy as a person – even as a brother – was found to be the experience also of Christians today. Given the mobility of people and the increasing cultural and religious plurality, communities are also challenged to transformation so that they will become more inclusive, welcoming the stranger, the foreigner, the former enemy.

STUDY 5: *Acts 10:1-48 – "God shows no partiality"*
The groups saw in the baptism of Cornelius – "a devout man who feared God" – an opening of the early church to the evangelization of the Gentiles, that is, of other peoples and cultures. The Holy Spirit enabled Peter to overcome his exclusive attitudes and to receive Cornelius into the community of believers. He learned the hard lesson for future mission that being a Jew does not have primacy over faith in the risen Lord, and that God's partiality extends beyond the Jewish people to others. Cornelius also had to cross religious and cultural barriers to take the step he did.

Again, the text and people's own experiences raised questions for discussion: How to overcome exclusive attitudes that exist in local congregations? How to help people to cross cultural barriers to welcome people of other cultures, and to cross religious barriers to relate with people of other religions? How can people today be bridges between different worlds, as Cornelius was between the Jewish and the Gentile world?

STUDY 6: *Acts 15:1-29 – "The apostles and the elders met together"*
The two controversial issues – were Christians bound by Jewish dietary laws and should Gentiles be received without first becoming Jews (that is, being circumcised)? – raised many questions and challenges: How to be authentically local and authentically Christian? How to preserve unity amid growing diversity? How to make peace in conflictive encounters? Paul and Barnabas were seen as being interested in the communion of the Gentile churches with the church in Jerusalem, regardless of cultural differences. The decision taken created a space where these differences could be lived with. It was seen in contrast with what still happens today where church leaders use their power to divide (even to found a new church), and where differences and divisions lead to wrangling and bitterness.

The method of resolving the problem also spoke to groups, as it highlighted the willingness to welcome all peoples with the salvific grace of the word of God and to walk together in diversity. Empowered by the Spirit, the church decided not to impose Jewish culture and unnecessary restrictions on the Gentiles. Unlike some parallel contemporary examples, there was no winning one another over by sheer argument or by insisting on what Jesus said or did not say on the subject.

The text also seemed to invite much reflection on the pain and struggle of churches to live with diversity today: some cultural groups in local congregations have been forced to worship separately, such as in South Africa, while others choose to do so for one reason or another; some have to accept worship that belongs to another culture, time or place with little or no relevance to contemporary daily life; some immigrants are expected to fit into a white middle-class worshipping community; sometimes youth are alienated by the imposition of a particular church culture; local congregations of a dominant culture can focus on oneness among themselves at the expense of enriching diversity.

STUDY 7: *Acts 16:11-24 – "On the sabbath day we went outside the gate"*
Less attention was given to this passage as, for reasons of time, it had to be combined with the study of Acts 10:1-48. Both dealt with

the gospel transforming persons and relationships. Here Lydia's openness to the Spirit and her hospitality were seen as a model for Christian community and integral to its witness.

The problems presented by the slave-girl "who had a spirit of divination" was for one group a reminder of the world of superstition some evangelists encounter today. There was sharing on the courageous efforts of Christians to challenge economic systems, the profit ethic, injustice and oppression so that the way of salvation may end contemporary forms of slavery.

Conclusion

The Bible studies were an invitation to participants to "come apart for awhile" each day to reflect on the word of God and to look from that vantage point at the local cultural contexts in which they are "called to be faithful witnesses". They were an opportunity to pray, reflect, discuss and celebrate the wondrous diversity of creative ways in which the gospel today – just as it did in the early church – affirms identity, creates community, challenges communities and societal structures, transforms relationships.

One group spoke of experiencing "a closeness to God" within their small group; another of becoming "a real community"; others of sensing the "power of God's word to draw into communion" beyond all differences of origin, age, culture, church denomination – and conference tensions and fatigue! Many testified to a deeper appreciation of what the Spirit is doing today in mission, in and through churches, mission agencies, groups and individuals.

The gathered community of Salvador dispersed on 3 December 1996, having been challenged, guided and strengthened by what God communicated during those days, including prayer and reflection on God's word. Through the living reality in Acts with which they engaged and through interaction with one another, they heard new calls to conversion, mutual encouragement and the "one hope". They received new invitations to live the gospel authentically in their own local contexts.

> For as the rain and the snow come down from heaven,
> and do not return there until they have watered the earth,...
> so shall my word be that goes out from my mouth;
> it shall not return to me empty,
> but it shall accomplish that which I purpose,
> and succeed in the thing for which I sent it (Isa. 55:10-11).

"Thuma Mina" – "Send Us, Lord": The Conference Closes

Christopher Duraisingh

The expressed purpose of a conference on world mission and evangelism is to enable the churches to be empowered for their mission locally and globally. Therefore, all that took place in Salvador was so that the participants might be sent out into the world in the power of the Spirit to share the gospel of one hope in their diverse cultures.

On Sunday 1 December most of the participants worshipped in local congregations and were thus able to observe first-hand the life and witness of the churches in the area. That afternoon participants worshipped with local Christians at downtown Sion Baptist Church in a "festival of faith" organized by the local churches, in which the preacher was an African American Baptist, the late Mac Charles Jones. These events helped participants to look beyond the conference to the church and world wherein Christians are to witness to the one hope to which they are called through the gospel of Christ.

Yet another conference event that was clearly aimed at the continuing renewal of churches in mission was a plenary hearing in which the participants shared their insights, vision and hopes for the shape of the mission of the church in the next decade and beyond. After a brief but powerful presentation by veteran missionary and ecumenical leader the late Lesslie Newbigin (UK) and further introductory comments from three persons representing diverse contexts (Nepal, the USA and Kenya), the participants shared their views on the nature, style and content of a fresh ecumenical statement on mission. Such a statement, intended to further reflection on and the practice of Christian witness in the next decade, was to be finalized by the Unit II commission and staff after the conference.

A further significant event was a business plenary in which the role of mission concerns and their structural expression within the life and work of the WCC, as well as the safeguarding of periodic ecumenical conferences on world mission such as the one in Salvador, were considered. In the light of the planned restructuring of the WCC, it was felt by many – most acutely by the CWME affiliated bodies (mainly ecumenical mission agencies and national/regional ecumenical organizations) – that the Salvador gathering ought to provide a clear mandate to request the WCC to continue to give visible structural expression of the mission agenda within the WCC and to give adequate representation of the affiliated bodies in such a structure. It was also felt that any such structure should include sufficient representation of those who are actively engaged in mission even outside the organized structures of the WCC member churches. After a lively discussion, the conference adopted resolutions which:

1. Requested the central committee:
    a) to set up a Board on World Mission and Evangelism to carry forward into the new structure concerns for mission and evangelism, and to provide for future meetings of the Conference on World Mission and Evangelism;
    b) to ensure substantial representation on the Board on World Mission and Evangelism of the affiliated bodies of the Conference on World Mission and Evangelism by seeking nominations from them, together with appropriate persons drawn from beyond the present constituency of the World Council of Churches and the Conference on World Mission and Evangelism;
    c) to have staff in the World Council of Churches assigned specifically to tasks of mission and evangelism.
2. Further requested the central committee to give the Board on World Mission and Evangelism an adequate place within the reorganized structure of the WCC.
3. Authorized the Board on World Mission and Evangelism to amend the constitution and bylaws governing the Conference on World Mission and Evangelism to take account of the new situation and structures, provided that notice of amendments be sent to the affiliated bodies not less than six months prior to their consideration by the Board.
4. Appointed a consultative group to assist and accompany the implementation of the above resolutions.

During the final two days the conference plenary heard, discussed and approved the message of the conference as well as a set of seven acts of commitment – specific and "do-able" affirmations pointing to possible concrete actions in mission by the participants and the churches beyond Salvador. It also went through the time-consuming process of reading the reports from the four sections. These reports, which had been adopted by the respective sections, were received by the conference plenary, which had opportunity to comment on them. As in past conferences, it was hoped that these written "products" would be shared widely with and studied carefully by Christians and churches everywhere.

There was a sense among the leadership of the conference that the Salvador gathering was only a way station, a point of refreshment, in the church's missionary journey. Like all past world mission conferences, it was intended to nourish the participants through mutual sharing of stories and the very life of the gathering and to send them back into the world with renewed energy and commitment for giving an account of the one hope of the gospel to which they are called.

It was fitting, therefore, that Sigrun Mogedal, co-moderator of the conference, should say in her closing address: "We have indeed been on a journey together. We have indeed been challenged. Right up to the end we have been struggling with decisive issues. But on this journey we have also been bound together and have been led to a fresh encounter with the gospel of Jesus Christ. We now leave with a new urge to witness to the whole body of Christ."

Dr Mogedal referred to the rich experience of an alternative form of globalization at the conference: "a globalization of togetherness without losing identity; where the spirituality and the hopes of each participant, from this rich global diversity, have been both affirmed and shared; where the anger, pain and guilt, the power and the powerlessness of each one of us has been exposed and heard; and where we now see our lives interdependent and woven together – still not without pain, but with much hard evidence from our experience that authentic sharing in mutual respect is possible, even when our concepts and worldviews and practices are in conflict". In this alternative vision of a global community of togetherness in diversity, she said, "We have been inspired by new and fresh curiosity as to the miracle of God's grace, the work of the Holy Spirit among us... We need to commit ourselves for genuine dialogue and sharing across cultures." Touched by the Holy Spirit, "we are urged to let the story of Jesus loose", not in a "triumphant and aggressive" manner but "reaching out in vulnerability".

Dr Mogedal then drew attention to what she perceived as "a striking feature of this conference", that

> the strongest testimonies to hope have come from situations of crisis, from poverty and marginalization: from the continent of Africa; from the spiritualities of indigenous people, sustained and nurtured in spite of forces of dominance and deprivation; from the tears and the drums – because they have witnessed to how Jesus Christ is alive and nurtures a costly hope, a confronting hope, a reconciling hope, an embracing hope in the midst of struggle and despair.

Equally striking to her was the fact that "dominant cultures, cultures choked by over-consumption and affluence, cultures of power and hierarchies have given testimonies to how hope rests in power given up, values turned upside down, in silence and letting go rather than in competitive influence". In this sense she felt there was "a convergence in insights" at the conference which pointed to the "need to examine the question of power and the question of hope together. We need to explore further how power and powerlessness exist together in any situation, the shifting dynamics between the two, and [recognize] that we all can make each other powerless or provide space for empowerment."

Voicing the feeling of the whole conference, Dr Mogedal concluded: "What has brought us together is mission, and it is with a renewed call to engagement in mission – more authentically, more vulnerably, more joyfully, more hopefully, more faithfully and more obediently – that now we return, each to our own context."

The thoughts and experiences of the participants were perhaps best encapsulated in the final paragraph of the conference message:

> With hearts set on fire with the beat of mission and a prayer on our lips that many will share with us in being "Called to One Hope" and take and find "The Gospel in Diverse Cultures", we commend the fruits of the conference to Christians and churches everywhere... to the glory of the triune God.

As it had begun, with the singing of "Laudate omnes gentes", so the eleventh conference on world mission and evangelism came to a close, with the chorus "Thuma mina", "Send us, Lord" – marking yet another step in the journey which the church began on the day of Pentecost, looking towards the eschatological hope of the gospel to which God calls all people in Jesus Christ.

Thuma mina – Send us, Lord.

Salvador: A Signpost of the New in Mission

Christopher Duraisingh

The official documents of the eleventh conference on world mission and evangelism in Salvador, Brazil, are now before us and the question about the legacy of Salvador for ecumenical mission thinking and practice looms large. The ten world mission conferences prior to Salvador have been significant milestones in the movement of Christian witness which began at Pentecost. They have functioned as events which energized the churches for looking at mission in new ways and for defining new frontiers of missionary obedience, and which called the churches to commitment to new forms of partnership and common witness. What then are the impulses for mission from Salvador? What may be its lasting significance? Its central message?

This essay is intended to initiate such an exploration. The following is my personal reading of Salvador – not just the proceedings of the meeting or the documents it produced, but also the entire preparatory process, including the four-year WCC study on gospel and cultures which I had the privilege of directing – and some of the impact and responses already evoked by the conference.

I seek to do three things: (1) to describe the significance of the nature of the gathering itself; (2) to reflect on the overall theme of the conference, pointing to its challenging relevance at the end of the millennium and suggesting a possible "interpretative clue" to understanding the thematic explorations at the event; and (3) to point to some of the salient features and insights from Salvador for the future of ecumenical mission thinking and practice.

There is no single memorable line, eye-catching phrase or slogan in the published statements that effectively sums up the Salvador meeting or can be cited as *the* mandate for mission from Salvador. Indeed, some have expressed their disappointment that such did not emerge. But was that the purpose? An ecumenical mission conference functions primarily as a lens: it gathers up the diffused rays of the world context as well as of the church's practice of mission at a particular moment and brings such diversities and even contradictions into focus so that the signs of the times may be accurately read and missionary thinking and practice appropriately advanced. Salvador sought to do precisely that. The preparatory processes, the nature of the participants, the choice of the venue, the flow of the programme and the exploration of the theme did bring the world context for mission today into focus – and in ways many were not prepared for.

The significance of the event

The tone and content of the conference message and the continuing testimonies of many participants suggest that the primary significance of Salvador may lie in the nature of the event itself. In fact, one might even say that those who have eyes to see and ears to hear can discern in the event the rumblings of a deep-down, ever-intensifying *seismological shift* in mission thinking and practice. Such a shift began in the early 1960s. In 1961, the International Missionary Council merged with the World Council of Churches and the ethos of the WCC began to be radically altered with the active participation of a large number of Orthodox churches and churches from the South. Early signs of the shift were seen in the ecumenical emphasis on the centrality of the local church in mission and in the "mission in six continents" motif at the 1963 world mission conference in Mexico City. Basic to all this was a foundational theological shift from a church-centred to a theocentric understanding of mission, which placed the emphasis on *the mission of the triune God in the whole of creation* as the source of and shaping power over the mission of the church.

The rumbling of the shifting plates was heard a little louder in Bangkok in 1972-73. How else could we understand the discussion there on culture and identity, the call by a few third-world church leaders for a "moratorium" on the sending of personnel and funds from North to South? As James Scherer puts it: "Bangkok was not simply pleading for a fuller recognition of cultural pluralism within the ecumenical movement. It was saying in no uncertain terms that the European model of Christianity was dead, and with it all Western claims to cultural dominance in the two-thirds world."[1] Bangkok was indeed a milestone in the rethinking of mission, led by a few third-world leaders from "anti-colonial" and "nativist" standpoints.

Further shifting of the plates was evident at the San Antonio conference in 1989, as the voices of marginalized people grew louder and clearer. Rather than accepting this as a sign of a positive turn in ecumenical mission history, many interpreted it merely as a crisis in the style of ecumenical gatherings.

It was however in Salvador that the shift in mission history was felt the most intensely. What is the nature of this shift? One striking way to explore this question is to contrast the Salvador meeting – the last world mission conference of this century – with the very first one in Edinburgh, in 1910.

Edinburgh took place at the pinnacle of colonialism, towards the end of a thirty-year period when the proportion of the earth's surface controlled by European powers rose from 67 percent (in 1884) to 84.4 per cent (in 1914). The participants in Edinburgh (all but a handful of them white, male and North Atlantic), its leadership and its confidence in the progress of the "Christendom" project are sure and certain tokens of the colonial era that shaped much of mission thinking at the turn of the century. At the heart of the conferences that followed Edinburgh – Jerusalem (1928) and Tambaram (1938) – was the continued conviction of an intrinsic relationship between Christianity and the history of Western civilization. The Eurocentric thinking which tended to interpret the European expansion of that period as a sign of the coming into being of a single universal history for all peoples everywhere would characterize the ecumenical vision and ventures in mission even into the late 1950s. Such a notion of "universal history" is spelled out in a statement from a Faith and Order meeting in Bristol in 1967:

> So God's history must sooner or later give birth to the conception of universal history, in the sense that all groups, tribes, nations, imperia, races and classes are involved in one and the same history... The universalizing and unifying history started in the ages of mission and colonialism, and is now in this generation penetrating human minds everywhere as never before.[2]

This idea has served within the ecumenical movement to justify the historical, cultural and theological dominance of the North Atlantic worldview.

Over against that picture of Edinburgh and its heritage, envision the meeting in Salvador, a city with a majority of people of African descent. The participants came from almost a hundred countries.

Salvador: A Signpost of the New in Mission 193

Seventy percent of them were from countries outside the North Atlantic region. The majority of those who had speaking or leadership roles at the conference were from the formerly colonized world. The descriptions in this report of the worship life, Bible studies and other aspects of the conference provide ample evidence of the emphasis upon diversity, post-colonial "de-centring" of cultural dominance, free expression of the gospel in a variety of cultural ways, and indeed a celebration of a "rainbow of cultures" throwing up the light of the gospel in a myriad of colours. Perhaps the most poignant reminder that we were on the threshold of something new was the visible and articulate presence of indigenous people from around the world. A group of them felt it important, for example, to challenge the policy of using in the conference proceedings five official languages which were all European.

The role played by indigenous people, women and youth, both in their preparatory meetings and during the conference itself, demonstrated that in a post-colonial and non-Eurocentric world, people "at the margins" and minority communities are not interest groups to be added on to a pre-existing nucleus, but fully active and generative participants. At times such a presence and claim brought a certain sense of conflict. For those given to a Eurocentric style and mind-set this probably was something of a problem. I was surprised to discover that those who have been for so long at the margins or reduced to being objects of mission history often had an "epistemological advantage" in handling conflictual issues and in "deconstructing" dominant and narrowly conceived claims to universality. In creative and subtle ways they exposed the myth of a "universal history" which had no place for their particular histories. Their presentations eschewed the sort of "binary", "either/or" thinking so characteristic of Eurocentrism. Their inclusive language had very little to do with expressions like "us/them" and "insider/outsider". This came home to me especially in some of the interventions by women and indigenous persons from Brazil and the Andean region in section IV.

The post-colonial mission agenda and the challenge to Eurocentrism were also manifested by the persistent calls from many participants from Europe and North America to acknowledge that the North Atlantic "Christendom" of an earlier day is no longer homogeneous. The traditional heartland of missionary movement to the rest of the world is itself a mission field. Its churches are captive to the debilitating dimensions of Western cultures shaped by consumerism, drugs and obsessions with sex and violence. One of the most popular presentations at the conference was by the late Lesslie Newbigin, who asked (among other things) how the Western churches which proposed to "evangelize the whole world in one generation" could be saved from their own cultural captivity. Within both Europe and the USA there are powerful networks around the "gospel and our culture" theme, calling the churches to liberation from cultural captivity and for inner renewal for mission. This indeed became a dominant issue at the conference and certainly will be crucial for the ecumenical mission agenda in the new millennium.

Salvador thus marks a *shift in mission thinking and practice from colonial to post-colonial and from Eurocentric to polycentric.* It dramatically portrays as never before that churches around the world have reached a critical point in the movement from being more or less homogeneous in faith, worship and life to a situation of theological and liturgical heterogeneity, rooted in a profound commitment to express Christian faith and witness in terms of particular local cultural idioms. This is accompanied by a refusal to allow distinct local formulations of the good news in Christ to be reduced or conformed to a single paradigmatic perspective shaped elsewhere. Many participants felt that a dominant trend at the conference was resistance to articulating the gospel in monolithic and homogeneous formulations, which tend to be abstract, general and universal. Instead, Salvador held forth the practice of diversity, multiplicity and heterogeneity born out of Christian experiences in concrete, specific and particular contexts. In their reports back home many participants vividly recall the enrichment of hearing a variety of very different understandings of the same biblical text or theological issue from others during the conference. In fact, the stories shared in the *Encontros* by indigenous people, Dalits from India and women about their encounter with God in Christ appeared to be "counter-narratives" to the traditional presentation of the gospel by "experts", which was often in European discursive style. The Bible studies and worship also pointed to the need for and potential of cross-cultural sharing of Christian experience, crossing cultural boundaries in order that what St Paul calls the "multi-coloured wisdom of God" (Eph. 3:10) may be witnessed to in all its richness.

The term "polycentric" points not only to the reality that there are many churches around the world but also to a systematic principle of *differentiation* – diversity in life and witness, theological formula-

Salvador: A Signpost of the New in Mission 195

tion, and dialogue and communion. It signifies a refusal to accord epistemological privilege and adjudicating power to any single church, whatever its intellectual, economic or political strength, however rich its historical background and heritage. A polycentric reality of churches as we move into the 21st century also entails genuine reciprocity among the churches – for no church in any culture has a unitary and fixed identity. All are bound together in a communion which allows them to be permeable, interactive, mutually enriching.

The two theme panels – one on interpreting the Bible across cultures and the other on evangelism in cultures – amply demonstrated the richness of diversity, the post-colonial and polyvalent meaning of texts and witnesses, as well as the potential for Christians crossing cultural borders to help each other to discern the "multi-coloured wisdom of God" in Jesus Christ.

The preparatory process and to some extent the conference itself made it evident that the differences in theological formulation and liturgical expression between participants from different traditions but the same cultural context are often much less than the differences between persons from the same denomination living in two different contexts. This raises a significant challenge to churches. One might conclude that the life and witness of the churches, certainly in the South, is being shaped less and less by denominational differences (mainly forged in the North and imported to the South during the colonial period) and more and more by the cultural and socio-political ethos shared by the churches in a given context. While the origin of many Protestant denominations may lie in a serious attempt to be contextual and indigenous, the original drive for "contextuality" became at some point static and frozen in a fixed denominational identity. The gospel and cultures focus in the Salvador conference seems to suggest that denominational boundaries may be transcended, the scandal of division may be overcome and churches may be united in common witness when *churches in a given place genuinely seek together to be contextual and rooted in their local cultures.*

Many participants, particularly those of African descent living in diaspora in the Americas, the Caribbean and Europe, expressed a strong desire not only to encounter Afro-Brazilian culture but also to dialogue with its religious expression in Candomblé. The presentation by leaders of the Afro-Brazilian community in Salvador offered a helpful introduction to this reality, but many participants were frustrated and even angry that the conference failed to provide adequate space and time for such dialogue and learning. This I take as further evidence of the post-colonial, polycentric shift in mission understanding. Contrast it with the tendency in mission circles earlier this century to demonize religious traditions other than Christian or to consider them as outside the realm of grace, a stance which grew out of an exclusivist understanding of God's revelation in the Christian faith. If Christianity alone rests on true revelation, then it follows – by the "either/or" logic of binary reasoning – that other faiths are false or illusory. When other religious traditions are conceived of as polar opposites to God's revelatory presence in Christ, they can be judged only as misdirected, even in their loftiest expressions.

For many at the conference, the single most memorable and moving event was the worship service at the slave dock of Solar do Unhão. The conference message spoke of "the solidarity of standing at the dockside in Salvador where, for three hundred years, the African slaves who were still alive after their capture and deportation were unloaded. By the 'stone of tears' together we wept tears of repentance." These tears of repentance were also tears of awareness – a recognition of the horrendous consequences of the Eurocentric devaluation of children of God from another culture and of a different colour. For some it was a painful – turned subversive – memory. But it was much more than that. For many, tasting the salt water by the sea and staring together across the ocean towards the continent of Africa were also marks of silent protest against the colonial and neo-colonial oppression that the church has often unthinkingly shared or supported. The embrace and the tying of a ribbon on the wrist of a brother or sister from another culture or race were indeed signs of solidarity in resistance and of commitment to a liberatory praxis against all forms of oppression. The increasingly faster and louder beat of the drums of Olodum became for many a public expression of the nascent hope of the coming reign of God.

I am aware that the printed reports of the Salvador conference do not make explicit this shift to a post-colonial and polycentric understanding of mission thinking and practice. Fundamentally, this may be due to the form and style of reporting that was expected. Perhaps those of us involved in envisioning the conference output were too concerned about producing polished consensus statements from the four sections, in the traditional style of ecumenical conference reports. Many who participated in the preparatory processes – particularly in the gospel and cultures study groups in many parts of the world – and in the conference itself have testified to the polyvalent, polysymbolic nature of their experiences. But the reports do not seem to capture the richness of this diversity. One wonders what might have resulted if the reports had instead been envisaged primarily as authentic expressions of actual experiences of the participants, in a variety of styles.

The post-colonial posture of many participants and the polycentric reality and overall direction of the conference made many restless and uncomfortable, particularly those accustomed to defining theology and the relation between faith and culture in a more static and essentialist manner. A variety of responses to the celebration of the rich diversity in the worship, the Bible studies, the "Rainbow" festival of gospel in cultures and the *Encontros* could be discerned. There were heated exchanges on such issues as the manner of God's presence in cultures, the role of indigenous cultures and spirituality, and human sexuality. In this sense, the conference ethos was fluid, pluriform, multivocal and even ineradicably untidy – leading, not surprisingly, to subtle and not-so-subtle clashes.

Some adopted a posture of defending the unity and integrity of the gospel above all else. Their starting point was the "one" gospel. Only when its nature has been explored and settled may one speak of its many expressions. Some in this group would also want to articulate (perhaps too quickly) a set of criteria drawing up limits to diversity – a safety net in relation to possible accusations of syncretism.

A second group seemed to be struggling for a transcendental description of the gospel – pure and simple, unaffected by history – which might be translated into cultural idioms. Herein was an understanding of culture as being primarily instrumental in value.

Others took what might be called a "liberal pluralist" stance, which tolerates a variety of forms of expression of the gospel. There is no commitment to adjudicate among the formulations; they are simply allowed to co-exist side by side. Since all historical knowledge is partial, all positions – even those which are conflictual – have their place.

A fourth group, fairly vocal and mainly from the South, affirmed that the only legitimate starting point is diverse contextual expressions of the gospel. The "one" gospel is an abstract notion which can only emerge from the dialogical sharing among all the diverse experiences and expressions of the love of God in Christ. It is the many "gospels" – stories of contextual experiences of the good news of God's loving and liberating presence in Christ – which can lead us to a perception of the common and shared truth of the gospel. Some participants spoke of "the gospel before the gospel", meaning the good news of God's presence in their histories even before Christian missionaries arrived among them. They would challenge the validity of the distinction often made in missionary history between the part of their history when they were "unreached" by God's love in Christ and the period since Christ became present among them.

Here again, how much richer would the proceedings of the conference and its report have been if these diverse positions could have been brought into sustained dialogue with each other and their encounters documented.

The theme: "Called to One Hope – The Gospel in Diverse Cultures"

As mentioned above, the theme of a world mission conference is intended to serve as a lens bringing to focus the diffuse and disparate elements of the global mission context at a particular moment, helping Christians to discern the possible nature of the church's missionary witness in that context. The organizers of the Salvador conference were convinced that the theme chosen did indeed capture diverse elements of the contemporary context. It speaks of hope at a time when (as one keynote speaker put it) "flirting with hopelessness" is the norm. While much of mission thinking emphasizes action and strategies, the Salvador theme invited us to *hope*. The timeliness of this emphasis is demonstrated by the focus on hope in the themes chosen for several recent regional and international Christian conferences, including the 1998 WCC assembly. Surprisingly, however, apart from the two keynote addresses, the deliberations in Salvador barely engaged with the first part of the theme at all. Follow-up reflections on the theme of the conference and its significance for the life and witness of the churches are thus critical.

The two keynote addresses draw our attention to a dual dimension of the call to hope: Christian hope is both personal and prophetic. It involves the renewal and transformation of persons as well as of communities and cultures. As the WCC's "Mission and

Evangelism – An Ecumenical Affirmation" (1982) suggests, one without the other is meaningless.

The theme also draws together two terms: "one" and "diverse". The word "one" within the biblical tradition need not mean a numerical oneness, unicity, but rather points to unity, integrity, communion – something which is unfragmented, unifying, shared.

The juxtaposition of "one" and "diverse" brings a certain sense of urgency to the exploration of the theme. The hopelessness everywhere today is due in part to increasing fragmentation – the struggle for particular cultural, ethnic, linguistic and religious identities. Often these searches for identity (so necessary to any human community) lead to promoting narrow group identities defined over against and pursued at the expense of other groups. All around us at this turn of the millennium we are witnessing the birth and development of violent and separatist tendencies. In the USA alone there are said to be no fewer than 400 "hate groups" with home pages on the Internet! At the same time dangerous alliances are being forged between religion/culture and exclusivistic expressions of national/ethnic identities. The legitimate search for diversity and difference, a hallmark of our post-modern age, has turned in many parts of the world into the nightmare of "killing fields".

It is in such a context that the church is called to be a sign and instrument of the hope of one shared communion of diversities, setting up pointers to the possibility of human community even as groups seek to affirm their own identity. As Philip Potter has said, a central ecumenical and missiological question is how the churches may "cooperate with God making the *oikoumene* an *oikos*, a home, a family of men and women... of varied gifts, cultures, possibilities, where openness, trust, love and justice reign".[3] In a world being torn apart by centrifugal forces of fragmentation, the churches are called to witness to God's call for the unifying, reconciling, one hope of the gospel. The conference's acts of commitment and section reports seem to imply that the juxtaposition of "one hope" and "diverse cultures" in the Salvador theme points towards a new paradigm for the mission of the church: witnessing to the promise of the gospel that *God in Jesus Christ wills a community of diverse identities*, distinct but bonded together in fellowship. If there is a singular interpretative clue to Salvador, I submit, it is this unifying hope of "otherness in communion" (to borrow a phrase from Metropolitan Zizioulas).

It could be said that the central problematic of our era is that of "the other", particularly those who are pushed to the periphery of society. Hence it is of paramount importance that Christians recapture the vision of the gospel story of God in Christ as that which gives hope both by affirming the "otherness", integrity and identity of peoples and groups and by building them into community. The synoptic gospels portray Jesus' eating and drinking with "tax collectors and sinners" as a central symbol of the coming of God's reign. Not only does Jesus free and name people, giving identity and worth to those whose identity has been systematically denied; he also draws them into a circle of companionship with himself and each other, binding them together in community. Liberation in and for community is the hope of the gospel of the coming reign of God in Christ. "Otherness in communion" is therefore a goal of Christian mission as well.

An exegetical study of the letter to the Ephesians (in which the phrase "called to one hope" occurs) indicates in no uncertain terms that the revealed secret of God in Christ, the hope of the gospel, is precisely the hope of reconciliation with God and with each other. Before stating that we are called to one hope, the author describes extensively how those who have been strangers and aliens – seen by the Jews as "the other" – are no longer strangers but are reconciled to God and to each other, the barriers having been broken down through Christ. The vision is clearly one of reconciled diversity, of "others" in communion. In recent times the churches have rediscovered the vision of the being of the triune God, a communion of three persons, as the ground of and pattern for human communion in "otherness". So the Salvador theme clearly leads us to envision the *missio Dei* as that act of God which unites all things to God and to each other. This is the heart of the gospel of hope, the hope that we are called to give an account of; it is also the essence of the church's mission. The gospel message is also that freedom and unity – otherness in communion – are made possible through the self-giving of Christ, who made himself vulnerable in love even unto death. Love which is ready to give itself for the other is the means of liberation and community. Those who know that they are accepted as they are, are also enabled to accept others, to bring freedom and embrace in fellowship. Is not all this and more implied in "called to one hope"? How appropriate and urgent, then, is the message of Salvador to a humanity torn asunder by all forms of oppression and fragmentation!

Salvador: A Signpost of the New in Mission

Another dimension which needs further exploration – though it was implicit in the stories shared in relation to the Bible study passages from the Acts of the Apostles and in the symbols used in the worship – is the *inseparability of hope and history* implied by the linking of the words "hope" and "cultures" in the conference theme. The hope that God offers in Christ is affirmed and discerned only within the processes of history – concrete interactions among persons, communities and nations in time and space. History is oppressive unless it is given meaning and purpose through the hope that God offers. More often than not, as Walter Brueggemann reminds us, "the temptation among us is to split hope and history. As a result, we hold to a religious hope that is detached from the realities of the historical process or we participate in a history which ends in despair because the process itself delivers no lasting victories for the participants."[4] There is no such thing as docetic, ahistorical hope. Hope is effective and real only in a particular historical, cultural context. There is no "meta"-hope, no master-narrative of hope outside of concrete hurts and sufferings, joys and aspirations of persons and communities in history. The missiological implications of this intertwining of "hope" and "cultures" are many.

It should also be noted that the theme uses the term "culture*s*" in the plural. This is a significant shift from earlier discussions of "gospel and *culture*", for at least two reasons. First, it implies that any transcendental or idealist approach to understanding the "gospel of hope" apart from its diverse and plural expressions is false and empty. Nor can we be satisfied with a generic discussion of "culture" or its relation to the gospel. In a sense, there is no "culture" in the abstract; there are only people who live, love, joke and experience and express meaning in particular ways which we call culture.

Second, the use of "cultures" in the plural suggests a different methodological approach: a shift from a primarily deductive to a more inductive method. The question of the relation between the gospel and cultures can be approached only *a posteriori* – after the experience. This is why the conference began with the phase of exposure to the diversity of expressions of the gospel in cultures, including the substantial period of presentations called the *Encontros*. It is as we grapple with the wondrous variety of ways in which Christians live, worship and witness that we may discern the gospel as the good news of unifying hope in a fragmented world.

A further aspect of the link between "hope" and "diverse cultures" is that hope is not hope unless it points to the *"not yet"* dimensions of the gift of God in Christ. In its historical and eschatological dimensions Christian hope involves a dual relationship between the gospel and cultures. On the one hand, as hope is rooted in history, there is an immediate relation, a belonging of the gospel to cultures; the gospel is never accessible apart from its enfleshment in particular cultures. On the other hand, since hope is also a critical principle and as such points to the "not yet" dimensions of God's promise to creation, the gospel stands at a distance from culture. This double-sidedness of belonging and distance, relation and strangeness, affirmation and transformation must characterize any Christian understanding of the relation between the gospel and cultures.

As Konrad Raiser suggests, "the ultimate horizon of Christian mission is the coming of God's reign. From the perspective of the kingdom of God the profile and contradictions of any particular context are being relativized. Contextual theology can remain authentic only if it recognizes the ultimate relativity and also the inseparable relatedness of all contexts if they are placed in this eschatological horizon of Christian mission."[5] Note the words "relatedness" and "relativity". It is in the perspective of the hope of the reign of God, a rule of freedom in community, that all cultures are destigmatized and affirmed as well as critiqued and transformed. The linking of "hope" to "cultures" in the Salvador theme enables us to speak about both the *inseparable relatedness and the relativity of all cultures* in the perspective of God's reign.

In pointing to the inseparable relatedness of all cultural expressions of the gospel and in relativizing each of them in the perspective of the reign of God, hope also *opens up each person or community to the other.* It helps to transcend the borders forged between diverse cultures in the past, and to create new relationships in dialogue and mutual illumination. Certainly the conference, in both its fourth act of commitment as well as the report of section IV, called for stepping beyond such exclusivist borders created out of "binary thinking" which construes the other as "them" over against "us". Such border-crossing facilitated by hope helps us to re-examine the partiality of our own understanding and to recognize our need for the other in order to discern the fullness of the love of God in Jesus Christ. Hope also opens Christians to working for those conditions where existing borders no longer disfigure communion across cultures but transfigure it for mutual enrichment.

An understanding of the gospel propelled by a sense of being called to a unifying and shared hope in Christ helps congregations and local churches to become "cross-border spaces", cross-culturally enriching places, where the "otherness" of the other may be understood on its own terms, and where new and holistic corporate Christian identities may be formed together in solidarity. Section III dealt with the role that congregations in increasingly pluralist societies might play in overcoming various phobias that develop when people view "the other" as threatening. It is only in and through hope in the coming reign of God that congregations may be able to overcome their temptation to remain "comfort zones" for their own members, and instead become open, hospitable and caring spaces in which people of diverse cultures and backgrounds may enter into open-ended and mutually illuminating dialogical relationship.

Indeed, stories and testimonies were shared in the small groups during Bible studies and section work about congregational experiences of border-crossing and becoming public spheres for nurturing "otherness in communion". Regrettably, much of what was shared in the small groups and experienced symbolically in the conference worship could not be documented.

Salvador's implications for mission

Let me now identify briefly some of the key features of the conference which need further attention and call for nurture for effective Christian witness in the decades ahead.

Evangelism within each culture

The very title of section I, "Authentic witness within each culture", is significant. While it calls for an unequivocal commitment to witness – "the voicing of the gospel", as the report puts it – the section speaks of the need to *witness from within.* Does this not suggest a very different way of relating to cultures? We are accustomed to hypostatizing culture "as something fixed and outside the gospel, like a selfsame, alien world 'into which' the Christian mission goes – like a divine intervention – in order to 'confront' and convert it by the proclamation of the gospel. But this is fair neither to the culture nor to the place of Christ in it."[6] How can churches and movements in mission challenge each other to discover authentic forms of witness *within each culture* that are true to the gospel of the incarnate love of God in Jesus Christ?

"Witness from within" is the only mode of evangelism which corresponds to belief in a God who does not control human history from without but rather enters into it, suffers with it and transforms it by participating in it fully and really. C.S. Song writes: "Christian mission in essence should be a love affair of the church with other human beings with whom God has already fallen in love... It is Christian believers building with them a community in the power of God's love. If this is what Christian mission is, then Christian mission is God's mission."[7]

This does not mean that witness from within a culture leaves that culture unchallenged. It is a life-style rooted and nurtured in one's history and culture which can pronounce the judgment of the gospel on that culture and bring radical transformation – change from the root.

Some participants (mainly from the South) wondered whether evangelism does not also include letting the gospel become the very hope of cultures from within – allowing the love of God in Christ to become the germinal element for the renewal of cultures from within, so that they become what God intended them to be: vehicles of justice and peace in which wholeness of life is promised for all. I am reminded of Paul Devanandan's definition of the evangelistic task in India as making known to Indians – Christians and others – the "inner-working of the Holy Spirit" in the renewal of the whole nation, its peoples and cultures. The idea that it is also the task of Christian mission to work and contribute towards the inner renewal of all cultures and religious traditions was expressed in a WCC consultation on gospel and culture in Riano, Italy, in 1984: "The gospel transforms people and cultures to bring to fruition the possibilities inherent in them; the best in them is realized when they have authentic self-identity and self-expression."[8]

The implications of this for the life and structure of a local church as a missionary congregation are many. As Krister Stendhal reminded the participants in the Melbourne world mission conference (1980), we have not sufficiently explored the implication for our evangelistic task if the church is to be the salt rather than making the whole world salt mountains, or to be the leaven in the bread rather than making the whole loaf a lump of leaven.

Such an exercise in mission will indeed be "mission in Christ's way" (to use part of the theme of the San Antonio conference). It is a mission method which implies neither displacement of the other nor elimination of all that is not Christian, but "enfleshment" from within. Mission in Christ's way does not seek the disappearance of another culture or religion but rather a "community of communities" which does not do away with differences but "holds them together within the living structure of a differentiated unity".[9] This approach demands a culture of dialogue – but dialogue in which Christians may give an unequivocal witness to God's love in Jesus Christ.

WCC statements over the past three decades have repeatedly affirmed that (in the words of the San Antonio conference) "both witness and dialogue presuppose two-way relationships... Witness does not preclude dialogue but invites it, and... dialogue does not preclude witness but extends and deepens it."[10] But while more than one section touched upon this issue, Salvador did not go beyond what San Antonio said. Nor did it spell out the practical ways in which a Christian group or parish may live creatively in the tension between dialogue and witness.

Mission in the context of ethnic violence and identity politics

Earlier ecumenical mission conferences have identified domination and oppression as frontiers for the mission of the church. Salvador, however, called the churches' attention to the increasing worldwide phenomenon of "violent and separatist ethnic struggles" as an urgent and critical area for Christian witness to God's reconciling and community-building love in Jesus Christ. The participants were acutely aware that even as they met, inter-ethnic conflict was escalating in many parts of the world, in extreme instances taking the form of ethnic cleansing or genocide. Violent struggles for separate states have led to a crisis in governability, challenging the viability of nation-states. Ethno-cultural definitions of nationality have led to the oppression of religious minority groups in many parts of the world. The conference also shared instances of churches which have themselves given uncritical support to ethnic nationalism and are thus complicit in the genocide of other culture groups.

So the conference asked how Christian witness to the gospel can be an articulation of a counter-culture in the face of a culture of violence and the exclusion of those who are ethnically, racially or religiously different. If racism is a cultural construct for the subjugation of one group by another, how may the gospel challenge racial assumptions, which many Christians are often unaware that they hold?

Salvador highlighted inter-ethnic conflicts and identity politics as aspects of a new missionary imperative of the churches, and exhorted them to seek adequate symbolic representations of "the other" in the light of Christian faith and ways of being credible signs and instruments of God's purpose to bring about a common humanity in justice and peace.

The life and mission of local congregations in increasingly pluralist societies

From different parts of the world, participants in section III shared their experiences of local congregations trying to learn how to live and witness in the midst of cultural plurality. Many communities are indeed unable to cope with the demands of cultural pluralism. The ethnically and racially "other" is suspect and frightening, not welcome. Xenophobia is an extreme response, but is being overtly expressed in many places. A more subtle but equally vicious expression may be seen in the tightening of immigration laws and in how refugees and asylum-seekers are treated by states in many parts of the world.

But strangers and aliens are key concepts in the biblical heritage. The Bible exhorts, "The alien who resides with you shall be to you as the citizen among you; you shall love the alien as yourself" (Lev. 19:34). Further, it is often the stranger who is God's messenger, bearing gifts from God. Yet many churches are unable to deal creatively with strangers or to engage in serious theological reflection on "the other" in the light of the gospel.

Kosuke Koyama argues convincingly that the gospel is essentially "stranger-centred", that an inclusive love for "the other" is at the heart of the biblical faith and is the defining characteristic of the early church's understanding of the person and work of Christ.[11] His reminder that "theology to be authentic must be constantly challenged, disturbed and stirred up by the presence of strangers" is timely. If we accept, with the ancient Greeks, that a touchstone of the quality of a civilization is the way in which it treats those who are different in culture or race, how do our congregations measure up today? The report of section III makes some valuable suggestions. Relevant education for mission at various levels of the church is critical in order that Christians may indeed live and witness to the inclusive communities that the gospel of Christ builds up, where "there is no longer Jew or Greek, there is no longer slave or free, there is no longer male or female; for all... are one in Christ Jesus" (Gal. 3:28).

Commitment to common witness and to renounce proselytism

Within the past ten years or so there have been new expressions of missionary commitment, particularly among many churches in the South – Korea and India, for example. The conference planning committee made provision for the leaders of some of these new missionary movements to share their stories in Salvador.

At the same time, competition among Christians and mission agencies in the name of evangelism has become rampant. The spirit of the free market seems to have infected the concern for evangelization, overcoming the spirit of unity and common witness among churches. Many churches in the South have adopted forms of missionary activity that are as culturally insensitive as were many of the missionary activities of the North in the 19th century. Since the fall of communism in Central and Eastern Europe, the fragmentation in mission structures and practice in those countries has been enormous. The Orthodox churches there describe this phenomenon as an "invasion". In such a context it is crucial to remember that any witness which is not common witness and does not promote community is a contradiction of the gospel.

So acute is the problem that the conference felt it important to address one of its seven acts of commitment to it. Thus the third commitment is "to promote common witness and to renounce proselytism and all forms of mission which destroy the unity of the body of Christ" and to seek "together with others a framework for responsible relationships in mission".

This search for authentic partnership and responsible relationships in mission has been with the ecumenical movement since its inception; and San Antonio had some powerful words to say on the subject. But the urgency is now greater than ever before. Therefore section IV studied and underlined the importance of a draft statement on common witness (subsequently commended by the WCC central committee to the churches for reflection and action). Difficult as it may be, a sustained effort to counter competition in mission is crucial; and promoting the reception of the third commitment from Salvador by churches and mission agencies must be given high priority. The role of the mission sector within the World Council of Churches will be critical to this task.

The unity that binds together diverse expressions of the one gospel
Among the thorniest questions in ecumenical discussions on the relation between the gospel and cultures are those concerning the nature of the unity that binds the diverse expressions of the gospel and the "limits to diversity". For some, indeed, these seem to be the *only* questions. While Salvador dealt with these issues, it did so along with other equally pressing issues directly related to the mission of the church. The conference preparatory processes made it clear that the first step ought to be listening to and learning from diverse local expressions of the gospel – for some had the feeling that even before they began to articulate the gospel in their cultural idiom others were raising the issue of the limits to inculturation.

Certainly there has been a crisis of language within the ecumenical movement. There is no broad common framework of language (hermeneutics) within which the churches may understand and affirm each other. In addressing this issue, Salvador found the interrelationship between "catholic" and "contextual" to be highly significant. As the section IV report puts it: "Catholicity requires that different contexts be in communion with each other and respect and challenge each other in the freedom of the Spirit. Together, contextuality and catholicity become signs of authenticity for the local as well as the global reality of the church."

While the section report does not fully capture the conflictual nature of the discussion on this topic, it does identify some of the factors that hinder the process of discerning together the unity which binds diverse cultural expressions of the gospel, including the uneven nature of power relationships among churches, group interests and different positions on ethical issues.

Salvador also rightly emphasized the communitarian nature of truth. The four criteria for testing the appropriateness of varied contextual expressions of the gospel identified by the report of section IV require further amplification and exploration of their proper use, as do the significant insights on the central question of syncretism. Discussions at Salvador showed that there are at least two opposing views on the issue. For some, syncretism is anathema. For many others, particularly from the South, syncretism is a normal, even essential, part of rooting the gospel in particular cultures.

My sense is that one's attitude to syncretism depends largely on how one understands the dynamics of religion and human religiosity. From within a Roman Catholic context Leonardo Boff has written:

> The value of syncretism depends on the viewpoint of the observer. If the observer sits in the privileged places within Catholicism – understanding it as a signed, sealed and delivered masterpiece – then he or she will consider syncretism to be a threat to be avoided at all costs. If, however, he or she is situated on a lower level, amid conflicts and challenges, in the midst of people who live their faith together with other religious expressions, on a level that understands Catholicism as a living reality and therefore open to other elements and the attempt to synthesize them, then syncretism is seen as a normal and natural process.[12]

Unfortunately, however, Boff adds, "our understanding of syncretism has come from those who have been afraid of it: the defenders of theological and institutional knowledge".

Where a religion is reduced to a set of doctrinal beliefs and fixed liturgical practices, so that the emphasis is on clearly identifiable content, syncretism is seen as an *unhealthy amalgam* of two or more disparate religions which denies the authentic "content" of one's own faith and practice.

But those who see the dynamics of religion primarily as a process of "integration" between a religious tradition and its cultural ethos – which is itself dynamic and changing – accept syncretism, the process of integration, as a necessary element in the development of religion. Such a process has gone on throughout the history of Christianity.

It can be argued that the formation of self-identity in general and religious identity in particular is inherently syncretistic – a process of growth which brings into being a radically new world of meaning. As Raymond Panikkar has written: "Such a growth means continuity and development, but also means transformation and revolution. Growth does not exclude mutation; on the contrary, there are moments even in the biological realm when only a real mutation can account for further life."[13]

Of course, not all integration is wholesome. During the discussions in Salvador a number of examples of false syncretism were shared. The unwitting accommodation of the gospel to individualism and capitalist consumerism by many Christians in the North is clearly a form of syncretism incompatible with the gospel. The uncritical acceptance of the attitudes of patriarchal cultures towards women in the life of many churches in the South is another clear case. What is important is for the churches to commit themselves irrevocably to mutual accountability and critique, to open themselves to each other across cultures so that they may "share a rich diversity of the Christian faith; discover the unity that binds these together; and affirm together the Christological centre and Trinitarian source of our faith in all its varied expressions".[14]

It is no wonder, therefore, that the second act of commitment urges Christians "resolutely to continue in dialogue together even when we substantially differ in the way we comprehend and use the term 'gospel' and understand the work of the Holy Spirit in all cultures". Such a commitment arises out of the affirmation that "it is only as churches seek together the truth of the gospel in dialogue with each other that they may discern the fullness of God's reconciling work in Christ and the one hope to which they are called".

* * *

The Salvador conference was a hopeful event, evoking anticipation of "that day" when "out of every tribe and nation" people will walk the walk of the reign of God. The eleventh conference on world mission and evangelism was indeed a significant milestone in the walk that began at Pentecost and leads on towards the fullness of God's reign, in the power of the Spirit of the risen Christ whose death on the cross opened for us the new way. As we dare to be open and vulnerable to each other, stripping ourselves of false securities, we shall discover the God of surprises[15] leading us on to radical and unforeseen vistas in mission in the decades ahead – as radical as the vision of Jesus of Nazareth himself: "Then people will come from east and west, from north and south, and will eat in the kingdom of God. Indeed, some are last who will be first, and some are first who will be last" (Luke 13:29-30). Not only are people of diverse cultures and contexts drawn into one communion at God's table but status and power relationships are reversed, with a clear bias for those who have been marginalized.

The visionary of the Isle of Patmos gives a captivating picture of the new order of God's reign:

I saw no temple in the city, for its temple is the Lord God the Almighty and the Lamb. And the city has no need of sun or moon to shine on it, for the glory of God is its light, and its lamp is the Lamb. The nations will walk by its light, and the kings of the earth will bring their glory into it. Its gates will never be shut by day – and there will be no night there. People will bring into it the glory and the honour of the nations. But nothing unclean will enter it, nor anyone who practises abomination or falsehood, but only those who are written in the Lamb's book of life (Rev. 21:22-27).

The vision is clear, and three aspects of it stand out. First, peoples and nations walk the highway of God's reign as fellow pilgrims. God is their light. There is community with God and each other. No longer is there neo-colonial force or a globalizing drive that destroys local identities or fragmentation that tears apart humanity – only otherness in communion, with all embraced in God's love. Second, nothing that harms even the weakest will have any place or power there. Finally, God is glorified and the relations among peoples and cultures are enhanced as the nations offer to God and share within their common life their heritages and honour. What a vision – humans beings and all of creation reflecting the splendour of the inner communion of the triune God!

Is God's dream not already unfolding in history? Was Salvador not a sign and portent of God's intent? Will this be the vision that spurs us on in our witness until the next milestone – and possibly another ecumenical world mission conference?

In seeking the fulfilment of God's will on earth we are called to pray, in the words of the conference prayer:

> Gracious God,
> who from the day of Pentecost
> has called to one hope all peoples everywhere
> through the embodiment of the gospel in diverse cultures:
> grant us, we pray, a vision of your love in Jesus Christ
> that embraces within its transforming power
> the rich plurality of the human race...
> Inspire in your church
> a rich sharing across cultures
> so that the heritages of all peoples may be offered to you, Triune God,
> who alone are worthy of glory and honour,
> at all times and in all places,
> through Jesus Christ. Amen.

NOTES

[1] James A. Scherer, *Gospel, Church and Kingdom: Comparative Studies in World Mission Theology*, Minneapolis, Augsburg, 1987, p.123.
[2] *New Directions in Faith and Order, Bristol 1967: Reports, Minutes, Documents*, Geneva, WCC, 1968, p.25.
[3] Report of the general secretary, WCC central committee, Geneva, July/August 1977, p.9.
[4] Walter Brueggemann, *Hope within History*, Atlanta, John Knox, 1987, p.3.
[5] Konrad Raiser, "Beyond Tradition and Context: In Search of an Ecumenical Framework of Hermeneutics", *International Review of Mission*, vol. 80, nos 319-320, July-Oct. 1991, p.354.
[6] Daniel Hardy, "The Future of Theology in a Complex World", in *Christ and Context*, Hilary Regan and Alan J. Torrance, eds, Edinburgh, T&T Clark, 1993, p.23.
[7] C.S. Song, *Tell Us Our Names*, Maryknoll, NY, Orbis, 1984, p.108.
[8] "Gospel and Culture: The Working Statement Developed at the Riano Consultation", May-June 1984, in *International Review of Mission*, vol. 74, no. 294, April 1985, p.266.
[9] Stanley Samartha, "Christian Community in a Pluralistic Society", in *Laity Focus and News*, a publication of the Church of South India Laity Congress, vol. 1, no. 17, 20 Nov. 1995, p.6.
[10] Frederick R. Wilson, ed., *The San Antonio Report*, Geneva, WCC, 1990, p.32.
[11] Kosuke Koyama, "'Extend Hospitality to Strangers' – A Missiology of *Theologia Crucis*", in *International Review of Mission*, vol. 82, no. 327, July/Oct. 1993, pp.283-95.
[12] Leonardo Boff, *Church, Charism and Power*, London, SCM, 1985, p.89.
[13] Raymond Panikkar, *The Intra-Religious Dialogue*, New York, Paulist, 1978, p.72.
[14] David Gill, ed., *Gathered for Life*, Geneva, WCC, 1983, p.33.
[15] These phrases are taken from *On the Way to Fuller Koinonia: Official Report of the Fifth World Conference on Faith and Order*, Thomas Best and Günther Gassman, eds, Geneva, WCC, 1994, p.234.

Appendices

Participants

Adams, Mrs Andrea
Delegate AB
Congregational Federation [UK]

Adiprasetya, Rev. Joas
Delegate FOM
Indonesian Christian Church (GKI)

Ador, Rev. Samuel Nyawelo
Delegated observer
Presbyterian Church in the Sudan

Aguirre Coli, Sr Gabriel O.
Delegate MC
Pentecostal Church of Chile

Ahlstrand, Rev. Dr Kajsa
Delegate MC, Church of Sweden

Ahonen, Rev. Dr Risto A.
Accredited visitor, Evangelical
Lutheran Church of Finland

Ajapahyan, Archimandrite Michael
Gevorg, Delegate MC (Italy)
Armenian Apostolic Church
(Holy See of Etchmiadzin)

Alcantara, Mr Pythagoras C.
Accredited visitor, Episcopal
Anglican Church of Brazil

Alemezian, Very Rev. Nareg
Manoug
Delegate MC (USA)
Armenian Apostolic Church
(Holy See of Etchmiadzin)

Alfeyev, Dr Hilarion
Delegate MC
Russian Orthodox Church

Altmann, Dr Walter
Delegated observer
Evangelical Church of Lutheran
Confession in Brazil

Anderson, Rev. Canon James R.
Accredited visitor
Church of England

Anthony, Monsignor Patrick A.B.
Delegated observer (Saint Lucia)
Roman Catholic Church

AB = CWME affiliated body
Commission = Programme Unit II Commission
FOM = Frontiers of mission
G&C coordinator = national/regional coordinator of Gospel and Cultures study
MC = Member church

The country of residence is given in brackets if this is different or not apparent from the name of the church; if the name of the church does not indicate the country, this follows in square brackets.

Aquino, Rev. Jorge Luiz F. de
Accredited visitor
Presbyterian Church in Brazil

Arnoso, Pastor Samuel
Accredited visitor
Spanish Evangelical Church

Arue, Rev. Tiaontin J.
Delegate MC
Kiribati Protestant Church

Arulampalam, Rev. S.S.
Delegate MC
Uniting Church in Australia

Attia, Mr Maged
Delegate MC (Australia)
Coptic Orthodox Church [Egypt]

Aubry, Rt Rev. Roger
Consultant (Bolivia)
Roman Catholic Church

Aykazian, Bishop Viken
Delegate Commission (Switzerland)
Armenian Apostolic Church
(Holy See of Etchmiadzin)

Ayo Ladigbolu, Bishop L.S.
Delegate MC
Methodist Church, Nigeria

Ayres Mattos, Bishop Paulo
Delegate MC
Methodist Church in Brazil

Azevedo Santos, Sra Mae Stella de
Delegated observer
Afro-Brazilian religion

Bader, Dr Dietmar K.
Accredited visitor (Germany)
Roman Catholic Church

Bailey, Rev. Dr Randall C.
Delegate FOM
Progressive National Baptist
Convention, Inc. [USA]

Bakker, Ms Ineke H.J.
Delegate MC, Reformed Churches
in the Netherlands

Balog, Rev. Margit
Delegate MC
Reformed Church in Hungary

Bamat, Dr Thomas P.
Accredited visitor (Brazil)
Roman Catholic Church

Bar, Mr Romulus
Delegate MC
Romanian Orthodox Church

Bastian, Dr Rainward
Delegate Commission
Evangelical Church in Germany

Belistri Giménez, Ms Ana Laura
Delegate FOM, Evangelical
Methodist Church in Uruguay

Bell, Sra Amalia
Delegate FOM
Moravian Church in Nicaragua

Bent Roland, Rev. Norman T.
Delegate FOM
Moravian Church in Nicaragua

Berglund, Deacon K. Annette
Delegate MC
Mission Covenant Church of
Sweden

Bernhard, Pastor Rui L.
Accredited visitor
Evangelical Church of Lutheran
Confession in Brazil

Best, Mr John R.
Accredited visitor
United Church of Canada

Best, Dr Marion S.
WCC Unit II Committee
United Church of Canada

Beyer, Oberkirchenrat Dr Ulrich
Delegate MC
Evangelical Church in Germany

Bhattacharji, Dr Sara
Delegate FOM, Mar Thoma Syrian
Church of Malabar [India]

Bisada, Mr Gamal Zekrie
Delegate FOM
Coptic Orthodox Church [Egypt]

Blaauw-Tijman, Ms Anneke M.
Delegate AB
Union of the Baptist Churches
in the Netherlands

Bolla Árpádné, Ms Helga
Delegate MC (Brazil)
Lutheran Church in Hungary

Bottoms, Rev. Ruth
Delegate Commission
Baptist Union of Great Britain

Braaksma, Ms Debra A.
Delegate MC (Kenya)
Reformed Church in America [USA]

Brown, Rev. Dr John P.
Delegate Commission
Uniting Church in Australia

Bulisi, Dr Pongo
Delegate Commission, Church
of Jesus Christ on Earth by His
Messenger Simon Kimbangu
[Democratic Republic of Congo
(Zaïre)]

Büntjen, Fräulein Christine
Delegate MC, Evangelical
Methodist
Church in Germany

Burger, Rev. Helmut
Accredited visitor (Germany)
Evangelical Church of Lutheran
Confession in Brazil

Burgie, Rev. Willette A.
Resource
Progressive National Baptist
Convention, Inc. [USA]

Butler, Rt Rev. Dr Thomas F.
Delegate MC, Church of England

Butselaar, Rev. Dr G. Jan van
Advisor, Reformed Churches
in the Netherlands

Byantoro, Archimandrite
Daniel Bambang
Delegate FOM
Indonesian Orthodox Church

Camba, Bishop Erme R.
Delegate Commission
United Church of Christ
in the Philippines

Campos Leite, Bishop Nelson Luiz
Host country observer
Methodist Church in Brazil

Campos Morante, Pastor Bernardo
Delegated observer
Pentecostal Church [Peru]

Camps, Rev. Dr Carlos M.
Resource, Presbyterian Reformed
Church in Cuba

Carol, Ms Anişoara
Delegate Commission
Romanian Orthodox Church

Carr, Rev. Dr Dhyanchand
Delegated observer (Hong Kong)
Church of South India

Carriker, Dr C. Timóteo
Accredited visitor (Brazil)
Presbyterian Church (USA)

Castañeta de Asila, Ms Maritza
Delegate FOM, Bolivian
Evangelical Lutheran Church

Castro, Rev. Prof. Clovis Pinto de
Host country observer
Methodist Church in Brazil

Castro, Pastor Emilio E.
Guest, Evangelical Methodist Church
in Uruguay

Cavalcanti, Rev. Prof. E.
Robinson de Barros
Resource, Episcopal
Anglican Church of Brazil

Centeno, Mr Sergio
Accredited visitor, Christian
Church (Disciples of Christ) [USA]

Chaplin, Rev. Fr Vsevolod
Delegate MC
Russian Orthodox Church

Participants 217

Charkiewicz, Mr Jaroslaw
Delegate MC
Autocephalous Orthodox Church
in Poland

Chávez Quispe, Ms María C.
Delegate MC, Evangelical
Methodist Church in Bolivia

Cheng Yang-En, Rev. Dr
Delegate MC
Presbyterian Church in Taiwan

Chevalley, Pasteur Geneviève
G&C coordinator, Reformed Church
of Alsace and Lorraine [France]

Cipriani, Padre Gabriele
Host country observer
Roman Catholic Church

Conde Conde, Pastor Claudio A.
Accredited visitor
Methodist Church of Peru

Couchell, Archimandrite Dimitrios
Delegate MC (USA)
Ecumenical Patriarchate
of Constantinople [Turkey]

Cowans, Rev. Dr Gordon E.
Delegate FOM, United Church in
Jamaica and the Cayman Islands

Crawley, Ms Gwen
Delegate Commission
Presbyterian Church (USA)

Crowe, Rev. Norman C.
Accredited visitor
Uniting Church in Australia

Cunha, Rev. Guilhermino
Host country observer
Presbyterian Church in Brazil

Cutimanco, Mr Goyo de la Cruz
Accredited visitor, Fraternity of
Evangelical Churches of Costa Rica

Dalmás Artús, Ms Mabel S.
Delegate MC (Argentina)
Evangelical Waldensian Church
of the River Plate [Argentina]

Darmaputera, Rev. Dr Eka
Delegate Commission
Indonesian Christian Church (GKI)

Davaine, Pasteur Christian
Delegate MC
Reformed Church of France

Deifelt, Rev. Wanda
Resource, Evangelical Church
of Lutheran Confession in Brazil

Delgado de Martín, Rev. M.
Griselda
Delegate FOM
Episcopal Church of Cuba

Demberger, Pfarrer Peter
Accredited visitor
Evangelical Church in Germany

Dias, Rev. Dr Zwinglio Mota
Delegate FOM, United Presbyterian
Church of Brazil

Didenco, Rev. Fr Victor
Delegate MC
Moldavian Orthodox Church,
Moscow Patriarchate

Dimitrov, Prof. Ivan Jelev
Delegate Commission
Bulgarian Orthodox Church

Ding, Pastor Andreas M.
Delegate MC, Evangelical
Presbyterian Church of Portugal

Discher, Ms Gudrun H.
Delegate MC
Evangelical Church in Germany

Domingues, Rev. Jorge Luiz F.
Advisor (USA)
Methodist Church in Brazil

Dos Santos, Pastor Batista Josefá
Host country observer
Episcopal Anglican Church of Brazil

Dotou, Mme Grâce
Delegate FOM, Protestant
Methodist Church of Benin

Dourado, Profa Nueza A.R.
Host country observer, United
Presbyterian Church of Brazil

Duff, Rev. John C.
Delegate MC
Presbyterian Church in Canada

Dumont, Rev. Dr Alfred A.
Delegate MC
United Church of Canada

Duraisingh, Mrs Suganthy
Accredited visitor
Church of South India

El-Masry, Ms Rania
Delegate FOM
Coptic Orthodox Church [Egypt]

Elliott, Rev. Donald W.
G&C coordinator
United Reformed Church
in the United Kingdom

Enns, Pfarrer Fernando
Delegate MC
Mennonite Church [Germany]

Evans, Rev. Melbalenia D.
Delegate MC
United Church of Christ [USA]

Fejo, Rev. Wali
Resource
Uniting Church in Australia

Fernando, Rt Rev. Kenneth
Delegate Commission
Church of Ceylon [Sri Lanka]

Ferrier, Drs Kathleen G.
Delegate MC
Netherlands Reformed Church

Fitzgerald, Rt Rev. Michael L.
Consultant (Italy)
Roman Catholic Church

Flores, Pastor Lucio P.
Host country observer
Presbyterian Church in Brazil

Flores Ponce, Mr R. Pablo
Accredited visitor
Methodist Church of Peru

Formilleza, Ms Prima S.
G&C coordinator
Baptist Church in the Philippines

Frýdl, Rev. David
Delegate MC
Czechoslovak Hussite Church

Füllkrug-Weitzel, Pfarrerin Cornelia
Resource
Evangelical Church in Germany

Gad, Mr Magdi M.
G&C coordinator
Coptic Orthodox Church [Egypt]

Gadiki, Rev. Vasi
Delegate MC
United Church in Papua New Guinea
and the Solomon Islands

Ganaba, Ms Olga
Delegate Commission
Russian Orthodox Church

García Ixcot, Sra L. Amanda
Delegated observer (Guatemala)
Roman Catholic Church

Gass, Rev. Dr Eric A.
Accredited visitor
Christian Church (Disciples
of Christ) [USA]

George, Rev. Dr K.M.
Delegate FOM, Malankara
Orthodox Syrian Church [India]

Glossner, Pfarrer Herbert
Accredited visitor
Evangelical Church in Germany

Godfrey, Canon David S.G.
Delegate AB, Church of Ireland

Gordun, Rev. Fr Sergey
Delegate MC
Russian Orthodox Church

Greene, Rev. Dr Colin J.D.
Accredited visitor (UK)

Grosse, Pfarrer Peter
Delegate MC
Evangelical Church in Germany

Gueorguieva, Ms Polina K.
Delegate FOM
Bulgarian Orthodox Church

Guldseth, Miss Ellen K.
Delegate MC
United Methodist Church [USA]

Günther, Pfarrer Dr Wolfgang
Delegate MC
Evangelical Church in Germany

Habib, Rev. Dr Samuel
Delegate Commission
Synod of the Nile
of the Evangelical Church [Egypt]

Hagesæther, Rt Rev. Ole D.
Delegate MC, Church of Norway

Halder, Ms Lila Sushama
Delegate MC
Church of Bangladesh

Hall Wynn, Rev. Prathia
Resource, American
Baptist Churches in the USA

Hallam, Mr Stuart P.
Delegate MC, Church of England

Halmarson, Rev. Cynthia G.
Delegate MC, Evangelical
Lutheran Church
in Canada

Hamilton, Ms Maggie E.
Resource
Church of England

Hamlin, Ms Heather L.
Delegate MC
Anglican Church of Canada

Hanna, Dr Labiba S.
Delegate FOM (USA)
Coptic Orthodox Church [Egypt]

Harman, Rev. Robert
Delegate Commission
United Methodist Church [USA]

Hauss-Berthelin, Pasteur Danielle
Delegate MC, Evangelical Church
of the Augsburg Confession
of Alsace and Lorraine [France]

Heckelmann, Fräulein Birgit
Delegate MC
Evangelical Church in Germany

Hendje Toya, Rev. Dr Jean-Samuel
Resource (Rwanda)
Evangelical Church of Cameroon

Hermansen, Ms A. Katrine
Delegate AB, Evangelical
Lutheran Church of Denmark

Hicks, Rev. Sarah M.
Accredited visitor, American
Baptist Churches in the USA

Hirano, Rev. Dr David Y.
Delegate MC
United Church of Christ [USA]

Hirsch, Rev. Alan
Delegate MC
Churches of Christ in Australia

Huang Po-Ho, Rev. Dr
Delegate FOM
Presbyterian Church in Taiwan

Hunsberger, Rev. Dr George R.
Delegate FOM
Presbyterian Church (USA)

Ibrahim, Metropolitan G. Yohanna
Delegate MC
Syrian Orthodox Patriarchate
of Antioch and All the East

Imbiri, Rev. Josias
Delegate MC
Evangelical Christian Church
in Irian Jaya [Indonesia]

Ioann of Belgorod, Bishop
Delegate MC
Russian Orthodox Church

Ionita, Prof. Dr Viorel
Delegated observer (Switzerland)
Romanian Orthodox Church

Itula, Mrs Talanoa D.
Delegate MC
Congregational Christian Church
in American Samoa

Ivliev, Archimandrite Jannuary
Resource, Russian Orthodox Church

Jakubeit, Frau Heike
Accredited visitor
Evangelical Church in Germany

James, Rev. Dr Emmanuel E.
Accredited visitor
Church of South India

Jarvis, Rev. Cortroy W.M.
Delegate MC
Moravian Church, Eastern
West Indies Province [Antigua]

Jeevan Babu, Rev. D.S.
Delegate AB
Church of South India

Jehu-Appiah, Rev. Jerisdan H.
Delegate FOM (UK), Musama
Disco Christo Church [Ghana]

Jensen, Rev. Dr Mogens
Delegate MC, Evangelical
Lutheran Church of Denmark

Jesudason, Miss Chandra C.
Delegate AB
Church of Ceylon [Sri Lanka]

Jiliaev, Archimandrite Nestor
Advisor (Switzerland)
Russian Orthodox Church

Johnsen, Mr Tore
G&C coordinator
Church of Norway

Johnston, Dr Alexandra
Delegate Commission
Presbyterian Church in Canada

Jonah of Bukoba, Bishop
Delegate FOM (Tanzania)
Greek Orthodox Patriarchate of
Alexandria and All Africa [Egypt]

Jones, Rev. Dr Mac Charles
Delegate Commission
National Baptist Convention
of America [USA]

Joshua, Mr M. Patrick
Consultant, Church of South India

Juárez de González, Sra Olivia S.
Delegate FOM
Baptist Church in Mexico

Justo de Oliveira, Rev. Ricardo
Host country observer, United
Presbyterian Church of Brazil

Kaminski, Herr Michael
Accredited visitor (Brazil)
Evangelical Church in Germany

Kanyoro, Dr Musimbi R.A.
Resource (Switzerland)
Evangelical Lutheran Church
in Kenya

Karadaglis, Dr Demetrios
Delegate Commission
Church of Greece

Karayiannis, Bishop Vasilios
Delegate MC, Church of Cyprus

Karibian, Archbishop O. Datev
Delegate MC (Brazil)
Armenian Apostolic Church
(Holy See of Etchmiadzin)

Kassab, Ms Najla A.
Resource
National Evangelical Synod
of Syria and Lebanon [Lebanon]

Kent, Miss Alida D.
Delegate FOM
Moravian Church in Suriname

Khatry, Dr Ramesh
Consultant, Aradhana Church
[Nepal]

Kim Dong-Wan, Rev.
Delegate AB
Korean Methodist Church

Kirill of Smolensk
and Kaliningrad, Metropolitan
Delegate MC
Russian Orthodox Church

Kishkovsky, Very Rev. Leonid
Delegate MC
Orthodox Church in America [USA]

Kivelä, Rev. Juhani
Delegate AB, Evangelical
Free Church of Finland

Klagba-Kuadjovi, Pasteur C. Charles
Delegate AB (France)
Methodist Church in Togo

Koria, Rev. Dr Paulo Tema
Delegate MC, Congregational
Christian Church in Samoa

Korotkov, Rev. Vladimir
Accredited visitor
Uniting Church in Australia

Koukoura, Dr Dimitra
Delegate FOM (Greece)
Ecumenical Patriarchate
of Constantinople [Turkey]

Kowo, Mrs Naomi
Delegate AB (Zimbabwe)
United Methodist Church [USA]

Krause, Pfarrer Dr Burghard
Accredited visitor
Evangelical Church in Germany

Kristensen, Ms Anne Karin
Consultant, Church of Norway

Laar, Rev. Drs Wouter van
G&C coordinator, Reformed
Churches in the Netherlands

Labi, Rev. Fr Kwame Joseph A.
Delegate Commission (Ghana)
Greek Orthodox Patriarchate of
Alexandria and All Africa [Egypt]

Lam, Pastor Holger
Delegate MC
Baptist Union of Denmark

Laoyan, Ms Frances K.
Delegate MC, Episcopal
Church in the Philippines

Larom, Mrs Margaret S.
Delegate MC
Episcopal Church [USA]

Larsson, Dr Birgitta
Delegate Commission
Church of Sweden

Lautmann, Rev. J. Fredrik H.
Accredited visitor
Church of Sweden

Lawrence, Ms Jackie
Delegate FOM
Baptist Church in Canada

Lazarus, Ms Lana
Delegate MC
Methodist Church of New Zealand

Lealaitafea, Rev. Paulo A.
Delegate FOM
Congregational Christian Church
in American Samoa

Lee Hong-Jung, Rev. Dr
Accredited visitor (UK)
Presbyterian Church of Korea

Léon de Pacheco, Pastora Maritza
Delegated observer
Koinonia Pentecostal
Evangelical Church [Venezuela]

Lettini, Rev. Gabriella
Delegate FOM (USA)
Waldensian Church [Italy]

Lewis-Cooper, Rev. Marjorie
Resource, United Church in
Jamaica and the Cayman Islands

Licayan, Ms Jezell Marie O.
Delegate MC
United Church of Christ
in the Philippines

Liggett, Rev. Julie
Accredited visitor
Church of the Brethren [USA]

Lima, Revmo Glauco S. de
Host country observer, Episcopal
Anglican Church of Brazil

Llewellyn, Ms Jennifer J.
Advisor
United Church of Canada

López-Lozano, Obispo Carlos
Delegate MC
Spanish Reformed Episcopal Church

Loswÿk, Rev. Edgar J.A.
Delegate MC
Moravian Church in Suriname

Lugo Morales, Bishop Gamaliel de J.
Delegated observer, Evangelical Pentecostal Union of Venezuela

Lugosi, Rev. Mihai
Delegate MC
Reformed Church in Romania

Luk Fai, Rev.
Delegate MC, Hong Kong Council of the Church of Christ in China

MacIver, Rev. Norman
Delegate MC, Church of Scotland

Madrid, Ms Maria Theresa M.
Resource (Philippines)
Roman Catholic Church

Magalhães, Rev. José Rômulo de
Host country observer
Independent Presbyterian Church in Brazil

Maluleke, Rev. Sekhetho Daniel
Delegate MC
Uniting Reformed Church in Southern Africa [South Africa]

Mansour, Bishop Damaskinos
Delegate MC (Brazil)
Greek Orthodox Patriarchate of Antioch and All the East [Syria]

Marín Bermúdez, Rev. Miriam
G&C coordinator
Baptist Church of Costa Rica

Maringa, Mrs Buyelwa Esther
Delegate MC
Evangelical Presbyterian Church in South Africa

Mason, Rev. J. Gary
Delegate AB
Methodist Church in Ireland

Massey, Rev. Dr James
Accredited visitor
Church of North India

Matsumoto Maori, Ms
Accredited visitor (Brazil)
United Church of Christ in Japan

Matsumoto Toshiyuki, Rev.
Delegate MC (Brazil)
United Church of Christ in Japan

Matthey, Pasteur Jacques
Delegate AB, Swiss Protestant Church Federation

Mbombe, M. Samuel
Delegate MC
Presbyterian Church of Cameroon

McGee, Rev. Dr Gary B.
Delegated observer
Assemblies of God (USA)

McKay, Rev. Nanette L.
Delegate MC
United Church of Canada

McLean, Rev. Father Colin
Accredited visitor (Brazil)
Roman Catholic Church

Mdoe, Pastor Ruth Kissah
Delegate MC, Evangelical Lutheran Church in Tanzania

Meissner, Oberkirchenrat Herbert
Delegate AB
Evangelical Church in Germany

Melanchthon, Dr Monica J.
Delegate FOM, United Evangelical Lutheran Churches in India

Meldrum, Rev. Siméa de Souza
Host country observer, Episcopal Anglican Church of Brazil

Melo, Rt Rev. José Carlos
Consultant (Brazil)
Roman Catholic Church

Méndez, Profa Oneida
Delegate FOM, Presbyterian Reformed Church in Cuba

Menezes de Souza, Rev. Capitan Maruilson
Delegated observer (Brazil)
Salvation Army

Mghwira, Ms Anna E.
G&C coordinator, Evangelical
Lutheran Church in Tanzania

Miller, Mr John
Accredited visitor
Christ Apostolic Church [Nigeria]

Mogedal, Dr Sigrun
Delegate Commission
Church of Norway

Mohanty, Most Rev. D.K.
Delegate MC, Church of North India

Moran, Sister Elizabeth
Resource (UK)
Roman Catholic Church

Morelli, Dom Mauro
Host country observer
Roman Catholic Church

Morgan, Rev. Enid R.
Delegate MC, Church in Wales

Morgan, Rev. Hampton
Accredited visitor
Moravian Church in America
(Southern Province) [USA]

Morgan, Ms Marion
Delegate Commission (Sierra
Leone)
Church of the Province
of West Africa [Ghana]

Moriana, Mr Ntsane Samuel
Delegate MC
Lesotho Evangelical Church

Motte, Pfarrer Dr Jochen
Accredited visitor
Evangelical Church in Germany

Moyer, Rev. John R.
Accredited visitor (Switzerland)
Presbyterian Church (USA)

Muita, Rev. Dr Isaiah W.
Delegate MC, Presbyterian Church
of East Africa [Kenya]

Mulbah, Mrs Elizabeth Sele
Delegate FOM (Liberia)
Church of the Province
of West Africa [Ghana]

Musomba, Rev. Angetile Yesaya
Delegated observer
Moravian Church in Tanzania

Mutiso-Mbinda, Msgr John
Consultant (Italy)
Roman Catholic Church

Mwerersa, Archbishop John G.K.O.
Delegate MC, African
Israel Church, Nineveh [Kenya]

Mwirabua, Rev. Mary Nkirote
Delegate MC
Methodist Church in Kenya

Nahas, Ms Maud
Delegate Commission (Lebanon)
Greek Orthodox Patriarchate of
Antioch and All the East [Syria]

Namwembe, Ms Despina
Delegate MC (Uganda)
Greek Orthodox Patriarchate of
Alexandria and All Africa [Egypt]

Nayap, Ms Dalila C.
Delegate FOM (Costa Rica)
Church of the Nazarene [Belize]

Ndeikwila, Mr Samson Tobias
Delegated observer
Evangelical Lutheran Church
in the Republic of Namibia

Nelson, Mr Corey A.
Delegate MC
Presbyterian Church (USA)

Nessibou, Rev. Dr Janice
Delegate FOM
Presbyterian Church of Ghana

Newbigin, Bishop J.E. Lesslie
Guest, United Reformed Church
in the United Kingdom

Nifon of Slobozia, Bishop
Delegate MC
Romanian Orthodox Church

Nikolla, Mr Andis
Delegate MC, Orthodox
Autocephalous Church of Albania

Nilsson, Rev. Dr Kjell Ove
Accredited visitor
Church of Sweden

Ninan, Ms Susan
Delegate MC, Malankara
Orthodox Syrian Church [India]

Nkulo, Mme Mpetsi
Delegate MC, Community of
Disciples of Christ [Democratic
Republic of Congo (Zaïre)]

Non, Rev. Janse Belandina
Delegate AB
Protestant Evangelical Church
in Timor [Indonesia]

Noort, Rev. Drs Gert
Delegate MC
Netherlands Reformed Church

Norgard, Rev. David
Delegate MC
Episcopal Church [USA]

Nygaard, Rev. Birger
Accredited visitor, Evangelical
Lutheran Church of Denmark

Nyomi, Rev. Dr Setriakor K.
Delegated observer (Kenya)
Evangelical Presbyterian
Church [Ghana]

Odurkami, Rev. Canon John Charles
Delegate MC
Church of the Province of Uganda

Ofstad, Rev. Kristin
Resource, United Reformed Church
in the United Kingdom

Oleksa, Rev. Fr Michael J.
Delegate FOM
Orthodox Church in America [USA]

Os, Ms Dini M. van
Delegate MC, United
Protestant Church of Belgium

Paavola, Rev. Hannu
Delegate MC, Evangelical
Lutheran Church of Finland

Padilha, Mr Anivaldo P.
Host country observer
Methodist Church in Brazil

Page, Rev. Dr Ruth
Delegate Commission
Church of Scotland

Panjaitan, Rev. Harry Riesman
Delegate MC
Indonesian Christian Church (HKI)

Papadakis, Ms Rebecca
Delegate MC (Greece)
Ecumenical Patriarchate
of Constantinople [Turkey]

Parris, Rev. Garnet A.
Delegate FOM
Baptist Union of Great Britain

Paul, Bishop
Delegate MC (South Africa)
Coptic Orthodox Church [Egypt]

Pauw, Prof. C. Martin
Delegated observer, Dutch
Reformed Church [South Africa]

Pawadee, Ms Janejinda
Delegate FOM
Church of Christ in Thailand

Perselis, Dr Emmanuel P.
Delegate MC (Greece)
Greek Orthodox Patriarchate of
Alexandria and All Africa [Egypt]

Petlyuchenko, Archpriest
Viktor Sergy
Delegate MC
Russian Orthodox Church

Petrecca, Pastor Hector O.
Delegate AB, Christian
Biblical Church [Argentina]

Phidas, Prof. Vlassios
Delegate MC
Church of Greece

Phillips, Miss Joan L.
Delegate FOM
Church in the Province
of the West Indies [Barbados]

Pierce, Mr Garland F.
Delegate FOM, African
Methodist Episcopal Church [USA]

Pihaatae, Pasteur François
Delegate MC, Evangelical Church
of French Polynesia

Pilusa, Mr Freddy
Delegate MC
Church of the Province
of Southern Africa [South Africa]

Plāte, Dean Modris
Delegate MC, Evangelical
Lutheran Church of Latvia

Poling-Goldene, Rev. Marta L.
Delegate MC, Evangelical
Lutheran Church in America [USA]

Porcile Santiso, Dr Maria Teresa
Consultant (Uruguay)
Roman Catholic Church

Prasad, Rev. Andrew
Accredited visitor (UK)
Church of North India

Prokopios of Philippi
and Neapolis, Metropolitan
Delegate MC, Church of Greece

Quack, Pfarrer Dr Jürgen
Accredited visitor
Evangelical Church in Germany

Quezada Escobar, Ms Fany
Delegate MC
Methodist Church of Peru

Rae, Rev. Dr Simon H.
Delegate MC, Presbyterian Church
of Aotearoa New Zealand

Raga, Mrs Bereberei
Delegate MC
Episcopal Church of the Sudan

Rakotonanahary, Mme Rojohery T.
Delegate MC (Madagascar)
Church of the Province
of the Indian Ocean (Seychelles)

Ralte, Dr Lalrinawmi
Delegate FOM
Presbyterian Church of India

Reed, Rev. Colin C.G.
Delegate MC
Anglican Church of Australia

Reeve, Rev. Dr Ted J.
G&C coordinator
United Church of Canada

Rey, Mr Victor
Delegated observer (Peru)

Ribeiro, Ms Dalva M. de Oliveira
Delegate MC
Methodist Church in Brazil

Richmond, Rev. Helen
Delegate MC
Methodist Church [UK]

Richter, Pfarrerin Ursula D.
Delegate MC
Evangelical Church in Germany

Rickard, Rev. John M.
Accredited visitor
Uniting Church in Australia

Rivera, Mr Angel Luis
Delegate FOM (Puerto Rico)
Christian Church (Disciples
of Christ)[USA]

Roberto, Ms Vera Maria
Accredited visitor, Independent
Presbyterian Church in Brazil

Rocha, Profa A. Violeta
Resource
Church of the Nazarene [Nicaragua]

Rocha Souza, Mr Enilson
Host country observer, United
Presbyterian Church of Brazil

Roest Crollius, Rev. Prof.
Dr Arij A.
Resource (Italy)
Roman Catholic Church

Rokaya, Dr Kali Bahadur
Accredited visitor
Sagarmaha Church [Nepal]

Ruiz, Ms Brenda Consuela
Delegate Commission
Baptist Convention of Nicaragua

Sam-Kpakra, Rev. Bob M.B.
Delegate FOM (Sierrra Leone)
United Methodist Church [USA]

Sampedro Nieto, Rev. Fr Francisco
Consultant (Chile)
Roman Catholic Church

Sangkhuma, Rev. Hmar
Delegated observer
Presbyterian Church of India

Scampini, Rev. Fr Jorge A.
Consultant (Argentina)
Roman Catholic Church

Schäfer, Rev. Dr Klaus
G&C coordinator
Evangelical Church in Germany

Schambach, Rev. Sonna Lee
Delegate MC
Moravian Church in America
(Northern Province) [USA]

Schmidt, Pastor Ervino
Host country observer
Evangelical Church of Lutheran
Confession in Brazil

Schmidt-Hesse, Pfarrerin Ulrike
Delegate FOM
Evangelical Church in Germany

Schünemann, Ms Silvia O.
Delegate MC, Evangelical Church
of Lutheran Confession in Brazil

Schwantes, Prof. Dr Milton
Resource, Evangelical Church
of Lutheran Confession in Brazil

Scouteris, Prof. Dr Constantine
Delegate MC
Church of Greece

Sharpe, Ms Wilma
Accredited visitor, American
Baptist Churches in the USA

Shibaeva, Ms Ekaterina
Delegate FOM
Russian Orthodox Church

Shishova, Mrs Marina I.
Delegate MC
Russian Orthodox Church

Silva, Rev. Lakpriya B.S. de
Delegate MC
Methodist Church [Sri Lanka]

Silva, Pastor Orlando
Delegated observer, Evangelical
Pentecostal Church [Brazil]

Silva Barbosa, Pastora
Silvia Maria
Accredited visitor
Methodist Church in Brazil

Singh, Rev. Dr Godwin R.
Resource
Methodist Church in India

Singh, Rev. Raymond S.
Delegate MC
United Reformed Church
in the United Kingdom

Sinner, Rev. Rudolf von
Accredited visitor, Swiss
Protestant Church Federation

Sitahal, Rev. Harold
G&C coordinator, Presbyterian
Church in Trinidad and Tobago

Siwu, Rev. Dr Richard A.D.
Delegate MC, Christian Evangelical
Church in Minahasa [Indonesia]

Slade, Rev. Dr Stanley D.
Delegate MC, American
Baptist Churches in the USA

Soares, Pastor André
Delegate MC, United Evangelical
Church "Anglican Communion
in Angola"

Soares, Prof. Sebastião A.G.
Accredited visitor, Episcopal
Anglican Church of Brazil

Soares de Souza, Pastora Zelia
Delegate FOM
Methodist Church in Brazil

Solang, Rev. Eduardo
Accredited visitor
United Church of Christ
in the Philippines

Sombrero, Rev. Tweedy Evelene
Delegate MC
United Methodist Church [USA]

Sone, Mrs Emilia
Delegate MC
Presbyterian Church in Cameroon

Sosa, Rev. Pablo
Resource, Evangelical Methodist
Church of Argentina

Speranskaya, Ms Elena S.
Delegate MC
Russian Orthodox Church

Sperb, Pastor Ulrico
Host country observer
Evangelical Church of Lutheran
Confession in Brazil

Spier, Rev. Patricia Tucker
Delegate MC, Christian Church
(Disciples of Christ) [USA]

Steuernagel, Rev. Dr Valdir R.
Delegated observer
Evangelical Church of Lutheran
Confession in Brazil

Stoica, Rev. Fr Costel
Delegate MC
Romanian Orthodox Church

Stoyadinov, Mr Mariyan
Delegate MC
Bulgarian Orthodox Church

Stright, Rev. Jeanne M.M.
Accredited visitor
United Church of Canada

Stright, Rev. H. Kenneth
Delegate MC
Presbyterian Church in Canada

Strub-Jaccoud, Ms Madeleine
Accredited visitor, Swiss
Protestant Church Federation

Stucker, Ms Agathe
Delegate MC, Swiss
Protestant Church Federation

Süss, Prof. Dr Paulo
Accredited visitor (Brazil)
Roman Catholic Church

Sugandhar, Mr Vimal Sukumar
Delegate MC
Church of South India

Suh Kwang-Sun, Rev. Dr David
Delegate FOM
Presbyterian Church of Korea

Suha, Ms Khasho
Delegate MC
National Evangelical Synod
of Syria and Lebanon [Lebanon]

Sumire Hanco, Pastor Valentin B.
Delegate FOM
Evangelical Church of Peru

Kang Sun-Chul, Mr
Delegate MC
Presbyterian Church of Korea

Supardan, Mrs E. Wilandari
G&C coordinator, Javanese
Christian Churches [Indonesia]

Suri, Rev. Ellison
Accredited visitor, Church
of Melanesia [Solomon Islands]

Šuvarská, Mrs Eva
Delegate FOM, Orthodox Church
of the Czech Lands
and Slovakia [Czech Republic]

Svensson, Rev. Bertil L.H.
Delegate FOM
Mission Covenant Church
of Sweden

Tahaafe, Ms Katalina
Delegate FOM
Uniting Church in Australia

Tananone, Mr Baw
Delegate MC
Church of Christ in Thailand

Tatarinov, Mr Vladimír
Delegate MC, Orthodox Church
of the Czech Lands
and Slovakia [Czech Republic]

Terwilliger, Rev. Dr Robert H.
Accredited visitor
Reformed Church in America [USA]

Thaler, Magister Willi
Delegate MC, Evangelical
Church of the Augsburg
and Helvetic Confessions [Austria]

Theodosius, Bishop
Geevarghese Mar
Delegate MC, Mar Thoma Syrian
Church of Malabar [India]

Tiel, Dr Gerhard Erich
Accredited visitor
Evangelical Church in Germany

Timbang, Rev. Fr Rhee M.
Delegate MC
Philippine Independent Church

Tolen, Dr Aaron
WCC president
Presbyterian Church of Cameroon

Topno, Most Rev. C.S.R.
Delegate MC
United Evangelical Lutheran
Churches in India

Toukkari, Ms Satu K.H.
Delegate FOM, Evangelical
Lutheran Church of Finland

Triebel, Pfarrer Dr Johannes
Accredited visitor
Evangelical Church in Germany

Turnipseed, Rev. R. Lawrence
Resource
United Methodist Church [USA]

Tuwere, Rev. Dr Ilaitia Sevati
Delegate FOM
Methodist Church in Fiji

Tuwere, Mrs Nina Taiviu
Accredited visitor
Methodist Church in Fiji

Ulloa Castellanos, Rev. Sergio
Delegate FOM
Baptist Church in Mexico

Urrea Viera, Rev. Fr Juan Carlos
Consultant (Colombia)
Roman Catholic Church

Usma Gómez, Rev. Fr Juan
Consultant (Italy)
Roman Catholic Church

Valim Filho, Mr José de Aguiar
Host country observer, United
Presbyterian Church of Brazil

Valle, Rev. Carlos A.
Resource (UK), Evangelical
Methodist Church of Argentina

Vandervelde, Prof. George
Accredited visitor (Canada)
Christian Reformed Church
in North America

Vasilescu, Dr Lucreţia M.P.
Delegate MC
Romanian Orthodox Church

Vasko, Rev. Dr Timo
Accredited visitor, Evangelical
Lutheran Church of Finland

Vavimaro, Pasteur Arlette
Delegate MC, Church of
Jesus Christ in Madagascar

Vis, Dr Jeroen L.M.
Accredited visitor (Netherlands)
Roman Catholic Church

Vogel-Mfato, Dr Eva-Sibylle
Delegate FOM
Evangelical Church in Germany

Vundla, Rev. Canon Themba Jerome
Delegate MC, Church of the
Province of Southern Africa
[South Africa]

Wapotro, M. Billy
Delegate FOM, Evangelical
Church in New Caledonia and the
Loyalty Isles [New Caledonia]

Watley, Rev. Dr William D.
Delegate Commission, African
Methodist Episcopal Church [USA]

Wehbe, Ms Maha M.
Delegate MC (Lebanon)
Greek Orthodox Patriarchate of
Antioch and All the East [Syria]

White, Rev. Bevon H.
Delegate MC
Moravian Church in Jamaica

Wihongi, Rev. Dawn Riria
Delegate MC
Anglican Church in Aotearoa,
New Zealand and Polynesia

Williams, Rev. Dr Lewin L.
G&C coordinator
United Church in Jamaica
and the Cayman Islands

Williamson, Rev. Dr Raymond K.
G&C coordinator
Anglican Church of Australia

Wilson, Rev. Dr Henry S.
G&C coordinator
Church of South India

Wilson, Rev. Sylvia D.
Delegate MC
Presbyterian Church (USA)

Wyatt, Rev. Dr S. Peter
Accredited visitor
United Church of Canada

Yamamoto, Mr Keith Akio
Delegate MC
Episcopal Church [USA]

Yeow Choo-Lak, Rev. Dr
G&C coordinator
Presbyterian Church in Singapore

Yong Ping-Chung, Rt Rev. Datuk
Delegate AB (Malaysia)
Church of the Province
of South East Asia (Singapore)

Yoo-Crowe, Mrs Seongja
Delegate MC
Uniting Church in Australia

Yoon Young-Sook, Ms
Delegate FOM
Orthodox Church of Korea

Zettel, Fräulein Mareike
Delegate MC
Evangelical Church in Germany

Zoé-Obianga, Dr Rose
Delegate Commission
Presbyterian Church of Cameroon

Zographos, Archimandrite Ambrose
Delegate MC (Greece)
Orthodox Church of Korea

Zwick, Pfarrer Rolf
Delegate MC
Evangelical Church in Germany

WCC staff and coopted staff

Ada, Pasteur Kokou Samuel
Evangelical Presbyterian Church
of Togo

Arx, Ms Denise von
(Ireland) Roman Catholic Church

Asante, Dr Rexford Kofi O.
Presbyterian Church of Ghana

Birchmeier, Pasteur Heinz
Swiss Protestant Church Federation

Black, Mr Christopher
United Church of Canada

Blancy, Dr Pasteur Alain
Reformed Church of France

The nationality is indicated in parentheses and the country of the church in square brackets, if not apparent.

Buss, Rev. Théo
Swiss Protestant Church Federation

Campos, Ms Sieni Maria
(Brazil) Roman Catholic Church

Campos Garcia, Ms Luzmarina
Evangelical Church of Lutheran
Confession in Brazil

Caytap, Ms Penelope B.D.
Episcopal Church in the Philippines

Coll, Ms Elena
Brazil

Conway, Dr D. Martin
Church of England

Cook, Rev. Dr A. Guillermo
(Argentina) Methodist Church
in Brazil

Cooney, Sister Monica F.
(Aotearoa New Zealand)
Roman Catholic Church

Delmonte, Ms M.C. Elisabeth
(Germany) Evangelical Waldensian
Church of the River Plate
[Argentina]

Drimmelen, Mr Robert W.F. van
Reformed Churches
in the Netherlands

Duraisingh, Rev. Dr Christopher
Church of South India

Edwards, Ms Donalie E.C.
(Antigua and Barbuda) Church
in the Province of the West Indies
[Barbados]

Freidig, Ms Marlise H.
Swiss Protestant Church Federation

Goertz, Pasteur Marc
Reformed Church of France

Isaac, Mr Samuel M.
Church of South India

Jenks, Mr Philip E.
American Baptist Churches
in the USA

Kaiser, Ms Helga A.C.
Evangelical Church in Germany

Langerak, Rev. Ana
(USA) Lutheran Church
in Costa Rica

Lundy, Ms Mary Ann
Presbyterian Church (USA)

MacArthur, Rev. Terry L.
United Methodist Church [USA]

McNiel, Ms Donna
Presbyterian Church (USA)

Mesa, Mrs Sheila M.
Church of Scotland

Meyer, Rev. Gérson
United Presbyterian Church of
Brazil

Meyer, Ms Romelia
United Presbyterian Church of
Brazil

Milano, Ms Catherine
(Switzerland) Roman Catholic
Church

Milosevic, Mrs Yvette A.
Church of England

Miranda, Ms Alice
Brazil

Mukarji, Dr Daleep S.
Church of North India

Mustaklem, Mr Costandi
Greek Orthodox Patriarchate
of Jerusalem and All Palestine

Newbury, Rev. John
Methodist Church [UK]

Nossova, Ms Zinaida I.
Russian Orthodox Church

Nottingham, Rev. Dr William J.
Christian Church (Disciples
of Christ) [USA]

Participants 231

Omulepu, Ms Sonia P.
Episcopal Church [USA]

Opitz-Chen, Rev. Dr Bettina
Evangelical Church in Germany

Osinga, Mr Lolke
Netherlands Reformed Church

Oxley, Rev. Simon J.
Baptist Union of Great Britain

Piakounova, Ms Olga M.
Russian Orthodox Church

Poma Añaguaya, Rev. Eugenio
Evangelical Methodist Church
in Bolivia

Pozzi-Johnson, Mr David L.
Evangelical Lutheran Church
in America [USA]

Raiser, Dr Elisabeth B.
Evangelical Church in Germany

Raiser, Rev. Dr Konrad
Evangelical Church in Germany

Reilly, Ms Joan G.
Church of Scotland

Ross, Ms Dawn M.
(Canada) Church of England

Rüppell, Dr Gert B.
Evangelical Lutheran Church
of Finland

Sabanes de Plou, Ms Dafne C.
Evangelical Methodist Church
of Argentina

Sander, Mr Luiz
Brazil

Sapsezian, Rev. Dr Aharon
(Brazil) Armenian
Evangelical Church

Sasson, Ms Margaret
Brazil

Sauca, Fr Dr Ioan
Romanian Orthodox Church

Sbeghen, Mrs Renate
Evangelical Church in Germany

Schmidt, Mr Ernst W.
Evangelical Church in Germany

Schüller, Ms Marilia
Methodist Church in Brazil

Smith, Mr Dennis A.
Presbyterian Church (USA)

Sovik, Dr Liv R.
Evangelical Lutheran Church
in America [USA]

Stromberg, Ms Jean S.
American Baptist Churches
in the USA

Stunt, Ms Heather
Church of England

Talvivaara, Ms Anu
Orthodox Church of Finland

Taran, Patrick A.
Society of Friends General
Conference [USA]

Tautari, Ms Tara
Methodist Church of New Zealand

Tierney, Ms Claire
(Ireland) Roman Catholic Church

Tkatchouk, Ms Lioudmila G.
Russian Orthodox Church

Tosat Delaraye, Ms Pilar
(Switzerland)
Roman Catholic Church

VanElderen, Mr Marlin
(USA) Christian Reformed Church
in North America

Varga, Mr Robert
(Switzerland)
Roman Catholic Church

Visinand, Mrs Elizabeth
Swiss Protestant Church Federation

Wieser, Dr Marguerite
Swiss Protestant Church Federation

Williams, Mr Peter
Evangelical Lutheran Church
of Denmark

Zierl, Ms Ursula
Evangelical Church in Germany

Stewards

Alves de Lima, Ms Natacha
Methodist Church in Brazil

Artigas, Mr Flávio H.R.
Methodist Church in Brazil

Attarian, Mr Douglas Vahe
(Brazil) Greek Orthodox
Patriarchate of Antioch
and All the East [Syria]

Beringui, Ms Eleni
Methodist Church in Brazil

Correia, Mr José Rubi
(Brazil) Roman Catholic Church

Dohir, Mrs Rana
(Brazil) Greek Orthodox
Patriarchate of Antioch
and All the East [Syria]

Fonseca, Mr Gustavo Celso da
Methodist Church in Brazil

García Langerak, Ms Olga
Lutheran Church in Costa Rica

Hofstätter, Mr Leandro Otto
Evangelical Church of Lutheran
Confession in Brazil

Mabeba, Mr Benny
Evangelical Lutheran Church
in Southern Africa [South Africa]

Magar, Ms Bimela T.
Gyaneshwar Church [Nepal]

Mantovani, Mr Ulisses L.
United Presbyterian Church
of Brazil

Mase Emi, Ms
Lutheran Church in Japan

Meyer, Mr Georg G.
Evangelical Lutheran
Church in Southern Africa
[South Africa]

Meyer, Mrs Renate U.
Evangelical Lutheran
Church in Southern Africa
[South Africa]

Milan, Ms Liliane Youssef
(Brazil) Greek Orthodox
Patriarchate of Antioch
and All the East [Syria]

Morrison, Rev. Terrance G.
Baptist Church [Bahamas]

Pereira da Silva, Ms Eufrida
Episcopal Anglican Church of Brazil

Pereira de Anchieta, Ms Marcia
Methodist Church in Brazil

Ramos da Silva, Ms Katia
Methodist Church in Brazil

Schultze, Ms Andrea
Evangelical Church in Germany

Shaheen, Ms Rasha
Syrian Orthodox Patriarchate
of Antioch and All the East

Shaw Ibañez, Ms Sandra K.
Evangelical Methodist Church
in Uruguay

Toledo, Ms Ana C.
United Methodist Church [USA]

Valera, Mr Demosthenes
Evangelical Presbyterian
and Reformed Church of Peru

Contributors

The Rt Rev. *E. Robinson de Barros Cavalcanti* (Episcopal Anglican Church of Brazil), at the time of the conference the director of the Centre for Philosophy and Human Sciences at the Federal University of Pernambuco in Recife, Brazil, has since become the Bishop of Recife.

The Rev. Dr *A. Guillermo Cook* (Methodist Church in Brazil) was the conference administrator. He has since retired in Costa Rica, where he is volunteer coordinator of Puentes/BRIDGES and visiting professor of missiology in several institutions.

Sister *Monica F. Cooney* smsm (Aotearoa New Zealand), at the time of the conference the Roman Catholic consultant in Programme Unit II of the World Council of Churches, is currently in Rome where she is engaged in research on the missionary spirituality of her religious congregation, the Marist Missionary Sisters.

The Rev. *Wali Fejo*, a leading Aboriginal churchman in the Uniting Church in Australia, is the principal of Nungalinya College in Darwin, Northern Territory, Australia.

The Rev. *Cornelia Füllkrug-Weitzel* (Evangelical Church in Germany) is responsible for the Education for World Mission desk in the joint mission agency of the Evangelical Churches in Berlin-Brandenburg, Pommern, Anhalt and Schlesische Oberlausitz, Germany.

The Rev. Dr *K.M. George* (Malankara Orthodox Syrian Church) is principal of the Orthodox Theological Seminary in Kottayam, India.

Dr *Musimbi Kanyoro* (Evangelical Lutheran Church in Kenya), at the time of the conference the executive secretary for Women in Church and Society of the Lutheran World Federation, is now general secretary of the World YWCA.

Metropolitan *Kirill of Smolensk and Kaliningrad* is the chairman of the Department of External Relations of the Russian Orthodox Church and a permanent member of the Holy Synod.

The Rev. *Marjorie Lewis-Cooper* (United Church in Jamaica and the Cayman Islands), at the time of the conference the general secretary of the Jamaica Council of Churches, is currently multiracial development worker for the United Reformed Church in the United Kingdom.

The Rev. *Kristin Ofstad* (Norway) is pastor in a United Reformed Church pastorate in North Cardiff, Wales.

Ms *Jean S. Stromberg* (American Baptist Churches in the USA) is director of the US office of the World Council of Churches in New York.

The Rev. Dr *Jean-Samuel Hendje Toya* (Evangelical Church of Cameroon) is Africa regional coordinator for Vereinigte Evangelische Mission (UEM), Germany, based in Rwanda.

The Rev. *Prathia Hall Wynn* (American Baptist Churches in the USA) teaches at United Theological Seminary in Dayton, Ohio, USA.